The
Stock Market

Theories
and
Evidence

The
Stock Market

Theories
and
Evidence

James H. Lorie
Graduate School of Business
University of Chicago

Peter Dodd
Australian Graduate School of Management
University of New South Wales

Mary Hamilton Kimpton
Formerly, School of Business Administration
Loyola University of Chicago

1985   Second Edition

RICHARD D. IRWIN, INC.
Homewood, Illinois   60430

The Irwin Series in Finance

Advisory Editor
Myron S. Scholes
Stanford University

ISBN 0-256-01917-7

Library of Congress Catalog Card No. 82–82309

A professional edition of this book is available from Dow Jones-Irwin, Inc.

Printed in the United States of America

1 2 3 4 5 6 7 8 9 0 ML 2 1 0 9 8 7 6 5

Foreword

It has been about 11 years since the first edition of *The Stock Market: Theories and Evidence* appeared. The foreword to the first edition still explains very well our purpose in writing this book. The reason for the second edition is that the world has changed somewhat and there have been numerous extensions and modifications of financial theory.

The most dramatic change in the financial world is probably the development of exchange markets for listed options. This has not only provided new opportunities for investors but has stimulated some fascinating research on the theory of option pricing, and by extension, the valuation of other assets.

By and large, the basic theory of finance remains intact. A few blemishes have appeared, but nothing so severe as to require the repudiation of any of the principles discussed in the first edition. The basic theories seem good for another 11 years and perhaps for a good deal longer than that.

October 1984

James H. Lorie
Peter Dodd
Mary Hamilton Kimpton

Foreword to the First Edition

Over the years there has been a large stream of popular articles and books about the stock market. This is not surprising since many millions of Americans have owned and do own stocks and since changes in stock prices have had a great direct impact on the net worth of investors and on the vigor of the national economy.

These articles and books have, with some notable exceptions, made one of two points. The first is that it is relatively easy for the individual investor to make very substantial returns by investing according to some simple rules. The second point is that the individual investor is manipulated or exploited by the denizens of the Wall Street jungle or the financial institutions to such an extent that investing in common stocks is intolerably hazardous.

The scientific literature about the stock market compellingly refutes both points. For reasons which this book tries to make clear, simple rules for selecting investments cannot be expected to produce extraordinary returns. Nor is the small individual investor at a substantial disadvantage as compared with the professional investor or the financial institution.

This book is about recent scientific research on the stock market, though much of it also applies to other investments. In the last 20 years, there has been an enormous change in what we know about the stock market and in the way we think about it. The changes have occurred primarily because of three things: (1) the publication in 1952 of Harry Markowitz's article on portfolio theory;[1] (2) the development of the theory of efficient markets and of its implications for security analysis and portfolio management; and (3) the development of high-speed computers and large files of financial information in machine-readable form, permitting the testing and extension of theories and a large volume of empirical findings. These related developments have increased our understanding of the ways in which investors should and do behave. We have also learned much about the functioning of our capital markets whose efficiency is important in channeling funds into their most promising uses.

Although in some fields academic work seems to have few general, practical implications, academic work in investments has practical implications which are basic and important. When the academic work is understood, it can be used to manage assets. Unfortunately, much academic work is written in ways that are difficult to understand, and much work depends for a complete understanding upon familiarity with numerous related articles and books which have appeared over many years in many places. This book attempts to organize, summarize, translate into simple language, and interpret the voluminous theoretical and scientific literature.

The book is divided into three sections. The first deals with the behavior of the stock market and in particular with the behavior of stock prices and rates of return on stocks. It includes a discussion of the theory of efficient markets, the evidence regarding its validity, and its implications for investors.

The second section deals with the valuation of securities. Since balance sheets and income statements for large numbers of companies for many years have been transformed into machine-readable form, there have been vigorous and persistent efforts to measure the forces which determine stocks prices in order to predict them more accurately. The use of formal models and empirical inquiry has provided new knowledge and has cast light on the validity of some old and new theories of security valuation. Among the topics covered in this section are the effect of capital structure and dividend policy on the value of the firm and the effects of the rate of growth in, and the stability of, corporate earnings.

The final section deals with portfolio theory. It includes an explanation of the principles of rational portfolio selection for investors who like high rates of return and dislike risk. Risk plays an important part in the theory of stock evaluation and in portfolio theory, and the book discusses current controversies about the definition and measurement of risk and current theories and findings about the relationship of risk to rates of return. The final section also includes a discussion of the way in which efficient markets would operate to determine the prices of risky assets, assuming that inves-

---

[1]Harry Markowitz, "Portfolio Selection," *Journal of Finance* 7, no. 1 (March 1952), pp. 77–91.

tors behave in accordance with the principles of modern portfolio theory. There is a concluding chapter on investment counseling. Modern developments in the field of investments have made counseling the dominant financial service, though it is probably the most neglected.

Acknowledgments

Hundreds of students and several colleagues in the academic and financial communities read the manuscript of this book and gave us helpful criticism. We wish to thank students in classes in investments at the Graduate School of Business of the University of Chicago during the fall, winter, and spring of 1971–72, and wish to thank especially our colleagues Fischer Black, Lawrence Fisher, Roger Ibbotson, David Kleinman, and Ralph Wanger.

Merrill Lynch, Pierce, Fenner & Smith, Inc. and the Graduate School of Business of the University of Chicago through its Center for Research in Security Prices provided generous financial support, and we thank them.

Domenica Moroney and Czatdana Baxter transformed our scattered thoughts and semilegible writing into clean copy. We are grateful.

February 1973   **J. H. L.**
                                                                M. H. K.

Contents

1. **The stock market and the national economy**   1
    Introduction. The stock market and the real economy. The
    determinants of the level of stock prices. Some descriptive
    statistics on the stock market and investors.

2. **Rates of return on investment—common stocks**   13
    and other securities
    A little financial arithmetic. Average rates of return on different
    securities: *Overview. Variability in rates of return. The market's
    trade-off of risk and return.* Rates of return and inflation. The
    effects of commissions, taxes, and weighting strategies.

3. **Stock market indexes and the market factor in stock returns** 33
    Introduction. The market model. Stock market indexes: *Some
    problems. Sampling. Weighting. Methods of averaging.* The
    major indexes: *The Dow Jones Industrial Average. The
    Standard & Poor's 500 Composite. The New York Stock Exchange
    Composite. The American Stock Exchange Price Level Index. The
    Value Line 1,400 Composite Average. The Wilshire 5,000. NASDAQ*

Composite Index. Investment-performance indexes. Stock index
futures. Concluding remarks.

4. The efficient market hypothesis   55
    Introduction. Some history: *Early beginnings.* Early tests of the
    weak form. Quest for a theory. Tests of the semistrong hypothesis.
    Tests of the strong form of the hypothesis: Professional investment
    managers: *Inside information.* Conclusions.

5. Implications of the efficient market hypothesis   80
    Introduction. Security analysis: *The state of the art. Implications.*
    Portfolio management: *The state of the art. Appropriate changes.*
    Investment counseling. Conclusions.

6. Dividends and stock valuation   88
    Introduction: *Basic principles.* Dividends and earnings: *The
    dividend and earnings hypotheses reconciled. Further comments
    on dividend policy.* The appropriate rate of discount. Conclusions.

7. Earnings   96
    Introduction: *Ambiguity in reported income because of numerous
    accounting options. Stock prices and accounting earnings.* Predicting
    earnings: *Historical earnings as a predictor of future earnings.
    Predictions of security analysts.* Conclusions.

8. The theory of portfolio management   108
    Introduction. The Markowitz contribution: *Portfolios and securities.
    The efficient frontier. Lending and borrowing.* Utility, risk aversion,
    and optimality. Conclusions.

9. Capital market equilibrium theory and evidence on the   132
    risk-return trade-off
    Introduction: *The assumptions. The realism of the model. Risk-free
    borrowing and lending. Efficient portfolios. Beta as a measure of
    risk. Additional risk measures. Extension of the CAPM. What does it
    all mean?* Conclusions.

10. Options   144
    Introduction: *Definitions and market procedures. Investment
    strategies using options. The pricing of options.* Concluding
    remarks.

11. Evaluating portfolio performance   154
    Introduction: *Rate of return. Risk. Combining measurements
    of rate of return and risk.* Measuring different parts of the portfolio:
    Diagnosing the causes of performance. Reaching a conclusion.

12. **A note on investment counseling** 167
   Introduction. The preferences and resources of investors. The
   specification of investment policy. Conclusion.

Glossary 173

Index 187

1

The stock market and the national economy

INTRODUCTION

Benjamin Friedman has remarked that a time-traveler from 1940, or even 1900, would probably feel closer to home on first disembarking in the financial markets than in most other areas of 1980 American economic activity.[1] And it is true that the basic functions of the financial markets and the major participants are little changed: Institutional investors, such as insurance companies, are investing in securities and spreading their risks; corporations are raising capital to finance their assets and newly developed products; and individuals are investing current savings to provide for future consumption.

Of course, the manner in which financial markets operate has changed dramatically. Technological changes often mask the inherent sameness and permanence of capital markets' primary roles. The basic functions are still to provide and allocate capital funds to firms with profitable investment opportunities and to offer an avenue of liquidity for individuals to invest current income or borrow against future income and thereby achieve their preferred time pattern of consumption. Because investing involves uncertainty, capital markets also provide a means for transferring risk among the parties to these transactions.

Of all the financial markets, the stock market probably has the greatest glamour and is perhaps the least understood. Some observers consider it a legalized haven for gambling, and many investors, including professionals, consider stock market investing as a game in which the sole purpose is picking winners. Such an outlook can lead to myopic concentration on short-run changes in stock prices, and it can lead to neglect of the extremely important role the capital markets play in the real economy. We shall exemplify that myopia for most of this book. Indeed, our objective is to explain, at a micro level, the workings of the stock market. In this first chapter, however, we consider the stock market as a whole.

THE STOCK MARKET AND THE REAL ECONOMY

As Figure 1–1 demonstrates, the stock market and economic activity move in similar cyclical patterns. This fundamental relationship has important ramifications. First, it is solid evidence that stock prices are meaningful in the sense of reflecting real economic variables and not simply random numbers driven by the psyche, sun spots, or the pronouncements of self-appointed seers. Second, it helps explain why the stock market is reported in so much detail by the media and why it is followed with concern by so many people.

The general correspondence between stock prices and the business cycle is evident in Figure 1–2, where a weighted moving average of a stock price index is mapped against the peaks and troughs of business cycles since 1948. The market has reflected all the recessions in the economy since 1948.

A number of studies investigating this relationship between stock prices and the national economy have found that changes in the stock market tend to precede changes in business conditions by an average of about four months. As a result, the stock price index is a major component of the index of leading economic indicators, which consistently provides a warning about changes in economic activity.[2]

Perhaps the clearest example of the leading characteristics of the stock market is the recession of 1974–75. This was one of the most severe recessions since World War II, and the decline in stock prices was the longest and steepest fall since the recessions of the 1930s. Note, however, that in Figures 1–1 and 1–2, the stock market decline began in 1973 and continued through 1974. Industrial production, on the other hand, continued to rise throughout most of 1973, and its collapse did not begin before late 1974.

In many ways the stock price index is the most exciting of the leading economic indicators. Unlike other components, the stock price index is available hourly and can be followed as closely as baseball or football scores. Preoccupation with hourly or daily fluctuations of individual stocks, however, can hide the consistent lead in the broad stock price index.

Downturns in business cycles occur when business decisions to expand are canceled or postponed and cost-cutting measures and layoffs are intro-

FIGURE 1-1   Industrial production and prices of common stock, 1953–1975

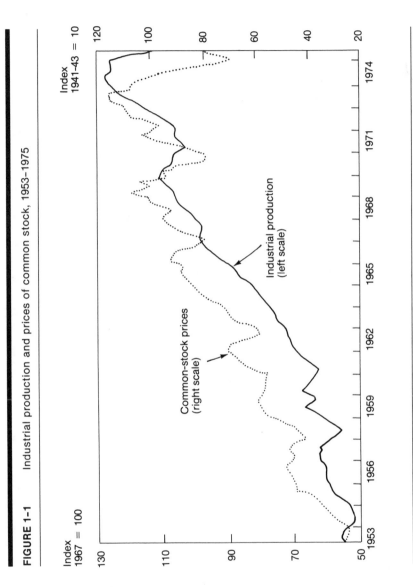

Source: Barry Bosworth, "The Stock Market and the Economy," *Brookings Papers on Economic Activity*, 1975, p. 259.

FIGURE 1–2   Stock prices and the business cycle, 1948–84

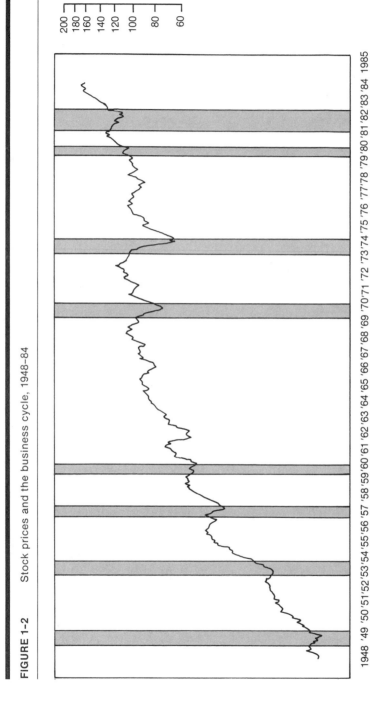

Scale L-2

200
180
160
140
120
100
80
60

1948 '49 '50 '51 '52 '53 '54 '55 '56 '57 '58 '59 '60 '61 '62 '63 '64 '65 '66 '67 '68 '69 '70 '71 '72 '73 '74 '75 '76 '77 '78 '79 '80 '81 '82 '83 '84 1985

Note: Stock prices, 500 common stocks (index 1941–1943 = 10). Shaded columns indicate a period of recession as designated by the NBER.
Source: *Business Conditions Digest*, January 1984, U.S. Department of Commerce, p. 13.

duced. These decisions are made when the prospects for profits diminish. Since the inherent motivating force is the expectation of profits, it is not surprising that the stock market is a leading indicator. Stock market prices are set by the interaction of investors backing their expectations of corporate profits. The rewards for being the first to identify changes in the corporate outlook are such that stock prices reflect an intense competition for information on future profits. The consensus of expectations regarding the stock market is consistently one of the best predictors of economic conditions.

THE DETERMINANTS OF THE LEVEL OF STOCK PRICES

The relationship between stock market indexes and real economic variables provides a clue about the determinants of stock price levels. The value of a corporation's stock is determined by expectations regarding future earnings of the corporation and by the rate at which those earnings are discounted. In a world of no uncertainty, all securities would offer a certain return equal to the real rate of return on capital. In a world of uncertainty, returns are not so easily explained. In our uncertain world, feelings about securities can be summarized by a personal estimate of the likelihood of various changes in future earnings. The weighted average or mean of these possible changes is called the *expected* change. (The weights are equal to the probabilities of occurrence.) The greater the mean or expected value of the possible changes, the higher the prices of stocks, other things being equal. And, in our risk-averse world, the greater the uncertainty, the lower the prices of stocks.

To reiterate, two determinants of stock price levels are the expected level of earnings and the degree of investor uncertainty in estimating what future earnings will be. The third determinant of stock price levels is the rate at which a prospective stream of *certain* earnings is discounted to determine its present value. The present value of any stream of earnings is affected by the rate at which it is discounted—the higher the rate, the lower the value. The rate at which earnings should be discounted is related to or determined by the rate of return that can be earned on alternative investments. Since, in the previous discussion, risk or uncertainty is explicitly taken into account—usually in estimating a risk premium—by consideration of the standard deviation of possible changes in earnings, the relevant rate of return on alternative investments is the rate of return on assets which do not entail risk.

The academic literature in finance often glibly discusses the "risk-free rate," and there are rates which seem to be virtually risk free, at least in nominal terms. For example, 180-day Treasury bills can be bought at a known price and will presumably be redeemed 180 days later at a known price. Indubitably, the federal government will have the power to redeem the bill, assuming the absence of nuclear holocaust, revolution, or fits of insanity, and thus—according to one's pessimism about catastrophe—the bills are risk free or virtually risk free. When the relevant period is longer—say, five years—there is no security which is equally risk free. Even if the market price is known and the probability of default is virtually nil, the total rate of return on a five-year government bond depends, in part, on the rates at which periodic interest payments can be reinvested, and these rates cannot be known with precision.

Most of the uncertainty in the total rate of return on the bond is due to fluctuations in the level of expected inflation. Following the classic analysis of Irving Fisher, perhaps the most distinguished American economist of the 20th century, the nominal risk-free rate comprises two elements: One is the real return on investment and is determined by the supply and demand for capital in the economy as a whole; the other is the expected inflation rate.[3]

Since all interest rates are interrelated, although in different ways at different business-cycle phases, it is convenient to say that the rate at which corporate earnings should be discounted is determined, in part, by interest rate levels. These levels have fluctuated widely in recent years. For example, at the end of 1960, the yield to maturity or rate of return on 90-day Treasury bills was about 2.25 percent, and the corresponding rate in mid-1984 was over 10 percent.

For risky assets, such as corporate securities, the appropriate discount rate is the risk-free rate plus a risk premium. In this sense, the discount rate is the rate of return that investors require from an investment of that particular risk level. The relevant definition of risk and the correct measure of the risk premium are important subjects in the latter parts of this book.

Forecasting changes in stock prices requires prediction of changes in expected profits and future interest rates. Accurate prophecy is extremely valuable and very rare. It requires identification of indicators that lead the leading economic indicators or at least lead the stock market. At different times, claims of prophetic powers are made, but subsequent research (and presumably the subsequent investment performance of the adherents) justifies extreme skepticism. A case in point is the hypothesized relationship between monetary variables and the stock market.

Since the publication of *A Monetary History of the United States*[4] by Milton Friedman and Anna Schwartz—and especially since Friedman's monetary theories have been so widely discussed, substantially confirmed by experience, and increasingly accepted—much attention has focused on money supply changes as precursors of changes in both general economic conditions and stock prices. Beryl Sprinkel, a true believer in the Friedman church, has written two interesting books on the relationship between changes in the money supply growth rate and changes in stock prices. In the second book, the major conclusions were:[5]

1. Changes in the money supply growth rate have a "usually decisive" effect on business conditions and stock prices.

2. Competent monetary analysis can detect relevant changes in monetary policy by reviewing Federal Reserve Board policy statements and by analyzing current changes in the money supply and other monetary statistics.
3. Understanding the relationship between the money stock and the real economy can contribute to solving the timing problem (that is, when to invest funds in or withdraw funds from the stock market), but finding the solution will continue to be difficult, and its value may diminish if cyclical fluctuations in stock prices diminish.

Other writers supported Sprinkle's claims and concluded that stock price changes resulted from monetary variable changes, that is, monetary changes lead stock prices.[6]

Subsequently, Rozeff[7] and Rogalski and Vinso[8] criticized these claims and refuted the hypothesis with rigorous empirical testing. Rozeff concluded:

> For the stock market, the lag in effect of monetary policy is essentially zero. Stock returns do not lag behind growth rates of the money supply. Still, changes in stock prices are related to monetary variables. A substantial fraction of current stock price change can be linked to current monetary policy. In addition, an important part of current stock price change appears to reflect stock market anticipation of future monetary growth.[9]

In sum, monetary variables influence the levels of stock prices, but do not lead the market as required for reliable prophecy. This result is not surprising.

Our common sense rejects the idea of a single time series of macroeconomic data which reliably leads the market, thus simply providing the secret of great wealth. Investors with common sense who play the timing game successfully must anticipate better than other investors the course of the general economy, corporate profits, and interest rates. This task seems to require a comprehensive and perceptive analysis of national and international economic, political, and social developments. The record of professionally managed portfolios indicates that many investors play the timing game and that few, if any, consistently win it.

SOME DESCRIPTIVE STATISTICS ON THE STOCK MARKET AND INVESTORS

The importance of the stock market to individuals in the economy is reflected in Figure 1–3, which shows the composition of the financial asset portfolios of American households in the post-World War II period. The investments of individuals are heavily weighted in corporate equities that trade on registered stock exchanges.

At the end of 1980, the market value of corporate equity securities in the United States was approximately $1,571 billion.[10] The value of shares listed

FIGURE 1-3   Financial asset holdings of U.S. households

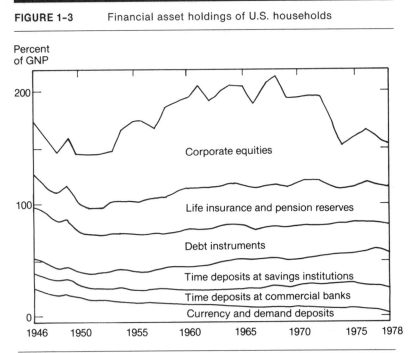

Source: Benjamin M. Friedman, "Postwar Changes in American Financial Markets," in *The American Economy in Transition*, ed. Martin Feldstein (Chicago: University of Chicago Press, 1980), p. 37.

on the New York Stock Exchange (NYSE) was over $1,242 billion, about four fifths of the total.[11] On the NYSE, there were over 33 billion shares listed in 2,228 issues of common and preferred stocks of 1,570 companies.

The next most important organized market in the United States is the over-the-counter market, which is also called the NASDAQ market because of the comprehensive OTC quotation service (National Association of Security Dealers Automated Quotation service) offered by the NASD. However, the NASDAQ market is clearly overshadowed by the NYSE. The share volume on the NASDAQ market in 1983 was just over 70 percent of the NYSE volume and more than seven times the volume on the next most important American market, the American Stock Exchange (ASE).

The dominance of the NYSE is evident in the total dollar volume of shares trades in the United States. In 1980, the total was $475 billion, of which 83.6 percent was on the NYSE, 7.3 percent was on the ASE, and the remainder was on the NASDAQ and regional exchanges.[12]

The number of issues on the NYSE is substantially less than 10 percent of the total publicly traded issues of stock in this country, but the value of stocks on the NYSE is over half the total. There is great concentration of value within the stock listings on the NYSE. For example, at the end of

1980, the market value of the common stock of International Business Machines was over $39 billion. The second most valuable stock was Exxon, with a value over $36 billion. To illustrate the degree of concentration, the five most valuable issues had a combined value equal to about 13 percent of the total value of all issues listed on the exchange, and the 50 most valuable issues had a value equal to about 40 percent of all NYSE issues.[13]

This great concentration of value has some implications for the construction of price movement indexes and the achievement of effective diversification, which are discussed in Chapter 3. Given the dominance of the NYSE, it is not surprising or alarming that most of the empirical research discussed in this book centers on stocks listed there.

In order to contribute further to a general feeling about the market's nature, it is worth noting who the investors are. One summary is given in Table 1-1.

Although individuals directly own about 72 percent of all outstanding equities, the influence of these stockholders in determining common stock prices is much less than that percentage might imply. First, many individuals have their holdings managed for them by financial institutions. In 1976, individuals accounted for only 22.2 percent of the total value of shares traded on the NYSE. Financial institutions and intermediaries accounted for 54.7 percent and members of the exchange, 23.1 percent. The relative importance of trading by institutions and intermediaries has risen rapidly. As recently as 1960, individuals accounted for more than half of the NYSE volume, as measured by shares traded, and more than 40 percent as measured by value.

The increasing role of institutions has had some dramatic consequences on financial markets. Throughout the 20th century, and especially in the years since World War II, there has been a shift away from direct transactions between nonfinancial borrowers and lenders toward the intervention of financial intermediaries. This is reflected in the earlier development of the commercial banking system, life insurance industries, and the later rise of nonbank deposit institutions and pension funds, both private and public.

The increasing use of financial intermediaries by individual investors reflects the lower transaction costs incurred by institutions and the diversification advantage associated with pooling many individuals' investments, which indirectly allows them to own interests in a large number of imperfectly divisible assets.

The dramatic growth of institutional stock holdings in the 1960s and 1970s has also had a significant effect on the structure of the investment industry and on the costs of investing in stocks. Prior to 1968, brokerage commissions charged to investors depended only on the stock's price and on the number of shares. During the 1960s, the structure of commissions fixed by NYSE regulation guaranteed that marginal revenues from large orders would exceed marginal costs of transactions. The fixed brokerage rates were sanctioned by the Securities and Exchange Commission (SEC), and

TABLE 1-1   Estimated holdings of NYSE-listed stock by selected institutional investors ($ billions)

Type of institution	Year-end					
	1949	1955	1960	1965	1970	1975
U.S. institutions:						
Insurance companies:						
Life	$ 1.1	$ 2.2	$ 3.2	$ 6.3	$ 11.7	$ 21.9
Nonlife	1.7	4.2	6.0	10.1	12.2	11.3
Investment companies:						
Open-end	1.4	6.3	12.4	29.1	39.0	35.2
Closed-end	1.6	4.6	4.2	5.6	4.1	5.4
Noninsured pension funds:						
Corporate and other private	0.5	3.4	14.3	35.9	60.7	82.2
State and local government	*	0.1	0.3	1.4	9.6	22.8
Nonprofit institutions:						
Foundations	2.5	6.9	8.0	16.4	17.0	22.1
Educational endowments	1.1	2.3	2.9	5.9	6.6	7.2
Other	1.0	2.5	4.4	7.7	9.0	8.7
Common trust funds	*	0.9	1.4	3.2	4.1	6.1
Mutual savings banks	0.2	0.2	0.2	0.5	1.4	2.3
Subtotal	$11.1	$ 33.6	$ 57.3	$122.1	$175.4	$225.4
Foreign institutions:† investment, insurance, and miscellaneous companies	—	—	—	—	—	$ 5.1
Total	$11.1	$ 33.6	$ 57.3	$122.1	$175.4	$230.5
Market value of all NYSE-listed stock	$76.3	$207.7	$307.0	$537.5	$636.4	$685.1
Estimated percent by institutional investors	14.5%	16.2%	18.7%	22.7%	27.6%	33.6%

* Less than $50 million
† Not included are foreign banks, brokers and nominees. This institutional group held an estimated $18.5 billion of NYSE-listed stocks at the end of 1975. Miscellaneous institutions consist of pension funds and other employee funds or trusts.
Source: *1981 NYSE Fact Book*, p. 50.

with limited membership and rules prohibiting price cutting and rebates by members, the NYSE operated, in effect, as a private cartel. As with all cartels, however, there were incentives for members to undercut indirectly and thus increase their respective shares of the lucrative trade at the cost of reduced margins.

During the 1960s, brokers devised many ingenious methods of competing using nonprice services, such as the "give up" system, wherein brokers gave portions of their commissions from an institution to another broker, who offered research services to the same institution. This system came under increasing criticism from the SEC and eventually led major exchanges to introduce modest volume discounts on orders of more than 1,000 shares.

The SEC, together with the Department of Justice, continued to press for the end of price fixing. Finally, on May 1, 1975, all fixed commissions were abolished. The resulting brokerage fee structure is presented in Figure 1–4.

In addition to declining commission rates, deregulation has substantially altered the entire structure of the brokerage industry. Brokerage firms

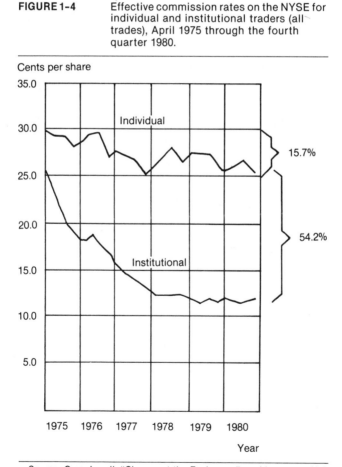

FIGURE 1-4   Effective commission rates on the NYSE for individual and institutional traders (all trades), April 1975 through the fourth quarter 1980.

Cents per share

Source: Greg Jarrell, "Change at the Exchange," working paper, University of Chicago, 1983.

have diversified, and commissions on securities are a declining fraction of their revenue. Discount brokerage firms have emerged, and there has been unprecedented merger activity and numerous bankruptcies in the securities industry.

The net result of changes in the securities industry is that the cost of stock market investing has been reduced since the 1960s.

NOTES

1. Benjamin M. Friedman, "Postwar Changes in the American Financial Markets," in *The American Economy in Transition*, ed. Martin Feldstein (Chicago: University of Chicago Press, 1980), pp. 9–78.

2. See Geoffrey H. Moore, "Stock Prices and the Business Cycle," *Journal of Portfolio Management* 1 (Spring 1975), pp. 59–64.

3. Irving Fisher, "The Theory of Interest: As Determined by Impatience to Spend Income and Opportunity to Invest It" (New York: Augustus M. Kelley, Publishers, 1965) originally published 1930.

4. Milton Friedman and Anna Jacobson Schwartz, *A Monetary History of the United States 1867–1960*, a study by the National Bureau of Economic Research (Princeton, N.J.: Princeton University Press, 1963).

5. Beryl W. Sprinkel, *Money and Markets* (Homewood, Ill.: Richard D. Irwin, 1971).

6. See K. E. Homa and D. M. Jaffee, "The Supply of Money and Common Stock Prices," *Journal of Finance* 26 (December 1971), pp. 1056–66; and M. W. Keran, "Expectations, Money and the Stock Market," *Federal Reserve Bank of St. Louis Review* (January 1971), pp. 16–31.

7. M. S. Rozeff, "Money and Stock Preces: Market Efficiency and the Lag in Effect of Monetary Policy," *Journal of Financial Economics* 1 (September 1974), pp. 245–302.

8. R. Rogalski and J. Vinso, "Stock Returns, Money Supply and the Direction of Causality," *Journal of Finance* 32 (September 1977), pp. 1017–30.

9. Rozeff, "Money and Stock Prices," p. 301.

10. Securities and Exchange Commission Staff Report on the Securities Industry in 1981, p. 13.

11. *1981 NYSE Fact Book*, p. 32.

12. Ibid., p. 50.

13. Ibid., p. 57.

2

Rates of return on investment—common stocks and other securities

Scientific progress in any field depends on accurate measurement. Many measurements are interesting in themselves, but their most important scientific role is to test the validity of theory. Since most financial theory is focused on an explanation of the level, structure, and behavior of rates of return, their accurate measurement is essential if the theory is to be tested and improved.

Of particular interest are the differences in rates of return across securities, since they provide valuable clues to the market's trade-off between risk and return. The unraveling of this fundamental, yet elusive relation, is central to the theory of finance. In essence, the problem is to identify and explain the long-term relation among rates of return. Unfortunately, this long-term relation is obscured by dramatic, short-term swings in market prices. Although fascinating to investors and market commentators, these short-term fluctuations complicate the search for the underlying risk-return relation. It is possible, however, with a long enough period of study and accurate measurements of historical rates of return, to reduce the effects of the short-term fluctuations and reveal the enduring risk-return relation.

The availability of such comprehensive studies is a relatively recent development, at least for stocks, and is closely associated with the advent of sophisticated computers. Satisfactory studies of the rates of return on bond investments can be found as early as 1938.[1] Refined measurements of the rates of return on common stocks, however, were first provided in 1964 by Fisher and Lorie.[2] They initially presented data on all stocks listed on the New York Stock Exchange for the period of 1926–60, and the detailed measures accounted for dividends and all relevant capital changes, such as stock splits. The study was updated and expanded in 1968 and 1976; and the availability of this data through the Center for Research in Security Prices (CRSP) at the University of Chicago has greatly stimulated the burgeoning empirical research in finance that has occurred in the past 15 years. The data are kept current by the CRSP.

Following the example of Fisher and Lorie, Ibbotson and Sinquefield updated the series to 1981 and included data on Treasury bills and corporate bonds.[3] In this chapter, both the Fisher-Lorie and Ibbotson-Sinquefield studies are discussed. Before presenting these data, there is a discussion of some common problems in computing rates of return.

A LITTLE FINANCIAL ARITHMETIC

All data on rates of return presented in this chapter are based upon changes in the market value of assets and on the value of payoffs received by the owners of those assets during the relevant period. The payoffs received are interest, dividends, rights, and occasionally other payments.

Computers deal most easily with rates of return compounded continuously, while most people seem to prefer rates compounded annually. Since this difference can cause difficulties and errors, it needs to be understood.

The annual rate of return compounded continuously on any investment is the natural logarithm ($\log_e$) of the ratio of the investment's year-end value to the beginning value. For example, if the investment was initially worth $100 and one year later was worth $110, the wealth ratio would be 1.1, and its natural logarithm would be 0.09531. The annual rate of return compounded continuously would be 9.531 percent. If the growth to $110 had taken only six months, the annual rate compounded continuously would have been twice as great, or 19.062 percent; if the growth had taken two years, the annual rate would have been half as much, or 4.765 percent.

The annual rate of return compounded annually is one less than the value of the exponential function e^x where x is the annual rate compounded continuously. For example, if the annual rate of return compounded continuously were 10 percent, the rate compounded annually would be given by the following expression:

$$e^{.10} - 1 = 1.1052 - 1 = .1052$$

Thus, the rate compounded annually would be 10.52 percent.* For all wealth ratios greater than 1.0, rates compounded continuously are less

---

*If y is the rate compounded annually, $y = e^x - 1$, where x is the rate compounded continuously. Values of e^x can be found in most books of mathematical tables.

than the corresponding rates compounded annually. For wealth ratios less then 1.0, the reverse is true.[4]

One common error in using rates of return is to assume that the average annual rate of return, compounded annually for several years, is equal to the arithmetic mean of the annual rates of return for the individual years. That is, if the annual rates of return compounded annually for a three-year period were 8, 10, and 12 percent, respectively, one might assume that the average rate of return for the three-year period was 10 percent. This is an error. The correct answer is found in either of two ways. The first is to calculate the geometric mean of the rates of return compounded annually.[*] The correct average annual rate of return for the three-year period would be the cube root of the annual rates as follows:

$$\text{Average annual rate} = (1.08 \times 1.10 \times 1.12)^{1/3} - 1 = 1.09988$$
$$= 9.99 \text{ percent}$$

The second calculation of the average annual rate of return compounded annually is to compute the arithmetic mean of the annual rates compounded continuously and then find the corresponding rate compounded annually. In the example, the successive annual rates compounded continuously are 7.696, 9.531, and 11.333. Their arithmetic mean is 9.52, and the corresponding rate compounded annually is 9.99 percent.

The point is illustrated by considering an initial investment of $100, which is worth $200 in one year and $100 in two years. The successive annual rates compounded annually are 100 percent and -50 percent. The arithmetic mean of the two rates is 25 percent. The true rate is clearly 0 percent. This is the result if we take the geometric mean as follows:

$$(2.0 \times 0.5)^{1/2} - 1 = 0$$

Another source of error in some rate of return calculations is the assumption that dividends, interest, or rights are received at the beginning, middle, end, or uniformly through the relevant time period rather than at the time they were actually received. Since there is strong seasonality in the distribution of interest and dividends, the simplifying assumptions which are sometimes used introduce small, but occasionally significant, errors into the calculation of actual rates of return. There are some special problems in calculating the variability of rates of return, which are discussed later in this chapter.

AVERAGE RATES OF RETURN ON DIFFERENT SECURITIES

Overview

Following the pioneering work of Fisher and Lorie, Ibbotson and Sinquefield have provided the most up-to-date study of returns to different se-

---

[*]In order to deal with negative rates of return, wealth ratios are used in computing the geometric mean. The average annual rate is then the geometric mean minus one.

TABLE 2-1   Year-by-year returns to different securities, 1926–1981

Year	Common stocks	Long-term corporate bonds	Long-term government bonds	U.S. Treasury bills	Consumer price index
1926	− 11.6	7.4	7.8	3.3	1.5
1927	37.5	7.4	8.9	3.1	− 2.1
1928	43.6	2.8	0.1	3.2	− 1.0
1929	− 8.4	3.3	3.4	4.8	0.2
1930	− 24.9	8.0	4.7	2.4	− 6.0
1931	− 43.3	− 1.9	− 5.3	1.1	− 9.5
1932	− 8.2	10.8	16.8	1.0	− 10.3
1933	54.0	10.4	− 0.1	0.3	0.5
1934	− 1.4	13.8	10.0	0.2	2.0
1935	47.7	9.6	5.0	0.2	3.0
1936	33.9	6.7	7.5	0.2	1.2
1937	− 35.0	2.8	0.2	0.3	3.1
1938	31.1	6.1	5.5	− 0.0	− 2.8
1939	− 0.4	4.0	5.9	0.0	− 0.5
1940	− 9.8	3.4	6.1	0.0	1.0
1941	− 11.6	2.7	0.9	0.1	9.7
1942	20.3	2.6	3.2	0.3	9.3
1943	25.9	2.8	2.1	0.4	3.2
1944	19.8	4.7	2.8	0.3	2.1
1945	36.4	4.1	10.7	0.3	2.3
1946	− 8.1	1.7	0.1	0.4	18.2
1947	5.7	− 2.3	− 2.6	0.5	9.0
1948	5.5	4.1	3.4	0.8	2.7
1949	18.8	3.3	6.5	1.1	− 1.8
1950	31.7	2.1	0.1	1.2	5.8
1951	24.0	− 2.7	− 3.9	1.5	5.9
1952	18.4	3.5	1.2	1.7	0.9
1953	− 1.0	3.4	3.6	1.8	0.6
1954	52.6	5.4	7.2	0.9	− 0.5
1955	31.6	0.5	− 1.3	1.6	0.4
1956	6.6	− 6.8	− 5.6	2.5	2.9
1957	− 10.8	8.7	7.5	3.1	3.0
1958	43.4	− 2.2	− 6.1	1.5	1.8
1959	12.0	− 1.0	− 2.3	3.0	1.5
1960	0.5	9.1	13.8	2.7	1.5
1961	26.9	4.8	1.0	2.1	0.7
1962	− 8.7	8.0	6.9	2.7	1.2
1963	22.8	2.2	1.2	3.1	1.7
1964	16.5	4.8	3.5	3.5	1.2
1965	12.5	− 0.5	0.7	3.9	1.9
1966	− 10.1	0.2	3.7	4.8	3.4
1967	24.0	− 5.0	− 9.2	4.2	3.0
1968	11.1	2.6	− 0.3	5.2	4.7
1969	− 8.5	− 8.1	− 5.1	6.6	6.1

TABLE 2-1 *(concluded)*

Year	Common stocks	Long-term corporate bonds	Long-term government bonds	U.S. Treasury bills	Consumer price index
1970	4.0	18.4	12.1	6.5	5.5
1971	14.3	11.0	13.2	4.4	3.4
1972	19.0	7.3	5.7	3.8	3.4
1973	− 14.7	1.1	− 1.1	6.9	8.8
1974	− 26.5	− 3.1	4.4	8.0	12.2
1975	37.2	14.6	9.2	5.8	7.0
1976	23.8	18.7	16.8	5.1	4.8
1977	− 7.2	1.7	− 0.7	5.1	6.8
1978	6.6	− 0.1	− 1.2	7.2	9.0
1979	18.4	− 4.2	− 1.2	10.4	13.3
1980	32.4	− 2.6	− 4.0	11.2	12.4
1981	− 4.9	− 1.0	1.9	14.7	8.9
Geometric mean	9.1	3.6	3.0	3.0	3.0
Arithmetic mean	11.4	3.7	3.1	3.1	3.1
Standard deviation	21.9	5.6	5.7	3.1	5.1

Source: Ibbotson and Sinquefield, *Stocks, Bonds, Bills and Inflation*, p.17.

curities. Their basic series consists of annual rates of return for common stocks, corporate bonds, U.S. government bonds and U.S. government Treasury bills over the period 1926–81. The common stock series is based upon the Standard & Poor's (S&P) Composite Index of 500 of the largest stocks (in terms of stock market value) in the United States.[5] The weight of each stock in the index is proportionate to its market value. Dividends are included and assumed to be reinvested in the same stock when received. The corporate bond series is based upon the Salomon Brothers' High-Grade, Long-Term Corporate Bond Index.[6] The CRSP U.S. Government Bond File is the source for both the long-term U.S. government bonds and the short-term U.S. Treasury bill series. Inflation is incorporated into the analysis and is measured by the consumer price index (CPI).

The results of the Ibbotson-Sinquefield study are summarized in Table 2–1. The table presents returns by year as well as geometric means, arithmetic means, and standard deviations (a measure of dispersion or volatility) for each of the basic series. The striking result is that common stocks clearly earned higher rates of return than the other securities. During the entire 56-year period, the average annual rate of return compounded annually on common stocks was 9.1 percent compared with 3.6 percent for corporate bonds and 3 percent for both U.S. government bonds and Treasury bills.

Table 2–2 presents cumulative wealth indexes for each of the securities, and these can be interpreted as the terminal value at the end of each year of

TABLE 2-2   Year-end cumulative wealth indexes for different securities, 1925–1981

Year	Common stocks	Long-term corporate bonds	Long-term government bonds	U.S. Treasury bills	Consumer price index	Inflation adjusted			
						Common stocks	Long-term corporate bonds	Long-term government bonds	U.S. Treasury bills
1925	1.000	1.000	1.000	1.000	1.000	1.000	1.000	1.000	1.000
1926	1.116	1.074	1.078	1.033	0.985	1.133	1.090	1.094	1.048
1927	1.535	1.154	1.174	1.065	0.965	1.586	1.195	1.215	1.103
1928	2.204	1.186	1.175	1.099	0.955	2.301	1.240	1.228	1.149
1929	2.018	1.225	1.215	1.152	0.957	2.105	1.278	1.267	1.201
1930	1.516	1.323	1.272	1.179	0.899	1.682	1.467	1.410	1.308
1931	0.859	1.299	1.204	1.192	0.814	1.056	1.590	1.474	1.459
1932	0.789	1.439	1.407	1.204	0.730	1.083	1.960	1.916	1.640
1933	1.214	1.588	1.406	1.207	0.734	1.660	2.151	1.903	1.634
1934	1.197	1.808	1.547	1.209	0.749	1.603	2.399	2.051	1.604
1935	1.767	1.982	1.624	1.211	0.771	2.297	2.553	2.090	1.559
1936	2.367	2.116	1.746	1.213	0.780	3.040	2.693	2.220	1.543
1937	1.538	2.174	1.750	1.217	0.804	1.915	2.682	2.157	1.500
1938	2.016	2.307	1.847	1.217	0.782	2.581	2.927	2.340	1.542
1939	2.008	2.399	1.957	1.217	0.778	2.590	3.056	2.486	1.549
1940	1.812	2.480	2.076	1.217	0.786	2.313	3.130	2.612	1.535
1941	1.602	2.548	2.095	1.218	0.862	1.861	2.928	2.401	1.398
1942	1.927	2.614	2.162	1.221	0.942	2.050	2.747	2.267	1.282
1943	2.427	2.688	2.207	1.225	0.972	2.505	2.737	2.242	1.246
1944	2.906	2.815	2.270	1.229	0.993	2.939	2.808	2.257	1.224
1945	3.965	2.930	2.513	1.233	1.015	3.921	2.857	2.445	1.201
1946	3.645	2.980	2.511	1.238	1.199	3.023	2.446	2.055	1.014
1947	3.853	2.911	2.445	1.244	1.307	2.927	2.188	1.832	0.934
1948	4.065	3.031	2.528	1.254	1.343	3.005	2.216	1.843	0.916
1949	4.829	3.132	2.691	1.268	1.318	3.634	2.330	1.997	0.943
1950	6.360	3.198	2.692	1.283	1.395	4.529	2.249	1.888	0.901
1951	7.888	3.112	2.586	1.302	1.477	5.309	2.065	1.712	0.864
1952	9.336	3.221	2.616	1.324	1.490	6.230	2.119	1.717	0.870
1953	9.244	3.331	2.711	1.348	1.499	6.129	2.178	1.768	0.881
1954	14.108	3.511	2.906	1.360	1.492	9.400	2.306	1.904	0.893

Year								
1955	18.561	3.527	2.868	1.381	1.497	12.325	2.309	1.872	0.903
1956	19.778	3.287	2.708	1.415	1.540	12.772	2.091	1.718	0.900
1957	17.646	3.573	2.910	1.459	1.587	11.061	2.206	1.792	0.901
1958	25.298	3.494	2.733	1.482	1.615	15.591	2.120	1.653	0.899
1959	28.322	3.460	2.671	1.526	1.639	17.197	2.068	1.592	0.911
1960	28.455	3.774	3.039	1.566	1.663	17.025	2.223	1.785	0.922
1961	39.106	3.956	3.068	1.600	1.674	21.459	2.314	1.790	0.935
1962	32.955	4.270	3.280	1.643	1.695	19.343	2.468	1.890	0.949
1963	40.469	4.364	3.319	1.695	1.723	23.369	2.481	1.882	0.963
1964	47.139	4.572	3.436	1.754	1.743	23.906	2.569	1.925	0.985
1965	53.008	4.552	3.460	1.823	1.777	29.680	2.509	1.902	1.005
1966	47.674	4.560	3.586	1.910	1.836	25.813	2.432	1.907	1.018
1967	59.104	4.335	3.257	1.991	1.892	31.065	2.242	1.680	1.030
1968	65.642	4.446	3.248	2.094	1.981	32.949	2.196	1.600	1.035
1969	60.059	4.086	3.083	2.232	2.102	28.390	1.901	1.431	1.039
1970	62.465	4.837	3.457	2.378	2.218	27.978	2.133	1.521	1.049
1971	71.406	5.370	3.914	2.482	2.292	30.951	2.292	1.666	1.060
1972	84.956	5.760	4.136	2.577	2.371	35.621	2.377	1.703	1.064
1973	72.500	5.825	4.090	2.756	2.579	27.866	2.209	1.547	1.046
1974	53.311	5.647	4.268	2.976	2.894	18.174	1.906	1.438	1.006
1975	73.144	6.474	4.661	3.149	3.097	23.323	2.043	1.467	0.995
1976	90.584	7.681	5.441	3.309	3.246	27.569	2.313	1.635	0.997
1977	84.076	7.813	5.405	3.479	3.466	23.947	2.203	1.520	0.982
1978	89.592	7.807	5.432	3.728	3.778	23.399	2.018	1.377	0.965
1979	106.112	7.481	5.277	4.115	4.281	24.464	1.703	1.199	0.940
1980	140.513	7.285	5.069	4.578	4.812	28.835	1.473	1.023	0.930
1981	133.615	7.215	5.162	5.251	5.242	25.129	1.337	0.955	0.979

Source: Ibbotson and Sinquefield, *Stocks, Bonds, Bills and Inflation*, p. 19.

TABLE 2-3   Percentage variability of returns to different securities, 1926–1981
(annualized monthly standard deviations)

Year	Common stocks	Long-term corporate bonds	Long-term government bonds	U.S. Treasury bills	Consumer price index
1926	11.74	0.90	1.76	0.31	2.05
1927	13.22	1.39	2.66	0.11	2.83
1928	17.35	1.82	3.21	0.59	1.73
1929	31.02	2.35	6.52	0.20	1.62
1930	26.26	2.21	2.25	0.29	2.15
1931	43.94	6.00	5.49	0.16	1.48
1932	68.02	7.00	10.31	0.29	1.93
1933	56.07	10.65	5.11	0.10	4.21
1934	22.22	2.75	4.12	0.04	1.99
1935	16.33	2.32	2.76	0.01	2.12
1936	14.40	1.11	2.10	0.02	1.54
1937	23.36	1.94	5.02	0.05	1.69
1938	41.19	2.26	2.23	0.07	1.83
1939	29.51	5.16	8.11	0.02	2.27
1940	26.70	1.96	4.92	0.02	1.08
1941	14.30	1.63	3.67	0.03	2.11
1942	14.71	0.71	1.38	0.03	1.28
1943	15.62	0.88	0.64	0.01	2.29
1944	7.86	1.28	0.36	0.01	0.95
1945	13.13	1.37	2.70	0.01	1.29
1946	18.70	2.12	2.74	0.00	5.70
1947	9.59	2.18	2.93	0.07	3.09
1948	19.94	2.12	1.90	0.07	2.83
1949	10.19	2.10	1.72	0.02	1.66
1950	10.79	1.05	1.45	0.03	1.72
1951	12.23	4.02	3.14	0.05	1.70
1952	11.32	2.76	3.20	0.07	1.14
1953	9.35	5.35	4.99	0.10	1.00
1954	12.95	2.24	3.25	0.06	0.74
1955	12.41	2.16	3.64	0.13	0.67
1956	14.76	3.20	4.50	0.10	1.05
1957	12.62	8.66	7.71	0.07	0.65
1958	6.27	4.65	6.64	0.26	0.88
1959	8.00	3.94	3.31	0.17	0.64
1960	13.42	3.63	5.72	0.26	0.70
1961	8.92	3.47	3.51	0.07	0.51
1962	20.09	2.12	3.48	0.08	0.66
1963	9.81	1.23	0.71	0.08	0.54
1964	4.02	1.40	0.88	0.06	0.40
1965	8.54	1.96	1.50	0.08	0.65
1966	10.89	4.79	7.78	0.11	0.69
1967	12.11	7.65	7.16	0.15	0.43
1968	13.02	7.20	7.92	0.09	0.40

TABLE 2-3 *(concluded)*

Year	Common stocks	Long-term corporate bonds	Long-term government bonds	U.S. Treasury bills	Consumer price index
1969	12.98	7.46	10.36	0.20	0.59
1970	20.29	9.61	13.42	0.21	0.42
1971	13.67	10.04	9.47	0.18	0.55
1972	6.63	3.01	5.55	0.16	0.40
1973	13.87	7.46	8.19	0.34	1.42
1974	23.93	11.68	8.28	0.34	0.82
1975	17.89	10.07	8.38	0.20	0.73
1976	13.72	4.44	4.71	0.13	0.46
1977	9.55	4.50	5.54	0.18	0.73
1978	16.64	4.45	4.46	0.33	0.61
1979	12.80	10.31	10.43	0.25	0.45
1980	17.53	19.91	20.42	0.85	1.25
1981	12.34	19.85	21.21	0.43	1.02

Source: Ibbotson and Sinquefield, *Stocks, Bonds, Bills and Inflation*, p. 35.

a $1 investment initially made at the end of 1925. A $1 investment in common stocks in 1925 grew to $133.62 by the end of 1981. This is, of course, in nominal dollars; after adjusting for inflation the terminal wealth is only $25.13.

Variability in rates of return

Investors in common stock were the big winners over the entire 56-year period from 1925 through 1981, but it is apparent that the higher level of returns was associated with substantially higher variability. The standard deviation of common stock annual returns was 21.9 percent, and the annual returns ranged from 54 percent in 1933 to −43.3 percent in 1931. Indeed, returns to common stocks were negative in 19 of the 56 years.

The relatively large dispersion of common stock returns is evident in Table 2–3, which presents estimates of the year-by-year volatility of different securities. Each year's standard deviation is calculated separately by annualizing the standard deviation of the 12 monthly returns. Note that the common stock returns were more variable in the pre-World War II period than in the postwar period.

Both King[7] and Blume[8] gave the first extensive documentation of the postwar decrease in the variability of common stock returns. Blume reported that of 251 NYSE stocks listed continuously from 1926 through 1960, 247 had higher variances of monthly returns for the period prior to 1944 than from 1944 through 1960. Officer later questioned the notion of a simple prewar versus postwar dichotomy and showed that the result was due solely to the 1930s.[9] He incorporated the Dow Jones Industrial Average as a

FIGURE 2-1   The one-year standard deviation of the market factor, industrial production relatives, and money (M2) relatives 1919–68

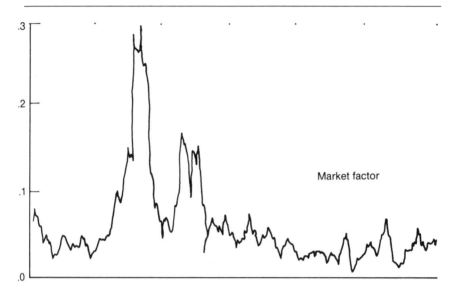

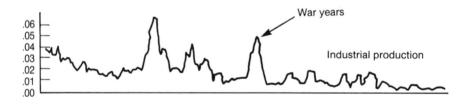

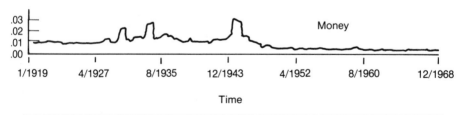

Time

Source: Officer, "The Variability of the Market Factor," p. 442.

market index of common stock returns for the period 1897 through 1925. He concluded that the variability of returns prior to 1929 was quite similar to the variability of returns after the 1940s, and that both of these periods greatly differed with the variability of returns in the 1930s. Officer's results are summarized in Figure 2–1, where the variability of common stock returns is compared to the variability of changes in industrial production. Both series show greatly increased volatility during the 1930s. Officer's results indicate that the decade of the 1930s was a period not only of low economic activity and stock prices but also of unusual volatility.

Another subject, which is discussed in subsequent chapters, is the effect of diversification on variability of stock returns. The standard deviation of common stock annual returns (Table 2–3) relates to the market portfolio as represented by the S&P 500. The variance of returns to individual stocks is much larger. This is evident in another Fisher and Lorie study.[10] Using data from 1926 through 1965, they found that there was about a 20 percent chance of losing 20 percent or more by investing in a stock for one year. With five-year holding periods, a stockholder lost at least 20 percent approximately 23 percent of the time and made at least 20 percent about half the time. For 10-year periods, a stockholder lost 20 percent or more of the investment less than one fifth of the time and made a profit of at least 20 percent about three fourths of the time.

Fisher and Lorie found that the market as a whole generally had 50–75 percent as much dispersion as one-stock portfolios. Conversely, one stock portfolios have roughly one and one third to two times as much dispersion as the market. Another interesting fact is how rapidly the possibility of reducing dispersion by diversifying is exhausted (see Table 2–4). That is, usually about 90 percent of all possible reductions in relative dispersion are achieved by the time the portfolio contains only 16 stocks.

Note, however, while much of the diversification risk can be eliminated in portfolios of relatively few stocks, some risk remains. Professional investment managers, wishing to achieve as much diversification as possible, spend considerable resources calculating the optimal combination of stocks for achieving the greatest diversification. Lorie has shown that the remaining diversifiable risk can be reduced by over one third using scientific techniques as opposed to a random selection of the same number of stocks.[11] Since professional managers are concerned that their well-diversified portfolios will perform significantly worse than the market, this reduction is important to them.

The market's trade-off of risk and return

The observed differences in both the levels and variability of the rates of return across securities are indicative of the underlying risk-return relation in the market. This is well-illustrated when Ibbotson and Sinquefield decompose the basic series to isolate both this risk-return trade-off and the

TABLE 2-4 Percent of possible reduction in relative dispersion achieved through increasing the number of stocks in the portfolio (based on portfolios of stocks from the NYSE for 1926–1965 or as specified.)

Measure of relative dispersion for holding period(s)	Number of stocks in portfolio						
	1	2	8	16	32	128	All (market)
Coefficient of variation							
40 one-year	0	43	84	92	96	99	100
20 one-year (1926–45)	0	43	84	92	96	99	100
20 one-year (1946–65)	0	43	84	92	96	99	100
8 five-year	0	42	83	91	96	99	100
4 10-year	0	38	79	89	94	99	100
2 20-year	0	40	81	90	95	99	100
Relative mean deviation							
40 one-year	0	42	84	91	95	98	100
20 one-year (1926–45)	0	45	87	94	96	99	100
20 one-year (1946–65)	0	39	80	89	94	99	100
8 five-year	0	37	79	89	95	99	100
4 10-year	0	35	79	90	96	100	100
2 20-year	0	43	91	99	100	100	100
Gini's coefficient of concentration							
40 one-year	0	41	81	90	94	98	100
20 one-year (1926–45)	0	39	79	87	93	98	100
20 one-year (1946–65)	0	40	81	89	94	98	100
8 five-year	0	36	76	85	91	97	100
4 10-year	0	28	65	76	84	93	100
2 20-year	0	29	66	76	83	92	100

Source: Fisher and Lorie, "Some Studies of Variability of Returns on Investments in Common Stocks," p. 116.

real-nominal properties of the securities. Their intuition is captured in Table 2–5, where different attributes of alternative securities, such as priority of payment, are used to define different risk elements. The differences in rates of return then reflect the premiums with which the market compensates those risks.

The evidence in Table 2–5 suggests that on the average U.S. government securities have been priced to compensate investors for expected inflation. Common stocks and corporate bonds have offered premiums for the risk of investing in the private sector and bearing the attached possibility of default.

RATES OF RETURN AND INFLATION

As shown in Table 2–1, the annual realized inflation rates measured by the consumer price index increased dramatically during the 1970s. These relatively high inflation rates introduced an additional element of uncertainty to investing. Since the ultimate goal of investing is increased consumption at some future date, investors are always concerned about the expected real rates of return on different assets. With inflation rates of 10 percent and more, investors focused on the inflation-hedging properties of different assets.

The most comprehensive study of the effects of inflation on security returns is by Fama and Schwert.[12] Beginning with the well-known hypothesis of Irving Fisher, Fama and Schwert predicted that all assets are priced so that the expected risk-adjusted nominal rate of return includes both a real return to the asset and the expected inflation rate. If the market prices assets in this fashion, all assets will be hedges against expected inflation. Fama and Schwert noted that some assets, however, can be better hedges against realized inflation than others. For example, consider an indexed bond whose price (and therefore nominal rate of return) is adjusted at the end of each period to compensate for that period's realized inflation. Such a bond offers a hedge against both the expected component of inflation, which is expected at the beginning of the period, and the unexpected component, which is the difference between the realized and expected inflation rates. On the other hand, a Treasury bill cannot be a perfect hedge against unexpected inflation, since its nominal return is set at the beginning of the period when unexpected inflation is zero.

Fama and Schwert find that government bonds, Treasury bills, and real estate compensate somewhat for unexpected inflation. The surprising result, however, is that common stock returns are negatively correlated with both expected and unexpected inflation. Rather than being compensated for inflation, investors in common stocks have been penalized.

This interesting result must be placed in perspective. It does not imply that common stocks have a negative expected real return; Table 2–5 shows that the real return to stocks over the 56 years 1925 through 1981 is 5.9 percent. As Fama and Schwert note, inflation is responsible for a small proportion of nominal stock returns, total variability.

The negative relation of common stock returns and inflation is, however, perplexing. Some clue as to why Fama feels that the Fisher hypothesis does not apply to stocks is provided in his later work.[13] He notes that stock price reflects the value of a corporation's underlying real assets. He then shows that the value of real assets is negatively affected by inflation and that the observed negative relation between inflation and stock returns mirrors the more fundamental relation between inflation and the value of real assets.

Not all economists agree with Fama's explanation, and several alternatives have been proposed. It has been argued that unanticipated inflation helps net debtors at the expense of net creditors, and firms that are net creditors are the only ones where equity returns are negatively related to unexpected inflation.[14] No empirical support for this explanation has been uncovered, however, and it is probable that most nonfinancial corporations are net debtors.[15] Summers has argued that firms reporting higher profits due to inflation and the use of historical cost accounting values are penalized by an extra tax burden.[16] Again, however, empirical support is lacking.

TABLE 2-5 Risk premiums and inflation adjusted returns to different securities, 1926–1981

Year	Equity and risk premiums on common stocks*	Default risk premiums on long-term corporate bonds†	Maturity risk premiums on long-term government bonds‡	Common stocks	Inflation long-term corporate bonds	Adjusted long-term government bonds	U.S. Treasury bills
1926	8.1	−0.4	4.4	13.3	9.0	9.4	4.8
1927	33.4	−1.4	5.6	40.1	9.6	11.1	5.2
1928	39.2	2.7	−3.1	45.1	3.8	1.0	4.2
1929	−12.6	−0.5	−1.3	−8.5	3.0	3.2	4.5
1930	−26.7	3.2	2.2	−20.1	14.8	11.3	8.9
1931	−44.0	3.6	−6.3	−37.3	8.4	4.6	11.6
1932	−9.1	−6.5	15.7	2.6	23.3	30.0	12.4
1933	53.6	10.7	−0.4	53.3	9.7	−0.7	−0.4
1934	−1.6	3.4	9.9	−3.4	11.5	7.8	−1.9
1935	47.4	4.4	4.8	43.3	6.4	1.9	−2.8
1936	33.7	−0.8	7.3	32.3	5.5	6.2	−1.0
1937	−35.2	2.3	−0.1	−37.0	−0.4	−2.9	−2.7
1938	31.2	0.6	5.6	34.8	9.1	8.5	2.8
1939	−0.4	−2.3	5.9	0.4	4.4	8.5	0.4
1940	−9.8	−2.7	6.1	−10.7	2.4	5.1	−1.0
1941	−11.6	1.7	0.9	−19.6	−6.4	−8.1	−8.9
1942	20.0	−0.6	2.9	10.1	−6.2	−5.6	−8.3
1943	25.5	0.7	1.7	22.2	−0.4	−1.1	−2.8
1944	19.4	1.9	2.5	17.3	2.6	0.7	−1.8
1945	36.0	−6.1	10.4	33.4	1.8	8.3	−1.9
1946	−8.4	1.8	−0.5	−22.9	−14.4	−16.0	−15.5
1947	5.2	0.2	−3.1	−3.2	−10.6	−10.8	−7.9
1948	4.7	0.7	2.6	2.7	1.3	0.6	−1.9
1949	17.5	−3.0	5.3	20.9	5.2	8.4	2.9
1950	30.2	2.0	−1.1	24.6	−3.5	−5.5	−4.4
1951	22.2	1.3	−5.4	17.2	−8.2	−9.3	−4.2
1952	16.5	2.3	−0.5	17.4	2.6	0.3	0.8
1953	−2.8	−0.3	1.8	−1.6	2.8	3.0	1.2
1954	51.4	−1.7	6.3	53.4	5.9	7.7	1.4

Year							
1955	29.6	1.7	-2.8	31.1	0.1	-1.7	1.2
1956	4.0	-1.4	-7.9	3.6	-9.4	-8.2	-0.4
1957	-13.5	1.1	4.2	-13.4	5.5	4.3	0.1
1958	41.3	3.9	-7.5	41.0	-3.9	-7.7	-0.2
1959	8.8	1.3	-5.1	10.3	-2.4	-3.7	-1.4
1960	-2.2	-4.3	10.9	-1.0	7.5	12.1	1.2
1961	24.3	3.7	-1.1	26.0	4.1	0.3	1.4
1962	-11.2	0.9	4.1	-9.9	6.7	5.6	1.5
1963	19.1	1.0	-1.9	20.8	0.5	-0.4	1.4
1964	12.5	1.2	-0.0	15.1	3.5	2.3	2.3
1965	8.2	-1.2	-3.1	10.3	-2.4	-1.2	2.0
1966	-14.2	-3.7	-1.1	-13.0	-3.1	0.3	1.4
1967	19.0	4.5	-12.9	20.4	-7.8	-11.9	1.1
1968	5.6	2.7	-5.2	6.1	2.1	-4.8	0.5
1969	-14.2	-3.6	-11.0	-13.8	-13.5	-10.6	0.5
1970	-2.4	4.9	5.3	-1.5	12.3	6.3	1.0
1971	9.5	-2.1	8.5	10.6	7.4	9.6	1.0
1972	14.6	1.3	1.8	15.1	3.7	2.2	0.4
1973	-20.3	2.2	-7.6	-21.8	-7.1	-9.1	-1.8
1974	-32.1	-7.0	-3.4	-34.8	-13.7	-7.1	-3.8
1975	29.8	5.1	3.2	28.3	7.2	2.1	-1.1
1976	17.9	1.6	11.2	18.2	13.2	11.4	0.3
1977	-11.8	2.3	-5.5	-13.1	-4.8	-7.0	-1.6
1978	-0.6	1.1	-7.8	-2.3	-8.4	-9.4	-1.7
1979	7.4	-3.0	-10.6	4.6	-15.6	-13.0	-2.6
1980	19.1	1.2	-13.7	17.9	-13.5	14.7	-1.1
1981	-17.3	-3.1	-11.3	-12.9	-9.2	-6.7	5.3
Geometric mean	5.9	0.5	0.0	5.9	0.5	0.0	0.0
Arithmetic mean	8.3	0.5	0.2				
Standard deviation	22.0	3.2	6.5				

*Equity risk premium = Common stock returns – Treasury bill returns
†Default risk premium = Long-term corporate bond returns – Long-term government bond
‡Maturity risk premium = Long-term government bond reteurns – Treasury bill returns
Source: Ibbotson and Sinquefield, Stocks, Bonds, Bills and Inflation, p. 30.

TABLE 2-6   Year-by-year returns to stock portfolios of different weighting schemes and different treatment of commissions and taxes

	1*	2†	3‡	4§	5‖	6¶
1926	1.4	10.4	0.3	0.8	0.8	0.8
1927	30.1	33.3	22.1	29.3	29.3	29.3
1928	46.7	39.2	39.7	45.7	45.7	45.7
1929	− 29.1	− 12.7	− 51.4	− 29.4	− 29.4	− 29.4
1930	− 37.5	− 28.0	− 38.1	− 38.0	− 38.0	− 38.0
1931	− 47.5	− 44.3	− 49.7	− 48.2	− 48.2	− 48.2
1932	− 7.9	− 7.6	− 5.4	− 9.8	− 9.8	− 9.9
1933	111.0	57.1	142.9	106.0	106.0	106.0
1934	17.0	3.7	24.2	15.3	15.3	15.2
1935	52.8	43.7	40.2	50.7	50.7	50.5
1936	48.4	32.6	64.8	46.8	46.8	46.3
1937	− 45.7	− 34.1	− 58.0	− 46.1	− 46.1	− 46.4
1938	32.3	27.1	32.8	30.7	30.7	30.3
1939	− 2.0	2.2	0.3	− 3.1	− 3.1	− 3.4
1940	− 8.9	− 7.6	− 5.2	− 9.9	− 10.1	− 10.6
1941	− 8.7	− 10.0	− 9.0	− 9.9	− 10.5	− 12.0
1942	33.0	16.5	44.5	30.8	29.7	27.3
1943	59.2	28.2	88.4	57.0	55.4	52.8
1944	40.1	21.3	33.7	39.0	37.4	35.0
1945	61.4	38.4	73.6	60.7	59.3	57.2
1946	− 9.3	− 6.2	− 11.6	− 9.5	− 10.4	− 11.7
1947	0.4	3.4	0.9	0.0	− 1.4	− 3.3
1948	− 2.1	2.0	− 2.1	− 3.1	− 4.2	− 5.8
1949	21.2	20.2	19.7	19.7	18.3	16.4
1950	37.6	30.6	38.7	35.9	34.3	32.1
1951	16.0	21.1	7.8	14.8	13.4	11.4
1952	10.1	13.4	3.0	8.9	7.6	5.5
1953	− 2.2	0.4	− 6.5	− 3.2	− 4.4	− 6.4
1954	57.2	50.8	60.6	55.2	53.8	51.4
1955	20.4	25.3	20.4	19.1	18.3	16.7
1956	7.7	8.9	4.3	6.6	5.8	4.2
1957	− 12.8	− 10.5	− 14.6	− 13.8	− 14.4	− 15.9
1958	60.1	44.2	64.9	58.1	57.1	54.9
1959	15.9	13.0	16.4	14.5	13.9	12.4
1960	− 0.8	0.6	− 3.3	− 1.9	− 2.6	− 3.8
1961	29.3	27.3	32.1	27.6	27.0	25.6
1962	− 12.4	− 9.2	− 11.9	− 13.4	− 14.0	− 15.0
1963	19.4	21.3	23.6	17.8	17.0	15.7
1964	18.0	16.1	23.5	16.5	15.8	14.7
1965	30.2	14.6	41.8	28.5	27.8	26.6
1966	− 7.1	− 8.8	− 7.0	− 8.2	− 8.8	− 9.8
1967	53.6	27.2	83.6	51.5	50.6	49.2
1968	30.0	13.6	36.0	28.5	27.5	26.5
1969	− 19.3	− 10.0	− 25.1	− 20.1	− 20.7	− 21.5
1970	− 3.1	1.8	− 17.4	− 4.4	− 5.2	− 6.4
1971	19.3	15.7	16.5	17.0	16.3	15.2
1972	8.7	18.1	4.4	6.7	6.0	5.1
1973	− 26.8	− 17.0	− 30.9	− 28.1	− 28.8	− 29.7
1974	− 25.2	− 27.0	− 19.9	− 27.2	− 28.2	− 29.4
1975	59.0	39.4	52.8	53.8	51.8	49.9
1976	44.0	26.0	57.4	40.1	38.5	36.9
Geometric mean	9.0	9.1	12.9	9.0	8.3	7.2

TABLE 2-6 (concluded)

	1*	2†	3‡	4§	5‖	6¶
Arithmetic mean	15.35	11.29				
Standard deviation	31.87	22.25				

*Year-by-year returns to an equal weighted portfolio of NYSE common stocks with dividends reinvested, no commissions, or taxes.
†Year-by-year returns to a value weighted portfolio of NYSE common stocks with dividends reinvested, no commissions or taxes.
‡Year-by-year returns to portfolio of small stocks (smallest quintile of NYSE stocks) with dividends reinvested, no commissions or taxes.
§Year-by-year returns to an equal weighted portfolio of NYSE stocks with dividends reinvested after commissions.
‖Year-by-year returns to an equal weighted portfolio of NYSE stocks with dividends reinvested after commissions and taxes (assumes low-tax-rate investor).
¶Year-by-year returns to an equal weighted portfolio fo NYSE stocks with dividends reinvested after commissions and taxes (assumes high-tax-rate investor).
Source: Fisher and Lorie, "Rates of Return on Investments in Common Stocks."

Another school of thought attributes the negative relationship between stock returns and the inflation rate to the effect of inflation on income generated by corporations. Inflation may increase the effective rate of the corporation, but it certainly increases the effective rate of personal income taxation on dividends and capital gains.

One widely publicized explanation is offered by Modigliani and Cohn, who believe that investors "are unable to free themselves from 'money illusion' and that as a result, (they) price equities in a way that fails to reflect their true economic value".[17] This view relies on irrational investor behavior, and it is inconsistent with the thrust of this book and modern finance in general. There is no sound economic basis for the argument based on the data—it is always possible to devise a theory to suit the facts and this does not constitute the testing of a theory. The Modigliani and Cohn conjecture remains just that. Moreover, it seems implausible that stock market investors are persistently foolish, while those in the bond market are not.

THE EFFECTS OF COMMISSIONS, TAXES, AND WEIGHTING STRATEGIES

The results of Ibbotson and Sinquefield provide an overall view of the investment performance of common stocks and other securities. It is interesting to contrast their results with those of Fisher and Lorie, whose analysis incorporates additional refinements. As well as using a broader index of common stocks, Fisher and Lorie specifically allow for the effects of brokerage commissions, taxes, and both equal weighted and value weighted portfolio strategies. Their results are summarized in Table 2-6.

Columns 1 and 2 of Table 2-6 present annual compounded rates of return for a portfolio of all NYSE common stocks from 1926 through 1976.

The equal weighted portfolio strategy of column 1 assumes equal investments annually in each listed stock and produces results similar to what would have been attained by selecting a large number of stocks for the portfolio by throwing darts at a newspaper page of stock quotations. Such an investment policy is possible for individual investors, but could not be carried out by all investors. The largest NYSE issues are worth a thousand times more than the smallest issue, and, therefore, the smallest issues would be completely taken up before an appreciable fraction of the largest issues had been absorbed. Note that this equal weighted strategy requires that the portfolio be rebalanced at the end of each period, since the prices of different securities will not have moved in tandem.

The alternative, value weighted strategy of column 2 requires an initial allocation of investment funds to each stock in proportion to its share of the total market value. The returns for each stock are the same for both portfolios, but they are weighted differently. Smaller valued stocks get a larger weight in the equal weighted portfolio than in the value weighted portfolio.

In Table 2–6, the geometric mean annual returns for both the equal weighted and value weighted portfolios are similar. Note that the arithmetic mean and standard deviation are quite different, suggesting a difference between the distributions of returns to small and large stocks. Column 3 of Table 2–6 presents annual compounded rates of return for a value weighted portfolio of the fifth, or smallest, quintile of NYSE stocks ranked by market value (that is, price times number of shares outstanding). The small-stock portfolio exhibits both higher mean return and higher standard deviation. Interestingly, the observed difference in the distribution of returns to small stocks prompted the marketing, in 1980, of an investment fund, made up of such small stocks, by Dimensional Fund Advisors of Chicago.

The remaining columns of Table 2–6 give returns adjusted for taxes paid on dividends and for brokerage commissions paid on the initial investment or on the reinvestment of cash dividends and proceeds of liquidations. In column 4, the results assume a tax-exempt investor, in column 5, the results assume a low tax rate investor, and in column 6, the results assume a higher-tax investor. Not surprisingly, the reported rates of return differ with these refinements.

There is an important message in Table 2–6: When estimating the profitability of alternative investment strategies, it is essential that the returns be measured consistently, net of all applicable costs. This is particularly well-illustrated in a study by Grier and Albin, who devised a trading-rule strategy that required buying stocks after a large block sale and selling them at closing that day.[18] They reported consistently large profits from their strategy over a number of years—even after allowing for average costs of 2 percent. Their study was later replicated by Dann, Mayers, and Raab, who incorporated the actual commissions and taxes that were incurred in following the strategy.[19] Not only did the large reported profits evaporate, they found that the strategy would clearly and quickly cause most investors to have large negative returns.

NOTES

1. W. Braddock Hickman, *Corporate Bond Quality and Investor Experience*, a study by the National Bureau of Economic Research (Princeton, N.J.: Princeton University Press, 1958); David Durand, *Basic Yields on Corporate Bonds, 1900–1942* (New York: National Bureau of Economic Research, 1942); David Durand and Willis J. Winn, *Basic Yield of Bonds, 1926–47: Their Measurement and Pattern* (New York: National Bureau of Economic Research, 1947); Frederick R. Macaulay, *The Movement of Interest Rates, Bond Yields and Stock Prices in the United States Since 1856* (New York: National Bureau of Economic Research, 1938).

2. Lawrence Fisher and James H. Lorie, "Rates of Return on Investments in Common Stocks," *Journal of Business* 37 (January 1964), pp. 1–24.

3. Roger G. Ibbotson and Rex A. Sinquefield, *Stocks, Bonds, Bills and Inflation: The Past and the Future* (Charlottesville, Va.: Financial Analysts Research Foundation, 1982).

4. For an excellent discussion of the relevent formulas, see Eugene L. Grant and William G. Ireson, *Principles of Engineering Economy*, 4th ed. (New York: Ronald Press, 1960), Chap. 6.

5. Standard & Poor's, *Trade and Security Statistics, Security Price Index Record* (Standard & Poor's Corporation, 1982).

6. Martin L. Liebowitz and Richard I. Johannseon, Jr., "Introducing the Salomon Brothers' Total Performance Index for the High-Grade Long-Term Corporate Bond Market," memorandum to portfolio managers, Salomon Brothers, November 1973.

7. B. F. King, "Market and industry Factors in Stock Price Behavior," *Journal of Business* 39 (January 1966), pp. 139–90.

8. M. E. Blume, "The Assessment of Portfolio Performance: An Application of Portfolio Theory," (Ph.D. diss. University of Chicago, 1968).

9. R. R. Officer, "The Variability of the Market Factor of the New York Stock Exchange," *Journal of Business* 46 (July 1973), pp. 434–53.

10. Lawrence and James H. Lorie, "Some Studies of Variability of Returns on Investments in Common Stocks," *Journal of Business* 43 (April 1970), pp. 99–134.

11. James H. Lorie, "Diversification Old and New," *Journal of Portfolio Management* 1 (Winter 1975), p. 25–28.

12. E. Fama and G. W. Schwert, "Asset Returns and Inflation," *Journal of Financial Economics* 5, (November 1977), pp. 114–46.

13. Eugene F. Fama, "Stock Returns, Real Activity, Inflation, and Money," *American Economic Review* 71, (September 1981), pp. 545–65.

14. Reuben A. Kessel, "Inflation Caused Wealth Redistributions: A Test of Hypothesis," *American Economic Review* 46, (March 1956), pp. 128–41.

15. Kenneth French, Richard Ruback, and G. William Schwert, "Effects of Nominal contracting on Stock Returns," *Journal of Political Economy* 91, (January 1983), pp. 70–96.

16. Lawrence H. Summers, "Inflation and the Valuation of Corporate Equities," National Bureau of Economic Research, Working Paper 824, 1981.

17. Franco Modigliani and Richard A. Cohn, "Inflation, Rational Valuation and the Market," *Financial Analysts Journal* (March–April 1979), pp. 3–23.

18. Robert Geske and Richard Roll, "The Fiscal and Monetary Linkage between Stock Returns and Inflation," *Journal of Finance* 38 (March 1983), pp. 1–33.

19. P. C. Grier and P. S. Albin, "Nonrandom Price Changes in Association with Trading in Large Blocks," *Journal of Business* 46 (July 1973), pp. 425–33.

20. L. Dann, D. Mayers and R. Raab, "Trading Rules, Large Blocks and the Speed of Adjustment," *The Journal of Financial Economics* 4 (January 1977), pp. 3–22.

3

Stock market indexes and
the market factor in stock
returns

INTRODUCTION

The investment industry generates a massive amount of information to
assist clients in their search for maximum, risk-adjusted returns. The potential investor has access to reams of analyses on firms, industries, and the
economy. Interestingly, the most popular piece of information is the daily
performance of market indexes, such as the Dow Jones Industrial Average,
which are regularly highlighted in news bulletins and newspapers.

The succinctness of these reports is deceptive, although the popularity of
stock indexes reflects their value as a single summary of complex economic
phenomena. As noted in Chapter 1, the stock market is a leading indicator
or barometer of the economy's health, and there is a demand for a summary
statistic to measure the market's current assessment of the economy. Also,
these indexes are used as benchmarks for judging the performance of investment portfolios.

The utility of stock market indexes relies upon a positive relationship between returns to different securities. If there were none, and different security returns were completely unrelated, aggregate measures of their performance would convey little information on returns to investors. Consider,
for example, the interpretation of an aggregate measure of the performance of football teams on any given Sunday when half do well and half do
poorly.

In fact, there is a positive relationship among stock returns, and stock prices tend to move in the same direction. This is not to say that on any given day every stock rises or every stock falls. Indeed, while events in the economy tend to leave a pervasive or general influence, there are other events that differentially affect stocks on any day. For example, there are congressional actions that only affect firms in one industry. Other events, such as oil discoveries and executive jet crashes, are often specific to only one firm.

Even if stocks tend to move in the same direction in response to macroeconomic events, there remains the question of whether some stocks tend to rise more or fall further than the market average. It is interesting to find out what proportion of the stock price variation is accounted for by market movements as a whole.

These questions interest both financial economists and investors. In fact, the cross-sectional dependency in stock price changes has been a crucial element in most empirical research during the past two decades that has, as we shall see in Chapter 4, substantially altered our understanding of the stock market. For example, in one of the classic empirical studies in modern finance, Fama et al.[1] investigated whether stock splits led to higher stock prices, as Wall Street folklore suggests. They noted that it is not sufficient to simply document the change in stock price around the time of a split. Suppose, for instance, that firms tend to split their stocks during market upswings. The unwary observer would erroneously infer that splits result in higher prices. On the contrary, even if the firms did not split, their stock prices would tend to rise with the market as a whole. An accurate assessment of the effect of stock splits requires that the researcher first account for price changes due to marketwide effects that are independent of the split, which will be discussed further in Chapter 4.

An equally cogent illustration of the importance of the market factor in stock returns, and one that is readily appreciable by investors, is the Kaplan and Weil study of the Value Line contest.[2] In the early 1970s, Value Line staged contests to attract investor attention. The contest on which Kaplan and Weil focused required contestants to select a portfolio of 25 stocks from the more than 1,400 stocks analyzed and ranked by Value Line. Contestant portfolios were ranked by the average percentage price increase of their 25 stocks for six months, beginning August 18, 1972. Value Line advertised that portfolios chosen from the stocks it ranked highest were expected to outperform those ranked lower. If that expectation was realized, Value Line hoped to attract more customers to its service.

Kaplan and Weil chose two portfolios. The first included all stocks that were estimated to have the greatest market volatility, that is, the stocks that rose and fell furthest with market upswings and downswings. The second portfolio included the 25 stocks with the lowest market volatility. They argued that if the market, as a whole, increased over the contest period, the first portfolio would record the largest gains and if the market fell, the second portfolio would record the smallest losses.

Over the contest period, the market (as represented by all the stocks ranked by Value Line) fell on the average of 6.65 percent. More than 89,000 entries were received, and the Kaplan and Weil low-volatility portfolio placed in the top 2–3 percent of all portfolios entered. Furthermore, the high-volatility portfolio placed in the lowest 1 percent of all entries. As we will see next, for portfolios of 25 stocks or more, most of the price change is due to marketwide factors.

THE MARKET MODEL

The tendency for stocks to move together is captured formally in the market model, which has played a central role in empirical finance and is widely used in applications of portfolio theory discussed in Chapter 8.[3]

Assuming we use monthly stock returns, the market model posits that the return in any month t to any stock j, R_{jt}, is linearly related to the return on the market portfolio in that month t, R_{mt}, where R_{mt} is the average return across all stocks,* and mathematically is described as:

$$R_{jt} = a_j + b_j R_{mt} + e_{jt}$$

The interpretation of the model is that the expected return to stock j in period t, given the expected return to the market is:

$$E(R_{jt}) = a_j + b_j E(R_{mt}).$$

The term $b_j E(R_{mt})$ captures the part of the total monthly return that is due to marketwide movements in stock prices. Any expected returns to stock j that are independent of the market are captured in a_j, and the model states that, *ex ante*, the best guess of the return to stock j in month t is $a_j + b_j E(R_{mt})$.

Like all models, however, it is neither a perfect nor a completely accurate representation. By chance alone, unexpected industry and firm-specific events will cause the actual return in any month t, R_{jt}, to be different from the expected return, and the difference is captured in the error term:

$$R_{jt} - E(R_{jt}) = e_{jt}.$$

There is no theory behind the market model. It is purely a statistical description of the association between returns on stocks and the market as a whole. As such, there is no formal definition of what a_j and b_j are, but it is possible to estimate these coefficients for any stock. This also allows us to provide some intuition for the model. Table 3–1 contains the monthly returns to Host International, Inc. and to the value weighted market portfo-

---

*The nuances of estimating the market return are discussed later in this chapter.

TABLE 3-1   Monthly percentage returns to Host International, Inc. and the
market, January 1975 through December 1979

Month	Host International	Market	Month	Host International	Market
January 1975	26.7	13.5	July 1977	– 4.2	– 1.5
February 1975	7.0	6.1	August 1977	2.2	– 1.4
March 1975	15.9	2.9	September 1977	3.1	0.1
April 1975	18.6	4.7	October 1977	6.4	– 3.9
May 1975	– 6.0	5.5	November 1977	11.0	4.2
June 1975	– 4.2	5.2	December 1977	– 1.0	0.5
July 1975	4.0	– 6.4	January 1978	– 2.7	– 5.7
August 1975	– 5.2	– 2.0	February 1978	10.4	– 1.2
September 1975	– 1.7	– 3.6	March 1978	10.2	3.2
October 1975	28.2	6.1	April 1978	15.6	8.3
November 1975	17.6	3.1	May 1978	5.4	1.9
December 1975	1.6	– 1.0	June 1978	1.2	– 1.3
January 1976	17.6	12.5	July 1978	22.3	5.7
February 1976	– 13.4	0.1	August 1978	3.1	3.8
March 1976	– 12.1	3.0	September 1978	– 13.6	– 0.6
April 1976	– 6.2	– 1.1	October 1978	– 28.8	– 10.2
May 1976	– 12.1	3.0	November 1978	19.0	3.1
June 1976	– 2.5	4.7	December 1978	– 2.1	1.6
July 1976	– 9.3	– 0.7	January 1979	– 7.8	4.7
August 1976	0.0	0.0	February 1979	– 10.1	– 2.9
September 1976	– 1.5	2.6	March 1979	11.4	6.2
October 1976	– 5.3	– 2.1	April 1979	– 5.5	0.7
November 1976	9.7	0.5	May 1979	– 6.6	– 1.5
December 1976	18.7	5.8	June 1979	19.6	4.5
January 1977	– 10.7	– 4.0	July 1979	3.7	1.5
February 1977	– 8.4	– 1.6	August 1979	7.9	6.3
March 1977	6.3	– 1.1	September 1979	– 3.2	– 0.0
April 1977	1.2	0.4	October 1979	– 10.4	– 6.9
May 1977	2.5	– 1.2	November 1979	– 12.4	6.0
June 1977	14.3	5.1	December 1979	– 4.2	2.3

Source: Center for Research in Securities Prices.

lio of all New York Stock Exchange stocks over the five years from January
1975 through December 1979. These pairs of returns are also plotted in Figure 3–1 together with the estimated market model (represented by the
straight line) for Host International estimated using that data. The estimated model is

$$R_{jt} = 0.11 + 1.63\,R_{mt}$$

Note that the interpretation of a_j and b_j is now easier: a_j is the intercept
on the vertical axis and represents the monthly return expected on Host International when the market return is zero; b_j is the slope coefficient of the
market-model line.

This slope coefficient, b_j, summarizes the sensitivity of R_{jt} to factors affecting the market. A value of b_j greater than 1 implies that the stock is
more volatile than the market and that its price moves proportionally up
or down farther than the market. A value of b_j less than 1 implies the stock

FIGURE 3-1   Market-model relationship of Host International, Inc., January
1975 through December 1979

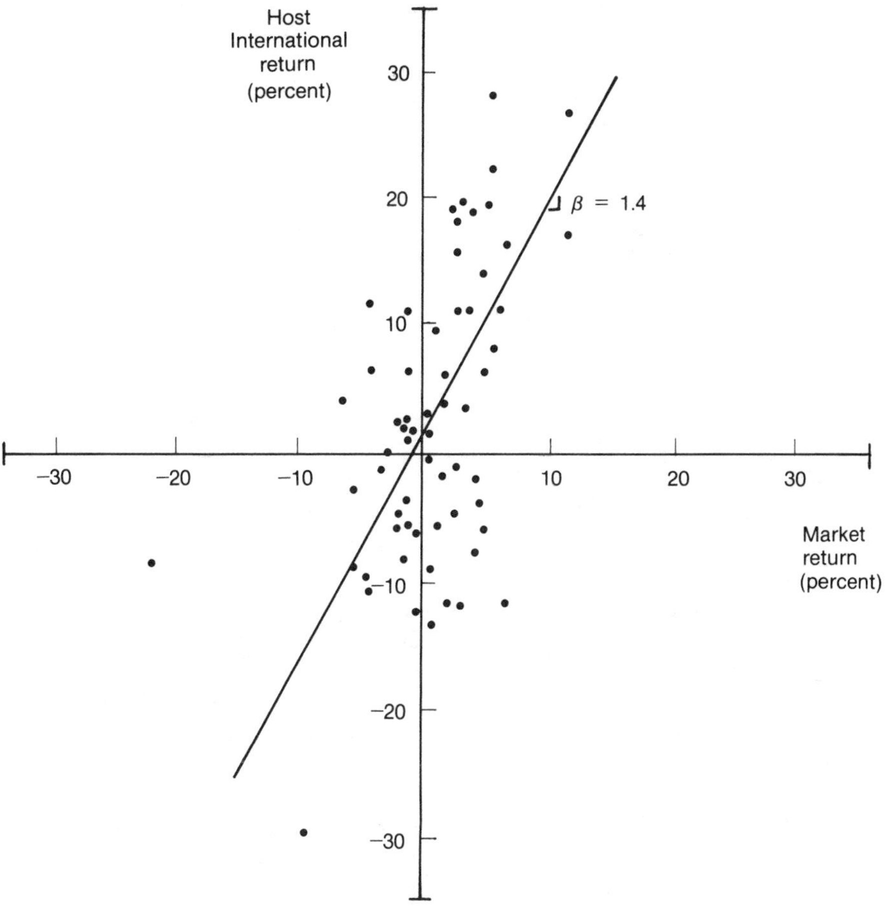

is less volatile than the market. Host International is a relatively volatile
stock.

The reasoning behind the model is made more obvious by noting that the
return on the market, R_{mt}, is assumed to capture the effects of economic
events and variables that commonly affect stocks in the market. Given this
interpretation, the return on stock j, R_{jt}, can be thought of as being a function of two factors: (1) part of the return, $b_j R_{mt}$, is presumed to be explained by marketwide events and variables, and (2) the other part of the
return, a_j and e_{jt}, is due to events and variables that are more specific to
stock j.

The part of a stock's variability of return that is due to marketwide factors in known as systematic risk. The notion is one of returns varying predictably or regularly with general moves of the market. The remaining variability of the stock return is its unsystematic risk. This variance is idiosyncratic and peculiar to the stock in question and is not predictable. The slope coefficient in the market model equation b_j can now be interpreted as an index of the systematic risk of stock j. This concept is central to modern portfolio theory, which is discussed in Chapter 8, and it is usual to refer to the slope coefficient in the market-model relationship as the beta (β) coefficient of the stock. Estimated beta (β) coefficients for most stocks are available commercially, and we will discuss some nuances of the estimations and uses of Beta in Chapters 8 and 9.

Although the market model applies to all stocks, the importance of the market factor in explaining the returns on particular stocks varies. As shown in Figure 3–1, there is an apparent association between the returns on Host International stock and the market (the data points tend to follow the line), and this is captured precisely by the market model. There is, however, substantial dispersion of the data points around the line. This dispersion indicates that the market model relation explains only some of the variation in R_{jt}. If each of the points lay on the line, it would mean that all variation in the 60 observations of R_{jt} is explained by the market factor $b_j R_{mt}$.

In statistical terms, the proportion of R_{jt} variation that is explained by the market factor is measured by the coefficient of determination or r^2. For Host International, the r^2 is 0.37, indicating that 37 percent of the total variation of returns over the five-year period is explained by market movements. The unexplained portion is captured in the error term e_{jt}, and by definition, these changes in R_{jt} are due to events that do not affect all stocks in the market.

Table 3–2 presents market-model summary statistics estimated over five years, ending December 1979, for 30 NYSE stocks selected at random. Note that the beta coefficients vary from 0.51 to 2.52, with an average of 1.3. The coefficients of determination vary from a low of 0.10 to 0.68, with an average of 0.36. the fact that more than half of the total variation in stock returns is unexplained by the market model should not be alarming. There is no absolute standard of acceptability for r^2, and the only test of the market model is how well it explains security returns relative to other models. To paraphrase George Stigler, it takes a model to beat a model. The evidence is that the market factor explains, on the average, over one third of the variation in stock returns, and for this reason, it has been widely used in financial economic research.

As well as being a useful tool for isolating firm-specific stock returns and abstracting from marketwide factors, the market model explains why stock market indexes are useful benchmarks for investment performance. The model explains, on the average, only about one third of the variation in re-

TABLE 3-2   Market-model statistics for 30 random stocks, 1975 through 1979

Firm	Slope coefficient (beta)	Coefficient of determination (r^2)
Allied Prods. Corp. Del.	0.64	0.11
American Nat. Res. Co.	0.66	0.32
Bankers Tr. N. Y. Corp.	1.11	0.46
Bard C. R. Inc.	1.78	0.56
Brunswick Corp.	1.52	0.41
Culbro Corp.	0.98	0.25
Damon Corp.	1.22	0.25
Dayco Corp.	1.09	0.29
Detroit Edison Co.	0.98	0.30
Donnelley, R. R. & Sons, Co.	1.09	0.48
Gateway Inds. Inc. Del.	1.88	0.19
Gray Drug Stores Inc.	1.24	0.31
H. M. W. Inds. Inc.	1.71	0.26
Harnishchfeger Corp.	1.63	0.15
High Voltage Engr. Corp.	2.40	0.47
Host Int'l. Inc.	1.62	0.39
Lear Seigler Inc.	2.15	0.66
Maryland Cup Corp.	1.17	0.31
Masco Corp.	1.82	0.68
Mays, J. W., Inc.	1.38	0.22
Mid-Continent Tel. Corp.	0.80	0.41
Middle South Utils. Inc.	0.63	0.28
Murphy, G. C. & Co.	1.17	0.31
National Semiconductor Corp.	2.52	0.45
Norfolk & Westn. Ry. Co.	1.00	0.43
Pacific Ltg. Corp.	0.51	0.22
Perkin, Elmer, Corp.	1.86	0.52
Popomac Elec. Pwr. Co.	0.71	0.30
Puget Sound Pwr. & Lt. Co.	0.79	0.42
Reeves Bros. Inc.	0.97	0.32
Average	1.30	0.36

turns on individual securities, but the importance of the market factor increases dramatically for portfolios of more than one security.

Table 3–3 presents summary market-model statistics for portfolios of increasing numbers of randomly selected stocks. Of course, if an investor held the market portfolio in total, the total variation of portfolio return would be due to the market and the r^2 would be 1. The marginal explanatory power of the model increases at a decreasing rate. It is perhaps surprising that for portfolios of as few as 15 stocks, the importance of the market factor is great, accounting for about 75 percent of the portfolio variance.

For investors with portfolios of as few as 15 stocks, the market return, as represented by some index, is a reasonable benchmark of performance. If, however, the investor's portfolio has a beta coefficient, (i.e. volatility measure) greater than 1, the returns on that portfolio can be expected to vary more than the market.

TABLE 3-3 Market-model statistics for randomly selected portfolios of increasing size

Number of firms	Beta	r^2
1	0.7615	.3001
2	1.0472	.3065
5	0.9994	.5518
10	1.1038	.6709
15	1.0468	.7685
20	1.0785	.7704
25	1.1709	.7395
30	1.1334	.7372
40	1.1330	.7552

Source: Center for Research in Security Prices.

The beta coefficient is central to modern investment theory and practice. As Kaplan and Weil have shown, investors who select portfolios with low betas will suffer less in a falling market and correspondingly do not do as well as the market when it rises. Those who are prepared to risk greater value declines in order to have a chance to earn higher expected returns will select relatively high beta portfolios. It is worth noting here that the market model does not offer a surefire way to investment success. The model gives us a best guess of the expected return to a stock or portfolio *conditional* on knowing the actual return to the market as a whole. Though some may argue that it is easier to accurately forecast marketwide returns than returns to individual securities, we argue *ad nauseam*, throughout this book, there is little evidence that either can be done consistently.

Earlier, we suggested that apart from marketwide factors, returns to individual stocks will be influenced by industrywide events. This statement is supported in a 1966 study by King, who used multivariate statistical tools to estimate the proportion of total stock return variability that is related to marketwide movements and the proportion that is due to industrywide factors.[4] Using data from 1927 to 1966, he found that slightly over 50 percent of stock's variability is explained by marketwide factors, and about 10 to 15 percent more variability is explained by events common to the industry. *

The slight marginal benefit from incorporating industry factors, together with the important problem of identifying the relevant industry for many large, diversified firms, has resulted in relatively few applications of the market-industry model. We will further investigate the volatility measure in Chapters 8 and 9, but the current message is that the market return is a surprisingly good performance benchmark for stock portfolios, even portfolios with only a few stocks. As yet, however, we have not explicitly

---

*Note that King used data from an earlier period and found that the market factor accounts for a greater proportion of stock return variability than was found in our later sample (Table 3-2). Fama has noted that there is a decline in the average r^2 of the market model since World War II.[5] Interestingly, both the return variance on the market portfolio and on individual stocks have declined. No satisfactory explanation for these results has been discovered.

discussed how the market return is measured. In practice, many measures of the market's performance are reported, and we will now consider the advantages and disadvantages of these indexes.

STOCK MARKET INDEXES

Some problems

We do not present a detailed, technical discussion on indexes in general, since such discussions are availabale in numerous statistics books.[6] Nevertheless, we shall discuss three important issues which arise in constructing indexes: selecting stocks for inclusion, determining the relative importance or wieght of each included stock, and combining or averaging included stocks. In briefer terms, these are the problems of sampling, weighting, and averaging.

Sampling

An index can be based on all stocks or just a sample of them. Movements in the New York Stock Exchange could be represented by movements of, say 100 stocks or by movements in the entire list. When indexes were first constructed, the burden of data processing made it impractical to include more than a few stocks. For example, when the Dow Jones Industrial Average was first published in 1884, only 11 stocks were included. Modern computers make it relatively easy to include a large number of stocks. As a result, newer indexes—such as those of the New York Stock Exchange and the American Stock Exchange—are based on all stocks listed on those exchanges.

Since there are indexes of the two major exchanges, which include all stocks, it may seem unnecessary to discuss the sampling problem. Such discussion, however, is helpful, since two important market measures, Standard & Poor's indexes and the Dow Jones Averages, are based on samples. The usefulness of indexes based on samples is influenced by the degree to which one can confidently infer movements in excluded stocks based on the movements in included stocks. For stocks on both the New York Stock Exchange and the American Stock Exchange, such inferences can be made with great confidence from both Standard & Poor's indexes and the Dow Jones Averages.

The adequacy of indexes calculated from samples is based on two things: (1) the fact that stocks of relatively few companies constitute a large proportion of the total stock value of all companies, and (2) the tendency of all stocks to move together.

For some purposes, the substantial concentration of value in relatively few companies contributes to the power of small samples. If each company is considered equally important, this concentration is of no help. If, however, large companies are considered more important than small companies, such as when one is interested in changes in the market value of all stocks, the value concentration is very helpful. (The extent of this concentration was discussed in Chapter 1.)

Earlier, we noted that between one third and one half of the variation in individual stock prices is explained by movements in the market. Obviously, if all stocks moved together in prefect lockstep, a single stock would represent the market with perfect fidelity. Although the degree of similar movement is not that high, it is still sufficient to help make relatively small samples valuable as indicators of general market movements.

If one tries to pick portfolios which are not representative, the degree of conformity will be much less. This is true of some mutual funds that are specialized by industry. Thus, the Explorer Fund of the Vanguard Group, which invests only in high-technology stocks, should not be expected to be representative of stocks in general. But, unless there is a deliberate attempt at specialization, almost any reasonably sized stock sample will well represent movements in all stocks. The best example is the Dow Jones Industrial Average.

When the purpose of the index is to represent changes in the value of all stocks, small samples can be used with great confidence. For example, in 1980, the stocks included in the Standard & Poor's 500 Stock Average constituted about 70 percent of the value of all stocks listed on the New York Stock Exchange. Even the widely quoted Dow Jones Industrial Average, which is based on only 30 stocks, included stocks with a value equal to about 23 percent of all stocks listed in September 1982.

Weighting

The prices of all stocks included in an index must be combined in order to determine the index's value. Therefore, each time the index is computed, it is necessary to determine the relative importance of each included stock.

Even if the persons computing the index do not recognize the weighting problem, they deal with it. For example, the Dow Jones Averages are constructed to give each included stock a weight proportional to its price. No one has ever devised a rational justification for this, except simplicity. Yet, the Dow Jones Averages are widely used and are valuable indicators of general market movements.

The reason for weighting is to ensure that the index reflects the relative importance of each stock in a way suited to the index's purpose. The two most common ways of weighting stocks are in accordance with market value or by assigning equal weights to equal relative price changes. The former method is appropriate for indicating changes in the aggregate market value of stocks in the index, while the latter is more appropriate for indicating movements in the prices of typical or average stocks. Changes in general market value are more important for studies of relationships between stock prices and other things in the national economy. Value weighted indexes

TABLE 3-4	Hypothetical average adjusted for stock split			
	Before split		After split	
Stock	No. shares	Price per share	No. shares	Price per share
A	10	$20	20	$10
B	10	10	10	10
C	10	6	10	6
Total	30	36	40	26
Divisor		3		2.1667
Average		12		12

*The divisor for the average after stock A splits is reduced from 3 to 2.1667 in order to preserve the value of the index.

also have the desirable property of "macroconsistency." That is, all investors are able to hold portfolios in which the individual stocks have a relative importance equal to the relative values of all outstanding shares.

On the other hand, indexes based upon equal weighting* are better indicators of the expected change in randomly selected stock prices. For some purposes, such an index is a more appropriate benchmark than a value weighted index.

An understanding of the major implications of the two most common weightings can be achieved by realizing that value weighted indexes attach a great deal of importance to large companies with stocks that may behave differently from the stocks of small companies. The main expected difference is greater volatility in fortunes and stock prices of small companies and the greater tendency for the price of large, diversified companies to be moved by general trends in the economy.

Although the stocks in the Dow Jones Averages are not value weighted, the selection produces almost the same results. That is, the stocks included are from very large companies. As a consequence, movements in the Dow Jones Averages are similar with respect to volatility and trend to indexes based on value weighting.

Another property of value weighting is the automatic adjustment for stock splits. If there is no change in aggregate market value of outstanding shares of the stock that is split, its relative importance remains the same, and the index is not affected. Indexes which are not weighted by market value have no such automatic adjustment. If the adjustment method changes the relative importance of the split stock, it may impart a bias to the index. When one of the stocks in the Dow Jones Average is split, adjustment is made by changing the divisor used in the calculation of the average value. The adjustment process is illustrated in Table 3–4.

---

*By equal weighting, we mean an index based on the assumption that equal dollar amounts are invested in each stock. We do not mean the process used in constructing the Dow Jones Averages in which the prices of included stocks are added up and divided by the number of stocks (adjusted for stock splits).

Although an adjustment is necessary to avoid the absurdity of causing a change in the value of the average in response to stock splits, the adjustment process and the method or weighting can produce a bias. Since stocks in the Dow Jones Averages are weighted according to their market price, the adjustment for a stock split reduces the relative importance of that stock. If stocks that split behave differently from other stocks, the Dow Jones Averages will be biased. There is some evidence that stocks which split are the stocks of companies that have been doing particularly well.[7] If such stocks continue to do well, the weighting and adjustment process for the Dow Jones Averages would produce a downward bias.

Methods of averaging

Given a group of common stock prices, either weighted or unweighted, one has to combine them into a single number to create a descriptive measure. Although statistics books list and discuss several averages or measures of central tendency, and although historically many different stockmarket index averages have been used, currently, only two kinds of averages are used in constructing the major U.S. stock market indexes. These are the arithmetic mean and the geometric mean.* All the widely used indexes, such as the New York Stock Exchange Indexes, the Standard & Poor's indexes, the Dow Jones Averages, and the American Stock Exchange Index are based on arithmetic means of prices or price changes. The only index based on a geometric mean is that of Value Line.

Before exploring averaging methods, it is worth noting that indexes, although typically based on averages, are not quite the same as averages. The difference is that an index is constructed by assigning some arbitrary, usually rounded number to the index value at subsequent (or previous) points in time. For example, many federal economic statistics are indexes which were arbitrarily assigned a value of 100 for the base period of 1967. The comsumer price index has a value of 258.4 in December 1983, which means that the index was 158.4 percent greater then than in the base period, 1967. The value of the Standard & Poor's 500 Stock Index in December 1980 was 100.97, and in the base period of 1941–43, the index value was 10. An average, on the other hand, does not involve selecting an arbitrary base-period value; it is simply an average. The Dow Jones Averages are not indexes, instead, they are simply the arithmetic means of stock prices included at each point in time and adjusted for stock splits. Table 3–5 illustrates the difference.

For some purposes, it is important to understand the differences which result from different averaging methods. The above example used an arith-

---

*Strictly speaking, an approximation of the geometric mean must be used, since it is computed by multiplication rather than addition. If the price of a stock falls to zero, the index would be zero.

TABLE 3-5

Stock	Base period price	Current period price
X	$100	$125
Y	50	75
Z	30	15
Average	60	71.67
Index	100	119.45

Note: The average of the stock prices was $60 in the base period. In the current period, the average is $71.67, or about 19 percent above the base average. The index is therefore 119.45. One additional point is worth noting. The index in the example refers to an unweighted arithmetic average of prices so the $25 or 25 percent increase in the price of stock X has the same effect on the index as the $25 or 50 percent increase in the price of Y.

metic average. If there is any variation through time in index prices, there will be a difference between the value of an arithmetic mean and a geometric mean of the prices. An index based on the geometric mean will increase more slowly and decrease more rapidly than an index based on the arithmetic mean. The degree of divergence increases with the degree of variability in the component prices. This is illustrated by an example of indexes based on three stocks which rise for two successive periods and then decline for two successive periods, as illustrated in Table 3–6.

Table 3–6 illustrates the differences between movements of arithmetic and geometric indexes when stock prices rise and fall and the methods of computing arithmetic and geometric means. The arithmetic mean is the sum of the individual prices divided by the number of prices; the geometric mean is the nth root of the product of the n prices.

Some people claim that the arithmetic mean has an upward bias, and others claim that the geometric mean has a downward bias. For example, if a $10 stock moves to $20, and a $20 stock falls to $10, the arithmetic average of the relative changes is 25 percent. If each stock returns to its original price, the arithmetic average of the relative change is still 25 percent. How-

TABLE 3-6 Indexes based on arithmetic and geometric averages of stock prices

			Period		
Stock	Base	1	2	3	4
X	$ 10	$ 12	$ 15	$ 10	$ 6
Y	10	15	20	15	2
Z	10	21	31	8	4
Average					
Arithmetic	10	16	22	11	4
Geometric	10	15.6	21	10.6	3.6
Index					
Arithmetic	100	160	220	110	40
Geometric	100	156	210	106	36

ever, the total value of the stocks is unchanged. The geometric mean adjusts for this, and the average return is zero. A corollary of this property of arithmetic averages is that over long periods of time, an arithmetic index outperforms most of the components. This is partially due, however, to the economic characteristics of stock prices. Since there is a lower, but no upper limit to price changes, their distribution will not be symmetric.* It is interesting to consider the magnitude of index differences that can be caused by the method of averaging. It has been estimated that a geometric average of Dow Jones stocks would have 2.4 percentage points less gain per year than the arithmetic average, whereas an arithmetic index of Value Line stocks would have increased on the average of 3 percentage points more per year than the geometric index. Similarly, Standard & Poor's 425 Industrial Average was about 17 in June 1950 and about 90 in July 1966. If a geometric average had been used, the index would have been only about 60 in July 1966.[8]

An interesting solution to the problem is the one used by Fisher.[9] For the period 1926–60, he computed both an arithmetic and geometric index of equally weighted relative price changes. When compared to the Fisher-Lorie rates of return (discussed in Chapter 2), he found the arithmetic index had an upward bias, and the geometric index had a downward bias with a greater magnitude. He therefore computed a combined index with weights of 0.56 and 0.44 for the arithmetic and geometric indexes, respectively.

THE MAJOR INDEXES

There is a variety of stock price indexes currently available. They differ both in construction and in purpose. We will limit our discussion to six of the most widely known indexes. We will also comment briefly on investment-performance indexes, which are a better measure of total returns.

The Dow Jones Industrial Average

The Dow Jones Industrial Average (DJI) is probably the most familiar of stock price measures and the measure most widely quoted by professional investors and taxicab drivers. At the same time, it is often the most misunderstood. Essentially, this measure is an arithmetic average of the prices of 30 industrial stocks, and a particular stock's influence on the change in the average is proportional to its price. For example, an increase of 10 percent in the price of a $100 stock has twice the effect of a 10 percent increase in a $50 stock. The average has changed both in composition and in computation since its 1884 appearance in a daily letter issued by Dow Jones & Com-

---

*More specifically, the distribution of price changes is positively skewed so that the median value falls below the mean value.

pany, Inc. At the time, it included 11 stocks. A 12th stock was soon added. In 1916, the sample was enlarged to 20 stocks, and in 1928, to 30 stocks. Occasionally, there have been substitutions in the stocks included to improve the representativeness of the average.

Originally, the average was computed by summing the prices of component stocks and dividing by the number of included stocks. Adjustments for stock splits or dividends of 10 percent or more were made by multiplying the new price of the affected stock by an appropriate factor.* For example, if a stock split two for one, the new price was multiplied by two in order to compute the average. In 1928, this procedure was changed. Since then, instead of summing the prices (some with multipliers) and dividing by the number of stocks, the price totals (with no multipliers) have been divided by a number adjusted so that the average is unaffected on the transition date. Each new stock split or dividend reduces the divisor so that by July 1984, the divisor was approximately 1.16. With this procedure, there is no exact equivalence between points in the average and dollars and cents. A $1 change for each stock in the index would cause the average to change by about 20 points.

A more important feature of the adjustment, however, is that the change in the divisor reduces the importance of the split stock relative to other stocks. The possibility of bias resulting from this computation was mentioned in the preceding section. The actual DJI stood at 192.91 at the end of 1945 and 969.26 at the end of 1965. If a constant divisor had been used throughout this period, with adjustments made in the original computation, the average would have been 1086.59 at the end of 1965.[10]

Despite the popularity of the Dow Jones Industrial Average, criticisms are abundant. A frequent, but superficial, objection is that it is widely misconstrued a being the actual stock price average. More fundamental criticisms are aimed at the representative sample and the computation method. The 30 stocks are of large, well-established companies. In 1982, they constituted about 23 percent of the market value of all New York Stock Exchange stocks. It has been argued that these so-called blue chips are not representative of an average portfolio and are therefore poor measures of market performance.

The major criticisms of the methodology focus on the whimsical system of implicit price weights, the possibility of bias resulting from the adjustments, and the failure to adjust for small stock dividends. The latter is usually added to the reported cash dividend total. For example, in 1964, the value of small stock dividends for which no adjustment was made constituted 19 percent of total dividends reported.[11]

Some (DJI) proponents who accept the sample have suggested changing the computational procedure by introducing explicit market value or equal weights. Some also argue for replacing the arithmetic mean with a geomet-

---

*Stock dividends of less than 10 percent were ignored.

ric mean. One proponent has actually recomputed the DJI using market-value weights and arithmetic and geometric means with equal weights. If the value of each of these variants was 192.91 at the end of 1945 (the actual value of the DJI), by the end of 1965, they would have the folowing values in comparison with the actual DJI of 969.26:[12]

Market value weights	1026.84
Equal weights—arithmetic average	1096.92
Equal weights—geometric average	813.40

The relationship between the 1965 value of the various averages is what one would expect with different computation methods. Over the 20-year period, the performance is quite similar, but for short periods, there can be considerable diversity in changes of the averages.

The Standard & Poor's 500 Composite

The Standard & Poor's 500 Composite includes 400 industrials, 40 utilities, 20 transportation and 40 financial. In contrast to the Dow Jones Averages, the relative importance of the component stock prices is determined by the value of shares outstanding. The index is officially described as a "base-weighted aggregative," but in fact, the weights are adjusted for stock dividends, new issues, and so forth. The aggregate market value of the stocks in the index is expressed as a percentage of the average market value in the period 1941–1943. This percentage is divided by 10, which was selected as the index value in the base period. This was done to put the index in line with the actual average of stock prices. *

The present daily price index was first published in 1957, although other less-comprehensive indexes were published before that. It has been extended back to 1928 on a daily basis. In coverage, it is considerably broader than the DJI. In 1982, the aggregate market value of the 500 stocks was almost 80 percent of all stocks on the New York Stock Exchange. The importance of individual stocks in the indexes can be very different. For example, the implicit weight of AT&T in the Dow Jones Industrial Average was 2.8 percent in 1965. Standard & Poor's 500 gave its market-value weight as 7.5 percent. If the Dow Jones Industrial Average used market-value weights, AT&T's weight would have been 18.6 percent.

A composite index, such as Standard & Poor's, has several advantages. The coverage is broad, and the weighting is explicit. Moreover, no adjustment for splits is necessary. Critics have argued that the index is dominated by large companies and that the value weights can create an upward bias.

---

*When the present index was first published in 1957, its value was 47; the average price of all shares on the New York Stock Exchange was $45.23.

These criticisms are much less universal than those criticisms aimed at the Dow Jones Industrial Average.

The New York Stock Exchange Composite

In 1965, the New York Stock Exchange inaugurated its own composite index covering all common stocks listed on the exchange. It is similar to the Standard & Poor's indexes in that it is an index of market value or, alternatively, a value weighted price index. It is intended to measure changes in the average stock price that result from market action alone. The aggregate market value is related to the value in the base period, December 31, 1965. On that date, the index was set at 50; the actual stock price average was $53.33.

No adjustment for splits is needed, but the base is adjusted to account for any changes in capitalization and new listings or delistings. The adjustment is such that the relationship between the adjusted base value and the current market value after the change is the same as that between the current market value before the change and the prior base value. Thus, the index is unaffected by factors other than price changes in the market. The index of daily closing prices has been extended back to May 28, 1964.

The American Stock Exchange Price Level Index

The American Stock Exchange also developed its first index in 1966. This was an unweighted index of price *movements* of all its traded stocks and warrants, derived by adding or subtracting the average net price change each day to the previous index value. It differed substantially from the usual stock market measures. Since only net changes were considered, the relationship of the net change to a stock's price was not considered. In this sense, it could be compared with the Dow Jones Averages.

The use of net price changes has several interesting features. It avoids the problem of splits in that the only time the index is affected is on the day after the split. In practice, the previous day's closing index is adjusted when stock splits, stock dividends, or cash dividends occur. When new listings appear, the divisor used to obtain the average net change is increased correspondingly.

The base price of the initial American Stock Exchange index was $16.88, the average price on April 29, 1966. Since values for other periods are calculated by adding or subtracting net price changes, this index was more appropriately called an average. It was available back to October 1, 1962.

The ASE index was changed in 1973 to a value-weighted index of prices. The index is identical in concept to the NYSE index.

FIGURE 3-2 The old American Stock Exchange Index and an index based on an average of actual prices, 1966–72

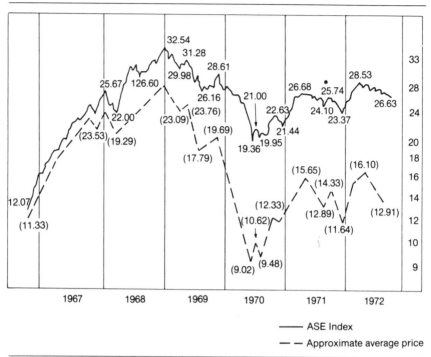

—— ASE Index

— — Approximate average price

Source: *Barron's*, September 18, 1972, p. 9.

The Value Line 1,400 Composite Average

The Value Line Composite Average, which first appeared in 1963, consists of 1,400 stocks in 60 industries. It is the only widely used index based on a geometric average of relative price changes of the component stocks. Although labeled an average, it is actually an index with a value of 100 on June 30, 1961. The adjustment for stock splits or dividends is made by adjusting the stock's closing price on the previous day to compute the relative change.

The Wilshire 5,000

The Wilshire 5,000 is a value weighted index of 5,000 stocks, including all issues on the New York Stock Exchange and the American Stock Exchange as well as stocks in the over-the-counter market on the NASDAQ system. In terms of the stocks covered, it is the broadest index available and is computed weekly.

NASDAQ Composite Index

The NASDAQ Composite Index is a value weighted index of more than 2,000 over-the-counter stocks. It has been available since 1971 and is reported daily. Being value weighted, and because of the large number of smaller stocks, the index is heavily influenced by the largest 100 or so stocks.

Investment-performance indexes

An investment-performance index is essentially an index of rates of return. It differs from a price index in that it accounts for cash dividends. Alfred Cowles was the first to publish a time series of this type.[13] Although no performance indexes are available on a current basis, the Center for Research in Security Prices at the University of Chicago offers indexes for all stocks listed on both the New York and American Stock Exchanges. Both an equal weighted index and a value weighted index are available on a daily basis from July 1962, with a current lag of about one quarter. Monthly indexes of all New York stocks are available back to January 1926.

The difference in price indexes and investment-performance indexes can lead the incautious to different conclusions. This is readily apparent in Table 3–7, taken from a study by Fisher.[14] For the period 1926–60, the price index indicates that rail stocks outperformed local and highway transportation stocks, while the more comprehensive investment-performance index indicates the reverse.

The preceding discussion raises an obvious question: Of what practical importance is the choice of an index? The answer is found in Table 3–8. The simple correlation between each pair of indexes measures the degree to

TABLE 3-7   Rates of change in two indexes of common stock performance

| | Period | | | | | |
| | 1/26–12/60 | | 12/40–12/60 | | 12/50–12/60 | |
Security Group	IPI*	PI†	IPI*	PI†	IPI*	PI†
Railroads	4.0	0.5	17.1	12.0	6.8	2.0
Local and highway transportation	5.6	− 0.4	16.7	8.6	11.6	5.5
Water transportation	4.4	− 1.7	14.2	5.3	9.4	1.4
Airlines	3.6	2.4	6.1	4.0	5.0	2.1
All common stocks	8.9	4.0	16.0	9.9	13.3	7.9

*Investment-performance index.
†Price index.
Source: Fisher, "Stock Market Indexes," p. 214.

TABLE 3-8 Daily correlations between various stock market indexes, January 1, 1980, through August 31, 1982

	S&P 500	NYSE	AMEX	Value Line	Wilshire 5000
Dow Jones	.93	.91	.74	.86	.94
S&P 500		.94	.78	.87	.97
NYSE			.79	.87	.95
AMEX				.84	.85
Value Line					.93

Source: Wilshire Associates, Santa Monica, Calif.

which they tend to move up and down together.* The correlations range from 0.74 through 0.97. Interestingly the smallest correlations are those with the American Stock Exchange. The American Stock Exchange Index's primary difference is that the firms covered are generally of smaller size. The lower correlations can be related to the discussion in Chapter 2, where it was noted that small stocks have behaved differently over time. One interpretation of the 0.74 correlation between the American Stock Exchange index and the Dow Jones Industrial is that more than 54 percent of the variance in one index is "explained" by the variation in the other. At the other end, the 0.97 correlation of the Wilshire 5,000 with Standard & Poor's 500 means that more than 94 percent of the variation in one is "explained" by the variation in the other.

STOCK INDEX FUTURES

The importance of marketwide movements to investment performance is no better illustrated than by the popularity of the relatively new futures contracts on market indexes. Investors now have the opportunity to trade futures contracts on the Value Line Composite index, Standard & Poor's 500, Stock Averages, and the New York Stock Exchange Composite index.[15]

The contracts are commitments to buy or sell 500 units of the underlying index for forward delivery. The final cash settlement price of the contract is pegged to the actual index value on the last day of trading for the expiring contract. Both the contract's buyer and seller must close out their positions by the end of the maturity month. As a practical matter, almost all futures transactions are closed out by an offsetting transaction (that is, a "round turn") before the contract expires or matures. At the close of trading on the last trading day of the expiring month, all contracts are "marked to market" (that is, marked to the "spot" index cash value). Convergence of the futures price with the cash market price is automatic in that the final settlement price equals the actual (spot) index value on the last trading day.

---

*The range of the correlation coefficient is − 1 to + 1. A value of + 1.0 or − 1.0 would indicate perfect correlation, while a value of 0.0 would indicate no correlation.

As well as allowing people to speculate or bet on movements in the market, the stock index futures offer valuable hedging possibilities for investors in common stocks. The most common motive for hedging is to guard against a market decline that would diminish the value of stocks already held. This is done by selling the futures contract short, so that the value of the short position and the value of the stocks will move in opposite directions. Unless, however, the stock portfolio is identical in composition to the market index being traded, the strategy will not involve a perfect hedge. Apart from transaction costs, the investor foregoes the potential capital gains on the stock portfolio, should the market rise.

The futures contract provides a relatively cheap form of protection against a loss on a portfolio of common stocks. This can be useful if the investor thinks the market is entering a period of substantial volatility but is uncertain which way it will turn. Perhaps there is a major federal election that is difficult to predict and whose outcome will have dramatic and opposite consequences for business fortunes in general. In this instance, a stock index futures contract can be valuable to an investment manager and is generally cheaper than liquidating the portfolio.

Similarly, an investor who believes that certain stocks will outperform the market will find the index futures useful. Although the invester is confident that these stocks will outperform the market, there is a possibility that the market will decline. The stock index futures contract enables the active investor to hedge out of the systematic risk of these stocks.

From the hedging perspective, lower transaction cost of the market index futures makes them attractive. For speculators, the contracts offer a convenient, readily marketable instrument for participating in market movements. With a 10 percent margin requirement or earnest money, the contracts offer a highly leveraged opportunity. Any investor with a stock portfolio wishing to protect that market value for a future commitment can use the index futures. One obvious use is by firms invloved in underwriting stock issues. After committing to a subscription price and before off-loading the new issue, the firm is vulnerable to marketwide declines.

CONCLUDING REMARKS

The well-founded observation that stock returns tend to move together in response to macroeconomic factors is central to modern investment theory and practice. As we will see in later chapters, the beta factor, which measures the sensitivity of a stock's return to these marketwide movements, is a simple concept that has powerful implications for asset pricing and portfolio management.

The relative importance of marketwide movements explains the popularity and abundance of stock market indexes. For some purposes, the construction of indexes can make a crucial difference in interpreting the results of research. For example, Irwin Friend et al. found that the average annual rate of return (compounded annually) on investment in 136 mutual funds was 10.7 percent for the period January 1960 through June 1968.[16] The rate from equal investment in all listed stocks was 12.4 percent, and the rate from investment in all stocks in amounts proportional to their initial market value was 9.9 percent. Is this mutual fund investment performance superior or inferior?

NOTES

1. E. Fama, L. Fisher, M. Jensen, and R. Roll, "The Adjustment of Stock Prices to New Information," *International Economic Review* 10 (February 1969), pp. 1–21.

2. R. Kaplan and R. Weil, "Risk and the Value Line Contest," *Financial Analysts Journal* (July–August 1973), pp. 1–6.

3. For a thorough discussion of the theory and estimation of the market model, see Eugene Fama, *Foundations of Finance*, New York: (Basic Books, 1976), Chapters 3 and 4.

4. Benjamin F. King, "Market and Industry Factors in Stock Price Behavior," *Security Prices: A Supplement, Journal of Business* 39 (January 1966), pp. 139–90.

5. Fama, *Foundations of Finance*, p. 131.

6. "Index Numbers," *Encyclopedia of Social Sciences* 7, pp. 154–69; Alfred Cowles III and Associates, *Common Stock Indexes, 1871–1937*, Cowles Commission Monograph (Bloomington, Ind: Principea Press, 1938); Irving Fisher, *The Making of Index Numbers: A Study of Their Varieties, Tests, and Reliability* (Boston: Houghton Mifflin, 1922).

7. Fama et al., "The Adjustment of Stock Prices,"pp. 1–21.

8. Paul Cootner, "Stock Market Indexes—Fallacies and Illusions," *Commercial and Financial Chronicle* 204 (September 29, 1966), p. 18.

9. Lawrence Fisher, "Some New Stock Market Indexes," *Security Prices: A Supplement, Journal of Business* 39 (January 1966), pp. 191–225.

10. Robert D. Milne, "The Dow Jones Industrial Average Reexamined," *Financial Analysts Journal* 22 (November–December 1966), p. 86.

11. Ibid., p. 86.

12. Ibid., p. 86.

13. Cowles, *"Common Stock Indexes."*

14. Fisher, "Some New Stock Market Indexes," *Security Prices: A Supplement, Journal of Business* 39 (January 1966), p. 214.

15. See Kansas City Board of Trade, *The Future is Here: The Value Line Composite Average, the Index Behind the Future* (1982).

16. Irwin Friend, Marshall Blume, and Jean Crockett, *Mutual Funds and Other Institutional Investors* (New York: McGraw-Hill, 1970), p. 19.

4

The efficient market
hypothesis

INTRODUCTION

During the 1960s, there was a curious and extremely important controversy about the process which determines common stock prices. Initially, the controversy focused on the extent to which successive changes in common stock prices were independent of each other. In more technical terms, the issue was whether or not common stock prices follow a random walk. If they do, knowledge of the past sequence of prices cannot be used to secure abnormally high rates of return.

As evidence accumulated that the walk is random, the academic attention shifted to an investigation of the kind of market-making process or price-setting process which would produce such a result. This led to the theory of efficient markets. An efficient market has been defined in many ways but perhaps the simplest, yet most general, statement of the proposition is offered by Fama: "Market efficiency requires that in setting the prices of securities at any time $t - 1$, the market correctly uses all available information."[1]

Another useful definition is from Jensen:

> A market is efficient with respect to a given information set if it is impossible to make profits by trading on the basis of that information set. By economic profits is meant the risk-adjusted returns net of all costs.[2]

Both Samuelson[3] and Mandelbrot[4] have proven rigorously that independence of successive price changes is consistent with an efficient market.

As the controversy and related works have progressed through the years, three forms of the efficient market hypothesis have been distinguished: (1) the weak form, (2) the semistrong form, and (3) the strong form. The weak form asserts that current prices fully reflect the information implied by the historical sequence of prices. In other words, an investor cannot enhance his/her ability to select stocks by knowing the history of successive prices and the results of analyzing them in all possible ways. The semistrong form asserts that current prices fully reflect public knowledge about the underlying companies and that efforts to acquire and analyze this knowledge cannot be expected to produce superior investment results. For example, one cannot expect to earn superior rates of return by analyzing annual reports, announcements of dividend changes, or stock splits. The strong form asserts that not even those with privileged information can make use of it to secure superior investment results.

If these startling hypotheses are true, their practical importance is enormous. They profoundly affect security analysis, portfolio management, and the selection of an investment strategy. One cannot assert for certain whether or not these hypotheses are true, but one can confidently argue that the evidence regarding their validity is persuasive enough so that all informed investors should be fully aware of the hypotheses, the evidence concerning their validity, and their implications.

This chapter traces the controversy, highlights the evidence relating to it, and discusses the general significance of the findings.

SOME HISTORY

Early beginnings

The term *random walk* has been of interest to statisticians for almost 70 years. It is believed that the term was first used in an exchange of correspondence appearing in *Nature* in 1905.[5] The exchange provided the proper answer to a common, vexing problem: if one leaves a drunk in a vacant field and wishes to find him at some later time, what is the most efficient search pattern? It has been demonstrated that the best place to start is the point where the drunk was left. That position is an unbiased estimate of his future position, since the drunk will presumably wander without purpose or design in a random fashion.

Even before the correspondence in *Nature*, Louis Bachelier had studied commodity prices and concluded that they followed a random walk, though he did not use the term.[6] Bachelier presented convincing evidence that commodity speculation in France was a "fair game." This meant that neither buyers nor sellers could expect to make profits. In other words, the current price of a commodity was an unbiased estimate of its future price.

Or, if each day's *expected* price were subtracted from the *actual* price, the sum of those differences on the average, would be zero.

Bachelier's earlier work was pregnant with meaning for investors, but the gestation period was one of the longest on record. There was some corroborating work in other contexts and with other data by Working,[7] Cowles,[8] and Kendall,[9] but modern work on this subject did not begin until 1959, when two original and provocative papers were published.

In one paper, Roberts indicated that a series of numbers created by cumulating random numbers had the same appearance as a time series of stock prices.[10] An observer with a predisposition to see familiar patterns in these wavy lines could detect the well-known head-and-shoulders formations and other patterns both in the stock price series and in the random series. Roberts also pointed out that the first differences of the numbers generated by the random process looked very much like the first differences of stock prices. Roberts' interesting pictures are given in Figures 4–1 and 4–2. Roberts suggested more research to see whether his tentative finding that stock prices appeared to be the result of a random process were confirmed by more detailed and exhaustive investigation.

The second work appearing in 1959, which provoked controversy and stimulated research, was by Osborne.[11] He was a distinguished physicist with the Naval Research Laboratory in Washington, D.C., when the article was published. Although Osborne has learned a great deal about the stock market since 1959, he professed (probably incorrectly) to be ignorant about the market at that time. He watched the numbers representing stock prices to see whether they conformed to certain laws governing the motion of physical objects. In particular, he was interested in seeing whether price movements were similar to the movements of very small particles suspended in solution—so-called Brownian motion. He found a very high degree of conformity between the stock price movements and the law governing Brownian motion. Specifically, the variance of price changes over successively longer intervals of time increases as the square of the length of time. This implies that the logarithms of price changes are independent of each other. Although Osborne's point of view is different, his findings are consistent with Roberts' work.

EARLY TESTS OF THE WEAK FORM

The work by Osborne and Roberts was taken seriously by only a small group of academics at first. Both pieces of work suggested, on the basis of preliminary and tentative investigation, that stock price changes were random. The first reactions in the academic community were to devise various ingenious tests of this randomness using bodies of data considerably more extensive than those used by either Osborne or Roberts. These tests by Moore (1962),[12] Fama (1965),[13] Granger and Morgenstern (1963),[14] and others provided substantial support for the tentative conclusions of

---

FIGURE 4-1   Actual and simulated levels for stock market prices of 52 weeks

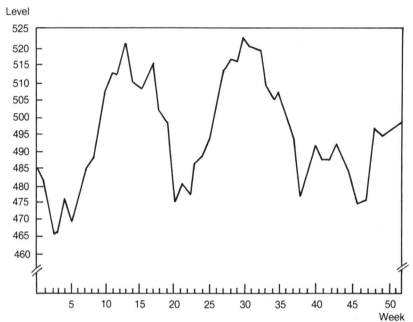

Friday closing levels, December 30, 1955—December 28, 1956, Dow Jones Industrial Average

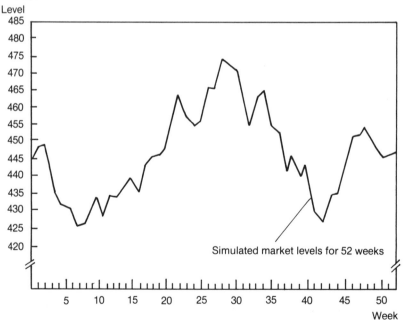

Source: Roberts, "Stock Market Patterns," pp. 5-6.

FIGURE 4-2   Actual and simulated changes in weekly stock prices for 52 weeks

Change

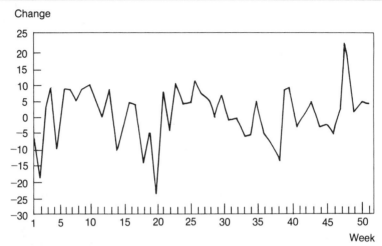

Changes from Friday to Friday (closing) January 6, 1956—December 28, 1956, Dow Jones Industrial Average

Change

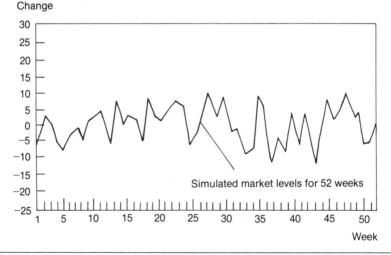

Source: Roberts, "Stock Market Patterns," pp. 5-6.

Osborne and Roberts. Based on measurements of serial correlations between price changes, through investigation of successive changes of a given sign, and in other ways, these workers tested the statistical independence or the randomness of successive changes in stock prices. They uniformly found only insignificant departures from randomness.

Since there is general agreement, we will present only a few highlights. Moore was one of the first to study the serial correlation between successive price changes of individual stocks. The interpretation of this sort of test is that a low coefficient suggests that previous price changes cannot be used to predict future changes. Moore examined weekly changes of 29 randomly selected stocks for 1951–58 and found an average serial correlation coefficient of -0.06. This value is extremely low, indicating that data on weekly changes are valueless in predicting future changes. Fama studied the daily proportionate price changes of the 30 industrial stocks in the Dow Jones Average for approximately five years, ending in 1962. The serial correlation coefficients for the daily changes are small, the average being 0.03. The investigation was extended to test the possibility that lagged price changes show some dependence. Again, the coefficients do not differ substantially from zero. Fama's results are shown in Table 4–1. The correlation coefficients are very low. While the evidence is impressive, correlation coefficients have an unfortunate attribute. They may be dominated by a few extreme and unusual observations.

To avoid this effect, Fama looked at the signs rather than size of successive changes to see if runs tended to persist. The daily changes in the prices of each of the 30 Dow Jones stocks were classified as zero, positive, or negative. A sequence of $+ + - + + + - - 0$, for example, would be made up of five runs. If runs tend to persist (that is, if there are trends), the total number of runs will be fewer and the average length of runs longer than if the series were random. Fama's findings are in Table 4–2. In general, the actual number of runs closely conforms to the numbers expected, although there is a slight tendency for runs in daily changes to persist. This is also suggested by the predominantly positive correlation coefficients for daily changes. The departure from randomness is negligible, however, and the evidence is strong support for the random-walk hypothesis. The financial community seemed to be unaware of or indifferent to this work.

Some advocates of technical analysis argued that these tests were unfair because they were too rigid and that possible complicated dependencies in successive price changes must be investigated. This led to an interesting effort to refute the implications of the work of Roberts, Osborne, Fama and others. Alexander tried to devise trading rules based solely on price changes that could produce abnormally high rates of return.[15] If he could find such rules, they would imply that price changes followed patterns and were not random. Alexander's trading rule was: Wait until stock prices have advanced by x percent from some trough and then buy stocks; next, hold those stocks until they have declined y percent from some subsequent peak, and then sell them or sell them short. Continue the process until bankrupt or satisfied.

Alexander's first efforts to refute the assertions of randomness appeared to be successful, and his results implied the existence of trends or persistence of movements in stock prices. His so-called filter technique produced enormous rates or return. On the basis of corrections in his work suggested and implemented by Fama[16] and Fama and Blume,[17] the profits disappeared. The major shortcomings of Alexander's early work were the failure to realize that dividends were a cost rather than a benefit when stocks were sold

TABLE 4-1   Daily serial correlation coefficients for lags of 1–10 days

Stock	Lag									
	1	2	3	4	5	6	7	8	9	10
Allied Chemical	.017	−.042	.007	−.001	.027	.004	−.017	−.026	−.017	−.007
Alcoa	.118*	.038	−.014	.022	−.022	.009	.017	.007	−.001	−.033
American Can	−.087*	−.024	.034	−.065*	−.017	−.006	.015	.025	−.047	−.040
A.T.&T.	−.039	−.097*	.000	.026	.005	−.005	.002	.027	−.014	.007
American Tobacco	.111*	−.109*	−.060*	−.065*	.007	−.010	.011	.046	.039	.041
Anaconda	.067*	−.061*	−.047	−.002	.000	−.038	.009	.016	−.014	−.056
Bethlehem Steel	.013	−.065*	.009	.021	−.053	−.098*	−.010	.004	−.002	−.021
Chrysler	.012	−.066*	−.016	−.007	−.015	.009	.037	.056*	−.044	.021
Du Pont	.013	−.033	.060*	.027	−.002	−.047	.020	.011	−.034	.001
Eastman Kodak	.025	.014	.031	.005	−.022	.012	.007	.006	.008	.002
General Electric	.011	−.038	−.021	.031	−.001	.000	−.008	.014	−.002	.010
General Foods	.061*	−.003	.045	.002	−.015	−.052	−.006	−.014	−.024	−.017
General Motors	−.004	−.056*	−.037	−.008	−.038	−.006	.019	.006	−.016	.009
Goodyear	−.123*	.017	−.044	.043	−.002	−.003	.035	.014	−.015	.007
International Harvester	−.017	−.029	−.031	.037	−.052	−.021	−.001	.003	−.046	−.016
International Nickel	.096*	−.033	−.019	.020	.027	.059*	−.038	−.008	−.016	.034
International Paper	.046	−.011	−.058*	−.053*	.049	−.003	−.025	−.019	−.003	−.021
Johns Manville	.006	−.038	−.027	−.023	−.029	−.080*	.040	.018	−.037	.029
Owens Illinois	−.021	−.084*	−.047	.068*	.086*	−.040	.011	−.040	.067*	−.043
Procter & Gamble	.099*	−.009	−.008	.009	−.015	.022	.012	−.012	−.022	−.021
Sears	.097*	.026	.028	.025	.005	−.054	−.006	−.010	−.008	−.009
Standard Oil (Calif.)	.025	−.030	−.051*	.025	−.047	−.034	−.010	.072*	−.049*	−.035
Standard Oil (N.J.)	.008	−.116*	.016	.014	−.047	−.018	−.022	−.026	−.073*	.081*
Swift & Co.	−.004	−.015	−.010	.012	.057*	.012	−.043	.014	.012	.001
Texaco	.094*	−.049	−.024	.018	−.017	−.009	.031	.032	−.013	.008
Union Carbide	.107*	−.012	.040	.046	−.036	−.034	.003	−.008	−.054	−.037
United Aircraft	.014	−.033	−.022	−.047	−.067*	−.053	.046	.037	.015	−.019
U.S. Steel	.040	−.074*	.014	.011	−.012	−.021	.041	.037	−.021	−.044
Westinghouse	−.027	−.022	−.036	−.003	.000	−.054*	−.020	.013	−.014	.008
Woolworth	.028	−.016	.015	.014	.007	−.039	−.013	.003	−.088*	−.008

*Coefficient is twice its computed standard error.

Source: Fams, "The Behavior of Stock Market Prices," p. 72.

TABLE 4-2   Total actual and expected numbers of runs for one-, four-, nine-, and 16-day periods

Stock	Daily		Four-Day		Nine-Day		16-Day	
	Actual	Expected	Actual	Expected	Actual	Expected	Actual	Expected
Allied Chemical	683	713.4	160	162.1	71	71.3	39	38.6
Alcoa	601	670.7	151	153.7	61	66.9	41	39.0
American Can	730	755.5	169	172.4	71	73.2	48	43.9
A.T.&T.	657	688.4	165	155.9	66	70.3	34	37.1
American Tobacco	700	747.4	178	172.5	69	72.9	41	40.6
Anaconda	635	680.1	166	160.4	68	66.0	36	37.8
Bethlehem Steel	709	719.7	163	159.3	80	71.8	41	42.2
Chrysler	927	932.1	223	221.6	100	96.9	54	53.5
Du Pont	672	694.7	160	161.9	78	71.8	43	39.4
Eastman Kodak	678	679.0	154	160.1	70	70.1	43	40.3
General Electric	918	956.3	225	224.7	101	96.9	51	51.8
General Foods	799	825.1	185	191.4	81	75.8	43	40.5
General Motors	832	868.3	202	205.2	83	85.8	44	46.8
Goodyear	681	672.0	151	157.6	60	65.2	36	36.3
International Harvester	720	713.2	159	164.2	84	72.6	40	37.8
International Nickel	704	712.6	163	164.0	68	70.5	34	37.6
International Paper	762	826.0	190	193.9	80	82.8	51	46.9
Johns Manville	685	699.1	173	160.0	64	69.4	39	40.4
Owens Illinois	713	743.3	171	168.6	69	73.3	36	39.2
Procter & Gamble	826	858.9	180	190.6	66	81.2	40	42.9
Sears	700	748.1	167	172.8	66	70.6	40	34.8
Standard Oil (Calif.)	972	979.0	237	228.4	97	98.6	59	54.3
Standard Oil (N.J.)	688	704.0	159	159.2	69	68.7	29	37.0
Swift & Co.	878	877.6	209	197.2	85	83.8	50	47.8
Texaco	600	654.2	143	155.2	57	63.4	29	35.6
Union Carbide	595	620.9	142	150.5	67	66.7	36	35.1
United Aircraft	661	699.3	172	161.4	77	68.2	45	39.5
U.S. Steel	651	662.0	162	158.3	65	70.3	37	41.2
Westinghouse	829	825.5	198	193.3	87	84.4	41	45.8
Woolworth	847	868.4	193	198.9	78	80.9	48	47.7
Averages	735.1	759.8	175.7	175.8	74.6	75.3	41.6	41.7

Source: Fams, "The Behavior of Stock Market Prices," p. 75.

short, the failure to take transaction costs into account, and the assumption that stocks could be bought or sold at the precise price when the signal to buy or sell was given. Fama and Blume demonstrated that filter schemes cannot, in general, provide returns larger than a naive policy of buying and holding stocks. Very small filters can generate larger profits before commissions, suggesting some persistence in short-term price movements. This is corroborated by some evidence persented earlier. However, the trends are so short that the profits are wiped out by commissions. The only ones to be enriched by using filter techniques to buy and sell stocks would be the brokers; the investors would be bankrupt.

All of these early investigations were tests of the so-called "weak form" of the random-walk hypothesis. That is, they tested the statistical properties of price changes themselves without reference to the relationship of these changes to other kinds of financial information. The evidence strongly supports the view that successive price changes are virtually independent. It also indicates that knowledge of the negligible dependencies, such as those implied by low serial correlation coefficients, cannot be used to enhance profits because of transaction costs.

QUEST FOR A THEORY

In the early 1960s, academic workers continued to investigate the randomness of stock prices, and the financial community continued to be indifferent, indignant, or only amused. The variety of opinion stemmed from disbelief in the validity of the findings or from the misconception that randomness implied a kind of senselessness in the determination of stock prices. After a substantial body of evidence had accumulated that stock prices did indeed seem to follow a random walk, the more inquisitive members of the academic community wondered about the economic process that could produce such results.

The explanation of the apparent randomness of stock prices lies in understanding the market-making mechanisms. In an efficient market, where information is freely available, the price of a security can be expected to approximate its intrinsic value because of competition among investors. Intrinsic values can change as a result of new information. If, however, there is only a gradual awareness of new information and its implications, successive price changes will exhibit dependence. If the adjustment to information is virtually instantaneous, successive price changes will be random. Although implicit in the work of Boness,[18] Sprenkle,[19] Moore,[20] and probably even Adam Smith, the first specification of efficient markets and their relationship to the randomness of prices for things traded in that market is attributable to Samuelson (1965)[21] and Mandelbrot (1966).[22] If a market has zero transaction costs, if all available information is free to all interested parties, and if all market participants and potential participants have the same time horizons and expectations about prices, the market will be efficient and, as Samuelson has proved, prices will fluctuate randomly.

The assertion that a market is efficient is vastly stronger than the assertion that successive changes in stock prices are independent of each other. The latter assertion—the weak form of the efficient market hypothesis—says that current stock prices fully reflect the historical sequence of prices so that a knowledge of that sequence is useless in forming expectations about future prices. The assertion that a market is efficient implies that current prices reflect and impound both the implications of the historical price sequence and all that can be publicly known about the companies whose stocks are being traded. This stronger assertion has proved to be especially unacceptable or unpalatable to the financial community, since it suggests the fruitlessness of efforts to earn superior rates of return by the analysis of all public information. Although some members of the financial community were willing to accept the implications of the weaker assertion about the randomness of price changes and thereby give up technical analysis, almost no community members were willing to accept the implications of the stronger form and thereby give up fundamental analysis.

One of the objections to the assertion of market efficiency and that current prices reflect all that is knowable about companies is the misconception that these assertions contradict an observable fact—the market has risen during almost all reasonable long time periods. How is it that current prices are unbiased estimates of future prices or that current prices impound all that is knowable about the future, if investors usually earn positive rates of return on common stocks as a consequence of their upward secular trend? The problem is not so vexing as it first seems. For example, it is possible to construct a coin that, on the average, comes up heads 6 times in 10. The sequence in outcomes from tossing the coin will follow a random walk, even though heads appears more frequently. The probability of a head on any toss is unaffected by the outcomes of previous tosses; it is always 0.6, no matter how many heads have been tossed before. Thus, the probability that the market will rise is greater than 0.5. At the same time, the probability that the market will rise in any day, week, or month is unaffected by the sequence of price changes in preceding days, weeks, or months. In other words, the distribution of price changes has a nonzero mean. Furthermore, the true probabilities of this biased coin, if generally understood, would not permit anyone to earn "abnormal" returns.

Perhaps a better explanation is provided by the reflection that investors would be willing to incur the risk of holding common stocks only if there was an expectation of positive rates of return. In addition, the expected rates would have to exceed the rates on less-risky assets, such as insured savings accounts. Efficiency in a market for such stocks would result in prices at each point in time which lead, on the average, to the expected rates of return. This modifies the earlier formula that current prices are unbiased estimates of future prices. The more reasonable assertion is that current prices produce rates of return that, on the average, will be positive after accounting for taxes, transaction costs, and other costs. It is not necessary that the expected rates of return for different stocks be the same. In fact, it would be astounding if they were. The rates of return that people antici- pate must be different for different stocks in order for investors to want to hold them. As will be demonstrated later, rates of return, on the average, are generally expected to be higher for stocks that supposedly subject the in- vestor to greater risk.

Once it was realized that the theory of efficient markets provided an ex- planation of the observed randomness of successive changes in stock prices, the controversy centered on the efficiency of the market. Efficiency implies much more than randomness in successive price changes; it implies the probable fruitlessness of analyzing public information to secure superior rates of return. This concept is known as the semistrong form of the effi- cient market hypothesis.

Testing the profit gained from the analysis of public information was made considerably easier by both the creation of the Compustat financial statement data base and the stock price data base of the Center for Research in Security Prices.* The Compustat tapes provide a particularly rich re- source for scientific inquiry into the usefulness of conventional financial in- formation that is found on balance sheets and income statements in identi- fying undervalued and overvalued stocks. Since many major financial institutions lease Compustat tapes at substantial cost, it can be presumed that many ingenious efforts have been made to interpret balance sheets and income statements for predicting changes in the price of the related com- mon stocks. It is quite possible that there is some secret method of looking at these data that produces superior investment results, but a large number of public efforts have uniformly resulted in failure.

TESTS OF THE SEMISTRONG HYPOTHESIS

The results of tests on the weak form of the efficient market hypothesis were consistent with market efficiency but did not test it directly. Investiga- tions of the semistrong form of the hypothesis are concerned with market efficiency and to what extent prices reflect public knowledge without bias. The focus of empirical tests is the speed of adjustment to new information. Fama, Fisher, Jensen, and Roll [23] looked at the effect of stock splits on stock prices. The folklore about stock splits was that the total value of an issue of common stock was increased by increasing the number of shares. Efforts to explain this apparent irrationality were numerous and untested. The var- ious explanations seemed to have in common the belief that investors, for various reasons, preferred stocks with low prices per share and that this

---

*Compustat tapes supplied by Investment Management Services, a subsidiary of Standard and Poor's, have been available since 1964. The tapes of the Center for Research in Security Prices (CRSP) are created and distributed by the center at the University of Chicago. These tapes also became available in 1964 after an initial grant from Merrill Lynch, Pierce, Fenner & Smith, Inc.

preference led to an increased demand for stocks at low prices, even though the level of earnings, volatility of earnings, and other underlying economic variables remained unchanged.

Believers in the efficiency of markets and the rationality of investors were skeptical about the folklore. There seemed to be no reason why splitting a stock should change its aggregate value unless the split implied something about the company future. Fama, Fisher, Jensen, and Roll subjected the folklore to its first comprehensive and rigorous scientific test. Their hypothesis was that splits, which are usually accompanied by dividend increases, were interpreted by the market as a predictor of a dividend change. A dividend change can convey information about management's confidence about future earnings. In an efficient market, the only price effects of a split would be those associated with the information implied by a possible dividend change.

Both the investigators' methods and findings are of considerable interest. They examined all stock splits of 25 percent or more on the New York Stock Exchange from January 1927 through December 1959. The investigators did not try to find out whether prices went up or down after stock splits; they determined whether stock prices went up or down more than could have been expected. This required that they abstract from the influence of general market conditions during months surrounding the time of the split.

For each of the 622 securities* in the study, the market model of Chapter 3 was estimated with the monthly rates of return for individual stocks and the rates of return for all listed stocks on the New York Stock Exchange. The estimated relationships were based on the 420 months during the 1926–60 period, with the exception of the 15 months before and the 15 months after the month of the split. These months were excluded because unusual price behavior in the months surrounding the split would obscure the long-term, market-model relationship.

Fama et al. then estimated the deviation of the actual return from the estimated market-model return for each security in each of the 29 months prior to the split and 30 months after the split. These deviations or residuals measure the unexpected or unusual returns to those stocks in those months. For each split, month 0 is defined as the month of the split, month − 1 as the month before the split, month + 1 as the month after the split, and so forth. Note that month 0 is not the same chronological month for all stocks, but the average residual in month − 1 across stocks is a measure of the unusual or abnormal return to stocks in the month before a split. These average residuals can be cumulated across months to measure the average abnormal return over that period relative to a stock split.

The study results are presented in Figures 4–3 through 4–5, which show the cumulative average residuals over the 60 months surrounding the splits.

---

*Some of the stocks in the sample split more than once, so the number of splits studied was 940.

FIGURE 4-3   Cumulative average residuals—all splits

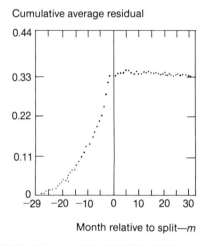

Cumulative average residual

Month relative to split—*m*

Source: Fama et al., "The Adjustment of Stock Prices, " p. 13.

Prior to the split, the average residuals are positive, and the stocks earn higher returns than predicted by their historical relationship with the market. After the split, however, there is no evidence of abnormal returns, and the return to the stocks are, on the average, as predicted by the market model.

Figures 4–4 and 4–5 summarize the data for stocks that had dividend increases within a year of the split. After the split, stocks that did not have a subsequent dividend increase had relatively declining rates of return. The authors interpret these findings as an indication that the announcement of a stock split implies the strong likelihood of a subsequent increase in dividends. In fact, 672 of the total 940 splits (71 percent) are followed by dividend increases. A dividend increase is likely, but not certain, and some stocks will not fulfill this expectation. When it is disclosed, after the split, that the expected dividend increase will not eventuate, the stock price falls to reflect this unexpected bad news. For stocks that increase dividends as expected, the confirmation is reflected in higher prices. The fact that there is normal postsplit stock price behavior for the sample of splits as a whole shows that the market makes an unbiased expectation of the dividend increase at the time of the split. These forecasts are fully reflected in securities prices by the end of the split month, and the evidence offers strong support for the efficient market hypothesis. Investors buying a sample of split stocks will earn normal returns from that investment strategy.

The conclusions of Fama et al. are reinforced in a subsequent study by Reilly and Drzycimski, who extended the earlier work by analyzing the

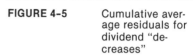

FIGURE 4-4 Cumulative average residuals for dividend "increases"

FIGURE 4-5 Cumulative average residuals for dividend "decreases"

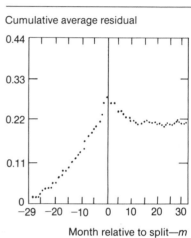

Source: Fama et al., "The Adjustment of Stock Prices," p.15.

Source: Fama et al., "The Adjustment of Stock Prices," p.15

stock price reaction to the public announcement of the split.[24] Results of this later study are summarized in Figure 4–6. Over the 15 days (that is, three trading weeks) prior to and including the announcement day, stockholders earn positive abnormal returns of 4.25 percent, indicating that some of the presplit positive performance observed by Fama et al. is associated with the announcement of the split. After the announcement, there is no evidence of abnormal returns. This strengthens the Fama et al. conclusion of market efficiency, and any information in the split is impounded in stock prices by the end of the announcement day.

A second ingenious research effort that provides evidence on market efficiency is the Scholes study of the price effects of large secondary offerings.[25] These are sales of large blocks of already outstanding corporate shares. Folklore contends that such sales will force the price of the stocks down because investors require a sweetener or inducement to purchase these additional shares. This lower price is the required sweetener, and it is quickly reversed after the block sale. Since the price pressure hypothesis presumes that the value of a corporation's outstanding stock is the same before and after the block sale, the hypothesized temporary price decline is inconsistent with market efficiency. As an alternative hypothesis, Scholes proposed that the block sale could release information to the market of an expected decline in a company's future performance. The information hypothesis predicts that any change in the stock price is permanent and, in an efficient market, rapidly impounded into the price.

FIGURE 4-6   Abnormal daily returns around the announcement of stock splits

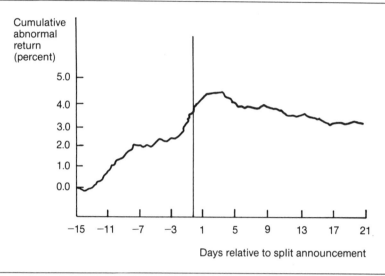

Source: Reilly and Drzycimski, "Short-Run Profits from Stock Splits," p. 67.

Using the market model and methodology similar to Fama et al., Scholes found that block sales were associated with an average decline in stock price of 1–2 percent. However, this decline was permanent and, therefore, inconsistent with the price pressure hypothesis. To further examine the information hypothesis, Scholes categorized block sales by type of seller and argued that large secondary offerings by corporate insiders, as well as investment companies, are more likely to be motivated by adverse information about future company performance than are sales by estates, trusts, and the like. The data supported his view, and the price decline is greater for the former categories. In his study, Scholes used daily closing prices and could find no evidence of temporary price depression associated with the block sale. However, Kraus and Stoll [26] used intraday prices and found some evidence of a price reversal after the block sale and before the close of trading. Their results confirm that there is a permanent price decline, but this decline is after some postsale gains have been earned on the sale day. These results were subjected to close scrutiny by Dann, Mayers, and Raab,[27] who collected transactions data for the day of a block sale. They calculated the returns to a trading rule of buying shares at the time of a block sale and selling at the end of the day. Dann, Mayers, and Raab were careful to calculate returns to this strategy net of all actual commissions and taxes. Their results are presented in Figure 4–7, where the net returns to the trading rule are calculated for stock purchases at varying times after the block trade. To earn a positive return, investors would have to make their

---

FIGURE 4-7   Rates of return to investing in large block sales*

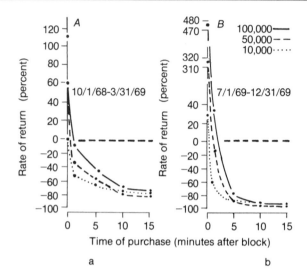

a   b

---

*Annualized † rates of return on initial wealth, −4.56 percent rule: purchase at first price at least *x* minutes after block, sell at close ‡ (using only first block per day). Gross returns less acutal commissions and N.Y. state transfer taxes (curves represent levels of initial wealth).

†Annualized rates of return are calculated by squaring the quantity one plus the respective six-month return.

‡Blocks occurring within *x* minutes of the close were assumed not to have been acted upon.

Source: Dann et al., "Trading Rules, Large Blocks, and the Speed of Adjustment," p. 16.

---

purchases within five minutes of the block sale. Within 15 minutes of the sale, the prices have completely adjusted to their subsequent closing levels. The speed with which the stock prices reach equilibrium following the block sales provides a good empirical measure of the market's efficiency.

Perhaps the transactions that best illustrate both the speed and unbiased nature of the efficient capital market are corporate takeovers and acquisitions. The economic consequences of mergers of public corporations have long been of concern to economists, regulators, and legislators. Also, the dramatic price effects of corporate combinations have fascinated investors. This fascination has intensified in the past 20 years with the arrival and increasing frequency of hostile tender offers. Unlike the negotiated merger agreement, a tender offer involves direct invitations to stockholders to exchange their shares for a stated cash or security consideration. If sufficient shares are tendered, control of the corporation is transferred. The tender offer has become a widely used alternative to the merger, and managements of targeted firms often heatedly oppose the offers and spend substantial resources to delay and defeat them.

FIGURE 4-8   Abnormal returns to stockholders of target firms in mergers

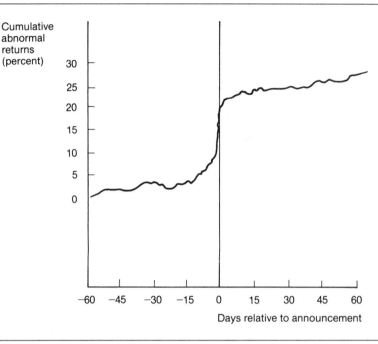

Source: Dodd, "The Effect on Market Value," p. 45–60.

The dramatic stock price consequences of attempted transfers in corporate control are evident in Figures 4–8 and 4–9. The data are a sample of New York and American Stock Exchange firms that were targets of tender offers and merger proposals between 1962 and 1978. The figures show the abnormal returns (i.e., returns net of marketwide price movements) to stockholders of the target companies over the 60 trading days (approximately three months) before and after the first public announcement of the acquisition attempt, which is defined as day zero. The striking results include the magnitude of the stock price effect and the speed with which the market reacts. The average gain for stockholders of target firms is 28 percent. This gain reflects the premium over market price offered by the bidders in these transactions.

Interestingly, the premiums offered to target stockholders have increased dramatically and persistently over the past 20 years. It is clearly profitable to hold shares in a firm that is the target of such offers, and many people have searched for a method of predicting these targets. However, studies utilizing published financial data from balance sheets and income statements have failed. This is not surprising since the evidence in Figures 4–8 and 4–9 indicates that the market is caught by surprise with these acquisi-

FIGURE 4-9   Abnormal returns to stockholders of target firms in tender offers

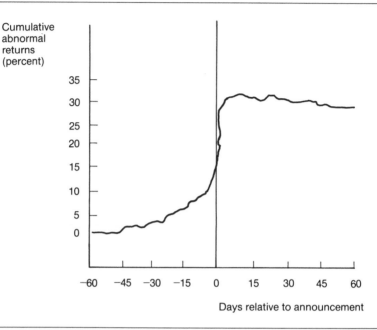

Source: Dodd, "The Effect on Market Value," p. 45-60.

tion proposals. Trying to predict target firms is, in essence, a game of trying to outperform the market.

It is important to note that at the time of the first public announcement of the acquisition, the transaction's outcome is unknown. In many cases, the first offer is followed by higher competing offers from other bidders and higher revised offers by the same bidder. In other cases, the transaction fails, control is not transferred, and the stock price falls dramatically when the failure is announced. Again, there are large returns to investors who can, at the time of the initial public announcements, predict the outcomes of these transactions. The potential for such gains has attracted an industry of arbitrageurs who effectively bet on the outcomes of acquisition transactions. If the stock market is efficient, the returns from this arbitrage game should be zero, on the average. If the market is efficient, the market reaction to the first public announcement will result in a price for target shares that is an unbiased estimate of the transaction's outcome. Investors who purchased all target shares of the sample in Figures 4-8 and 4-9, and the day after the announcement of the offers held those shares through the date of the final outcome, earned zero abnormal returns.[28] Of course, anyone with private information about the subsequent outcome in any particular transaction stands to make large abnormal returns. Ironically, it is the competition for such information among arbitrageurs that ensures the market is efficient.

There have been many other studies that provide evidence of semistrong market efficiency and some are discussed in later chapters. The evidence has become so persuasive that it is fair to conclude that semistrong form market efficiency is now an accepted working assumption in financial economics research.

TESTS OF THE STRONG FORM OF THE HYPOTHESIS: PROFESSIONAL INVESTMENT MANAGERS

After discussion of the weak and semistrong forms of the efficient market hypothesis, it is time to examine the strong form—namely, that stock prices reflect not only what is generally known through public announcements, but also what may not be generally known. Certain groups have monopolistic access to information. Also, the ardent quest for original insights and small revealing clues by legions of security analysts could confer superior ability to predict the future course of stock prices. Analyses of the performance of portfolios managed by groups that might have special information constitute tests of strong form market efficiency.

These tests consist of an examination of the performance of professionally managed portfolios. The argument is that the performance of professionally managed portfolios, which were consistently superior to market performance as a whole or to relevant subsets of stocks in that market, would indicate an element of inefficiency in the price-setting process. Consistent superiority would suggest that some people have superior access to relevant information not reflected in stock prices.

The most visible of the professionally managed portfolios are the mutual funds. They are required by law to present all of the information necessary to compute rates of return on their portfolios. Fortunately for the brevity of this discussion, the results of investigations of mutual fund performance are rather uniform. The first reasonably comprehensive and serious study of mutual fund performance was done by Irwin Friend and his associates at the Wharton School of Finance and Commerce at the University of Pennsylvania.[29] This study was undertaken at the request of the Securities and Exchange Commission and was published under their auspices. The study covered 189 funds from December 1952 to September 1958. The major conclusion, in the context of this chapter, was that, on the average, the performance of the mutual funds studied was insignificantly different from the performance of an unmanaged portfolio with similar asset composition. Rates of return on the latter were measured by the Standard & Poor's Indexes. About half of the funds performed worse and half of the funds performed better that the unmanaged portfolios. There was no evidence of consistently superior performance by any of the funds. Comparisons with rates of return on an unmanaged portfolio fully invested in common stocks, as represented by the Standard & Poor's Composite Index, indicated that few of the funds did as well. Those which did were shares in specialized funds.

The next major study differs in design and coverage from the first, but the conclusions are consistent. William E. Sharpe studied the performance of 34 mutual funds for the period 1954–63.[30] Unlike the earlier study, the Sharpe study accounts for rates of return and risk, as measured by variability in rates of return for individual funds. (The analytic framework of the study is the "capital asset pricing model" developed by Sharpe[31] and Lintner.[32] This is discussed in detail in Chapter 9.)

Sharpe found that, if the funds' expenses are ignored, 19 of the 34 outperformed the Dow Jones Industrial Average, after taking risk into account. If expenses are considered, only 11 funds did better than the Dow Jones "portfolio," and 23 did worse. Sharpe estimates that the odds are more than 100 to 1 against the possibility that these results were affected by the particular sample.[33] There were some persistent, measurable differences in the performance of individual funds, but these were mainly differences in expenses incurred. This finding lends "support to the view that the capital market is highly efficient and that good managers concentrate on evaluating risk and providing diversification, spending little effort (and money) on the search for incorrectly priced securities."[34] Sharpe's major conclusion, therefore, is that mutual fund performance provides evidence that the market for common stocks and other financial assets is highly efficient. Even the professional managers of mutual funds failed consistently to outperform a comprehensive market index.

A more comprehensive study of mutual fund performance by Michael Jensen[35] covered the performance of 115 mutual funds for the period 1955–64. He followed Sharpe in that he did not take account of rates of return alone. Recognizing that variations in fund performance could be expected based on the degree of risk assumed, Jensen compared the performance of individual mutual funds with the expected performance from randomly selected portfolios of equal riskiness.[36] There is a serious problem in defining the benchmark against which performance of mutual funds is evaluated, and this problem is discussed at length in Chapter 9.

In effect, Jensen compared the performance of mutual funds with that of randomly selected portfolios of equal riskiness. Assuming the funds had no expenses other than brokerage commissions, he found that about half performed better and half performed worse than the control portfolios. When the incurred expenses are accounted for, only 43 of 115 mutual funds had superior performance. For the 10-year period, the average terminal value of mutual funds would have been about 9 percent less than the terminal value of the randomly selected portfolios, assuming reinvestment of dividends and interest. When loading charges are accounted for, the comparisons are even less favorable. At the end of the 10-year period, the average terminal value of the funds was 15 percent less than that of the randomly selected portfolios.

Although Jensen's results indicate that mutual funds, on the average, did not outperform randomly selected portfolios of equal riskiness, there remains the possibility that some mutual funds consistently outperform randomly selected portfolios. Jensen looked into this matter to some degree, though he admitted that further investigation is warranted. Based on his preliminary inquiry, he found that a mutual fund that was superior to a randomly selected portfolio in one period was superior to a randomly selected portfolio in a subsequent period about half the time. Jensen also sought to determine whether any fund was more often superior to randomly selected portfolios during the 10-year period than would be expected on the basis of chance alone. He found no evidence of such superiority. In sum, Jensen's investigation of mutual fund performance provided additional support for the strong arm of the random-walk hypothesis. Mutual fund managers did not appear to have a monopolistic access to information. Moreover, large expenses were not associated with high rates of return.

The results of these earlier studies of mutual fund performance have been replicated in more recent periods. Becker Securities Funds Evaluation Service reported that between 1968 and 1977, the performance of more than 83 percent of all mutual funds was worse than Standard & Poor's 500 index.

One can readily imagine that such findings as those of Friend, Sharpe, and Jensen did not create strong euphoria in the mutual funds industry. The least happy interpretation of the findings cited above was that mutual fund managers were incompetent. Even if one avoided this *misinterpretation*, it was possible to conclude—although erroneously—that mutual funds provided no useful function. In fact, neither charges of incompetence nor of uselessness are justified.

The fact that mutual funds did not outperform randomly selected portfolios probably means that mutual fund managers compete in an efficient market with other portfolio managers of approximately equal competence. Mutual fund managers must compete with commercial bank trust departments with professional individual investors, and with other professionals in investment counseling firms, insurance companies, and elsewhere. Since mutual fund managers must maintain a portfolio of at least 20 securities, and since these portfolios are usually widely diversified, it is not surprising or indicative of incompetence that, on the average, these portfolios do not perform much differently from portfolios of equal riskiness selected from the whole market.

Even if this is true, mutual funds have important functions to perform. Perhaps the most important function has been persuading large numbers of individual investors that common stocks are an appropriate investment for ordinary people of modest wealth. The long history of rates of return on common stocks, compared with other financial investments, suggests that this persuasion by managers of mutual funds has proved beneficial to the investing public. In addition, mutual funds provide a very efficient way for a relatively small investor to achieve effective diversification, which is highly desirable. Mutual funds also provide useful bookkeeping and custodial services, and they are increasingly able to buy brokerage services on relatively favorable terms. Thus, we can conclude that evidence on mutual fund performance supports the strong form of the efficient market hypothesis, but it does not indicate either lack of competence by mutual fund managers or the foolishness of individual investors who use mutual funds as an outlet for their savings.

Inside information

In its strictest sense, the strong form of the efficient market hypothesis is clearly refuted. To the extent that announcements by corporate officials convey information to the stock market, these insiders can profit by trading before making the announcements. For example, Patell presents evidence that public earnings announcements forecast by corporate managements are associated with positive stock price movements, and management could earn substantial positive returns by trading in their firm's stock prior to announcing the forecast.[37] In general, trading by insiders is monitored by the Securities and Exchange Commission (SEC), which publishes details of the trades in the *Official Summary of Insider Trading*. Jaffe studied the trades published in this *Official Summary* and found that insiders earned abnormal returns from their trading.[38]

Some insider trading is illegal, and one area of concern to the SEC and the exchanges has been trading information of impending corporate acquisitions. As discussed earlier, announcements of tender offers and merger proposals by bidding managements have dramatic effects on target stock prices. Generally, the announcements are the culmination of substantial analysis and planning. Bidding firms are at pains to prevent leakage of the proposed acquisitions as are the financial intermediaries who assist in the planning. In fact, the discovery that some employees had been trading on information of impending takeovers led some investment banking firms to substantially alter their organizational structures in an attempt to protect their credibility and reputations.[39]

Another example of the value of inside information is the trading performance of specialists on major exchanges. Niederhoffer and Osborne[40] found that specialists make profits by trading on information on executed orders. Of course, entry to the specialist industry is not free, and the price for specialist seats reflects the profits that can be earned.

There is no doubt that access to inside information, such as that available to corporate officials and specialists, enables investors to beat the market. This is not surprising and explains why market efficiency is usually restricted to the weak and semistrong forms.

CONCLUSIONS

This chapter has traced the development of the random-walk hypothesis. At first, investigators studied the properties of changes in stock prices and found them substantially independent. This independence caused stock prices to follow a random walk. This result was surprising and interesting. The quest for an explanation led to the theory of efficient markets, which has implications far beyond the mere statistical independence of successive changes in stock prices. An efficient market is one in which many buyers and sellers react through a sensitive and efficient mechanism to cause market prices to reflect fully and virtually instantaneously what is knowable about the future of companies whose securities are being traded. This view caused a transformation from the so-called random-walk hypothesis to the so-called efficient market hypothesis, which now dominates most discussion of this subject.

The importance of market efficiency must not be understated. The efficiency of the capital market is one powerful reason investors are so willing to invest in that market: they are protected by this efficiency and can be confident when buying or selling shares that they are not at a disadvantage, since the price they trade at incorporates all that is publicly knowable about those stocks.

It must be noted that the results discussed in this chapter apply on the average, and individuals with superior skill in generating and processing investment information can earn substantial economic rents. In light of the accumulated evidence, individual investors should be skeptical about others' proclaimed abilities at selecting stocks and humble about their own. However, the search for superior investment performance is continual, and for those with the necessary skills, the rewards are great.

NOTES

1. Eugene F. Fama, "Reply," *Journal of Finance* 31 (March 1976), pp. 143–44.
2. Michael C. Jensen, "Some Anomalous Evidence Regarding Market Efficiency," *Journal of Financial Economics* 6 (June–September 1978), pp. 95–101.
3. Paul A. Samuelson, "Proof that Properly Anticipated Prices Fluctuate Randomly," *Industrial Management Review* 6 (Spring 1965), pp. 41–49.
4. Benoit Mandelbrot, "Forecasts of Future Prices, Unbiased Markets, and Martingale Models," *Security Prices: A Supplement, Journal of Business* 39 (January 1966), pp. 242–55.
5. Karl Pearson and the Right Honorable Lord Rayleigh, "The Problem of the Random Walk," *Nature* 72, (1865), pp. 294, 318, and 342.
6. Louis Bachelier, *Théorie de la Spéculation* (Paris: Gauthier-Villars, 1900).

7. Holbrook Working, "A Random Difference Series for Use in the Analysis of Time Series," *Journal of the American Statistical Association* 29 (March 1934), pp. 11–24.

8. Alfred Cowles and Herbert E. Jones, "Some Posteriori Probabilities in Stock Market Action," *Econometrica* 5 (July 1937), pp. 280–94.

9. Maurice G. Kendall, "The Analysis of Economic Time Series, Part I: Prices," *Journal of the Royal Statistical Society* 96 (1953), pp. 11–25.

10. Harry V. Roberts, "Stock Market 'Patterns' and Financial Analysis: Methodological Suggestions," *Journal of Finance* 14 (March 1959), pp. 1–10.

11. M.E.M. Osborne, "Brownian Motions in the Stock Market," *Operations Research* 7 (March–April 1959), pp. 145–73.

12. Arnold B. Moore, "Some Characteristics of Changes in Common Stock Prices," in Paul H. Cootner, *The Random Character of Stock Market Prices* (Cambridge, Mass.: MIT Press, 1964), pp. 139–61.

13. Eugene F. Fama, "The Behavior of Stock Market Prices," *Journal of Business* 38, (January 1965), pp. 34–105.

14. Clive W. J. Granger and Oskar Morgenstern, "Spectral Analysis of New York Stock Market Prices," *Kyklos* 16 (January 1963), pp. 1–27.

15. Sidney S. Alexander, "Price Movements in Speculative Markets: Trends or Random Walks," *Industrial Management Review* 2 (May 1961), pp. 7–26; also by Alexander, "Price Movements in Speculative Markets: Trends or Random Walks, No. 2," *Industrial Management Review* 5 (Spring 1964), pp. 25–46.

16. Fama, "The Behavior of Stock Market Prices," p. 80–83.

17. Eugene F. Fama and Marshall E. Blume, "Filter Rules and Stock Market Trading," *Security Prices: A Supplement, Journal of Business* 39, (January 1966), pp. 226–41.

18. A. James Boness, "A Theory and Measurement of Stock Option Value," (Ph.D. diss., University of Chicago, 1962).

19. Carl Sprenkle, "Warrant Prices as Indicators of Expectations and Preferences," *Yale Economics Essays* 1 (Fall 1961), pp. 178–231.

20. Arnold B. Moore, "Statistical Analysis of Common Stock Prices," (Ph.D. diss., University of Chicago, 1962).

21. Samuelson, "Proof that Properly Anticipated Prices Fluctuate Randomly."

22. Mandelbrot, "Forecasts of Future Prices."

23. Eugene F. Fama, L. Fisher, M. Jensen, and R. Roll, "The Adjustment of Stock Prices to New Information," *International Economic Review* 10 (February 1969), pp. 1–21.

24. Frank K. Reilly and Eugene F. Drzycinski, "Short-Run Profits from Stock Splits," *Financial Management* (Summer 1981), pp. 64–74.

25. Myron S. Scholes, "The Market for Securities: Substitution versus Price Pressure and the Effects of Information on Share Prices," *Journal of Business* 45 (April 1972), pp. 179–211.

26. Alan Kraus and Hans R. Stoll, "Price Impacts of Block Trading on the New York Stock Exchange," *Journal of Finance* 27 (June 1972), pp. 569–88.

27. L. Dann, D. Mayers, and R. Raab, "Trading Rules, Large Blocks, and the Speed of Adjustment," *Journal of Financial Economics* 4 (January 1977), pp. 3–22.

28. See Peter Dodd, "The Effect on Market Value of Transactions in the Market for Corporate Control," *Proceedings of Seminar on the Analysis of Security Prices*, Center for Research in Security Prices (Chicago: University of Chicago, May 1981).

29. Irwin Friend, F. E. Brown, Edward S. Herman, and Douglas Vickers. *A Study of Mutual Funds*, prepared for the Securities and Exchange Commission by the Securities Research Unit, Wharton School of Finance and Commerce, University of Pennsylvania (Washington, D.C.: U.S. Government Printing Office, 1962).

30. William F. Sharpe, "Mutual Fund Performance," *Security Prices: A Supplement, Journal of Business* 39 (January 1966), pp. 119–38.

31. William F. Sharpe, "Capital Asset Prices: A Theory of Market Equilibrium under Conditions of Risk," *Journal of Finance* 19 (September 1964), pp. 425–42; also by Sharpe, "Risk Aversion in the Stock Market: Some Empirical Evidence," *Journal of Finance* 20, (September 1965), pp. 416–22.

32. John Lintner, "Security Prices, Risk, and Maximal Gains from Diversification," *Journal of Finance* 20 (December 1965), pp. 587–616.

33. Sharpe, "Mutual Fund Performance," p. 137.

34. Ibid., p. 138.

35. Michael C. Jensen, "The Performance of Mutual Funds in the Period 1945–64," *Journal of Finance* 23 (May 1968), pp. 389–416.

36. Michael C. Jensen, "Risk, The Pricing of Capital Assests, and the Evaluation of Investment Portfolios," *Journal of Business* 42 (April 1969), pp. 167–247.

37. James R. Vertin, "Passive Equity Management Strategies," in *Readings in Investment Management*, ed. Frank J. Fabozzi Homwood, Ill.: Richard D. Irwin, 1983), p. 19.

38. James M. Patell, "Corporate Forecasts of Earnings Per Share and Stock Price Behavior: Empirical Tests," *Journal of Accounting Research* 14 (Autumn 1976), pp. 246–76.

39. J. Jaffe, "The Effect of Regulation Changes on Insider Trading," *Bell Journal of Economics and Management Science* (Spring 1974), pp. 93–121.

40. See *The Wall Street Journal*, March 16, 1982, p. 25.

41. Victor Niederhoffer and M. F. Osborne, "Market Making and Reversal on the Stock Exchange," *Journal of the American Statistical Association*, 61 (December 1966), pp. 897–916.

5

Implications of the efficient
market hypothesis

INTRODUCTION

In the previous chapter, we presented substantial evidence regarding the validity of the various efficient market hypotheses. The conclusion is not that superior performance is impossible, but merely that consistently superior performance for a given risk level is extremely rare. If that conclusion is generally true, the value of security analysis and portfolio management would be quite different than if it were not.

This is a curious paradox. In order for the hypothesis to be true, it is necessary for many investors to disbelieve it. That is, market prices will promptly and fully reflect what is knowable about the companies whose shares are traded only if investors seek superior returns, make conscientious and competent efforts to learn about the companies whose securities are traded, and analyze relevant information promptly and perceptively. If that effort were abandoned, the efficiency of the market would diminish rapidly.

The paradox is striking, but it barely differs from the paradox of all effectively competitive markets. Entrepreneurs search for ways to create a competitive advantage over their rivals, and this rivalry results in prices of goods and services lowered so as to offer no promise of abnormal returns to potential rival firms. Investors continue to compete in an effort to arrive at superior judgments. The likelihood of being consistently superior is apparently quite small, but the rewards for success can be enormous. Clearly, it is a game worth winning, although it may not always be a game worth playing.

This chapter discusses appropriate strategy for investors who accept the major conclusions of the preceding chapter. The next two sections of this chapter cover the implications of the efficient market hypothesis for security analysis and for portfolio management.

SECURITY ANALYSIS

The state of the art

Security analysis is carried out by almost all investors and financial institutions. The individual investor typically makes casual inquiry about securities through conversation with brokers, scrutiny of the financial pages of the press, reading annual reports, and so forth. Financial institutions are more systematic and professional in their approach. They employ thousands of security analysts whose credentials entitle them to hold membership in the various financial analysts' societies. Although amateur and professional security analysts' methods differ substantially, they both attempt to identify undervalued and overvalued securities. Implicit in this identification process is the notion of intrinsic value. The security analysts try to assess the magnitude of negative and positive differences between current market prices and what the prices *should* be—that is, intrinsic value.

Various theories of security valuation are used and most attach great importance to the level of earnings per share, expected growth in earnings per share, riskiness, and dividend payments. The impact of these different variables upon intrinsic value varies according to the statistical techniques or the types of intuition used on the problem. Security valuation is carried out with the belief that portfolios resulting from the process will provide rates of return superior to those produced by any other process, especially random selection. As indicated earlier, there is substantial evidence that the classical process of security evaluation for identifying undervalued and overvalued securities does not produce the superior rates of return which are sought. This seems true even though some financial institutions perform the task of security evaluation extremely well. With the use of large files of financial information in machine-readable form and highly trained staffs of economists and statisticians, sophisticated models of security valuation are created and large numbers of securities are evaluated. Unfortunately, all of this, competent though it be, seldom produces the desired results.

Implications

The most general implication of the efficient market hypothesis is that most security analysis is logically incomplete and valueless. A typical analytical report is based on public information, perhaps supplemented by a company visit, and indicates the prospects for either improvement or deterioration in the company's profitability. After what is often a detailed, lucid, accurate, and perceptive analysis, the analyst concludes with a recommendation that the stock be bought, held, sold, or sold short. The logical incompleteness consists of failing to determine or even consider whether the stock's price already reflects the substance of the analysis. For believers in efficient markets, a recommendation to buy or sell cannot rest solely on one's opinion about a company; it must be based on a significant difference between that opinion and the opinion of other investors who determine the stock's current price. A very optimistic forecast of a company's future earnings is no justification for buying the stock; it is necessary that the analyst's forecast be signifcantly more optimistic than other forecasts. Such marked differences in opinion are the basis of abnormal gains and losses. A proper analytical report includes evidence of the existence of such a difference and support for the analyst's own view.

The evidence indicates that stock prices react when information that alters the expectation of a firm's future earnings is released. Clearly, one legitimate function of security analysis is to discover such information before the competition and reap the reward when the market learns of it.

Indeed, it is this competition for information that limits the opportunity for above-average returns and ensures market efficiency. As we shall see in Chapter 7, security analysts' forecasts of corporate earnings are more accurate than time-series projections of past earnings. Through company visits and aggregation and disaggregation of industry data, analysts make forecasts of the expected profitability. These forecasts generate abnormal investment performance only if they are better than the consensus of all other analysts and investors. This search and analysis is costly, and higher-than-average returns are required to compensate for these costs.

The importance of allowing for the costs of inquiry and analysis when assessing investment performance is illustrated in a study of 70 mutual funds by Mains.[1] Before operating expenses and transaction costs, he found that 80 percent of funds outperformed the market. After allowing for expenses, the funds' performance was no better than the market. The funds were able to outperform a naive investment strategy, but only enough to cover the costs of their research and analysis.

It is extremely unlikely that superior rates of return can be consistently earned by analyzing public information in conventional ways. Although originality may be coupled with unsoundness and unproductivity, the only hope for superiority in results lies in seeking unique ways of forming expectations superior to others in the market.

Another implication of an efficient market is the possibility of economies of scale in security analysis and portfolio management. The quest for undervalued and overvalued securities costs about the same whether the amount available for investment is $1,000 or $1 billion. If the occasional success of the quest—and nothing has been said to suggest its inevitable failure—could produce superior returns of, say 0.5 percent, this would produce an additional $5 return on the $1,000 investment and a $5 million return on the $1 billion investment. Clearly, the quest might make sense for large financial institutions with billions of dollars to manage, while it would not make sense for investors with smaller sums.

A belief in an efficient market is not exactly equivalent to a disbelief in the possibility of superior security analysis. There are individuals who have a quicker or more profound understanding of the economic consequences for individual firms of changes in the economic environment or changes within the firm. Truly talented professional portfolio managers try to make sure they can identify such rare and valuable talent when it is encountered. This requires a systematic effort to assess the quality of advice or predictions made by security analysts. Sometimes, analysts work for the same firm as the portfolio managers; sometimes, they work for brokers and investment counselors, with whom the professional manager has contact.

An interesting method of assessing the value of predictions has been developed by a firm with a large staff of analysts. Each analyst is responsible for expressing an opinion about a group of stocks in his industry. These opinions are classified in one of six categories: (1) The stock should be bought because of its very bright prospects. (2) It is acceptable to buy the stock. (3) The stock may be held but should not be acquired. (4) It is acceptable to sell the stock if it is held. (5) The stock must be sold. (6) No opinion. This categorizing of analysts' opinions enables the portfolio manager to ascertain whether or not individual analysts can discriminate among the stocks for which they are responsible. Perhaps some analysts have great discriminatory powers and other analysts do not. Either judgment should be reached only after the passage of considerable time, at least three years.

The ultimate purpose of assessing the value of the information and predictions of security analysts is to improve the analysis—that decisions are based upon. This is achieved in two ways. The most obvious way is to pay more attention to analysts whose record is superior, and pay less attention—if any—to analysts with inferior records. Successful discrimination reduces the enormous flow of information that comes to portfolio managers and increases the usefulness and profitability of their advice.

Of course, an analyst who is consistently wrong in predictions is just as valuable as one who consistently wins. High-investment returns are earned by simply reversing the predictions, selling on buy signals, and buying on sell signals.

A second way in which the evaluation of security analysis can lead to its improvement is by changing the methods of analysis. The simplest changes would consist of diminishing the ambiguity of predictions or advice which is conveyed. A basic and more difficult change is altering how security analysts look at the world in order to derive their data and other basic information, and how they interpret the information to select promising invest-ments. Discrimination among security analysts provides rich material for identification of the best security analysis evaluation methods.

PORTFOLIO MANAGEMENT

The state of the art

Currently, portfolio management as practiced by professionals in finan-cial institutions is fairly easily described. Security analysts classify securities in categories according to their attractiveness as investments. Investment committees consider the recommendations of security analysts and create a list of securities, which are approved for purchase by portfolio managers. These lists vary in length from time to time and from institution to institu-tion, and it would not be unusual to find an approved list of 200 securities in a large financial institution.

Portfolio managers then select securities from the approved list as a re-sult of their own appraisals and in response to individual preferences of cli-ents, whose funds are being invested. In creating the individual portfolios, the portfolio manager is often constrained by general policies specifying the minimum number of securities which must be held, the maximum propor-tion of the portfolio which can be in any single security or industry, the minimum number of industries in which investments must be held, and so forth.

Adjusting portfolios to the tastes of the individual investor is amusingly described by Brealey:

> It is a commonly held view that the mix of common stock maintained by an investor should depend on his willingness to bear risk. According to this view, a broker or investment counsellor is a kind of financial interior decorator, skillfully designing portfolios to reflect his client's personality.[2]

Appropriate changes

Those who believe, as Brealey does, in the efficient market hypothesis would change the process of professional portfolio management. Except on rare occasions, no money or energy would be expended in predicting the rates of return on individual securities. The rare occasions would arise when a portfolio manager had strong reason to believe that the security an-alyst or some other member of his/her financial institution had either confi-dential information or an especially original and valuable insight into a corporation's prospects. On other occasions, the professional portfolio manager would consider the following things:

The degree of diversification. This means that the portfolio manager should ensure that virtually all of the fluctuations in rates of return on the portfolio are determined by fluctuations in the general market for common stocks. As is discussed later (Chapter 9), the market on the average provides superior rates of return for risk which cannot be avoided (risk of owning securities in general) but does not provide superior returns for risks which can be avoided (risks caused by the independent fluctuations in the value of a group of common stocks apart from market fluctuations as a whole). The task of achieving substantial diversification is easy. As indicated in Chapter 3, even simple random selection leads to portfolios which approximate the market very closely when only 16 or 20 stocks are held. Recall, however, that optimal diversification requires more effort.

Interestingly, a number of mutual funds have been established which attempt to closely monitor the performance of specified market indexes. These index funds are an outgrowth of the increasing awareness and acknowledgment of market efficency evidence. The index fund offers small investors the opportunity to diversify virtually to the market's limit at low cost.

The riskiness of the portfolio. The level of risk that the client or beneficiary should assume must be determined either by consultation with the client or independently by the professional advisor when the client's views are of no value, such as when the client is an infant or a senile person. The appropriate level of risk is determined by the client's resources, needs, tastes, and whether the client is an individual, a corporate trustor, or an endowed institution.

The maintenance of the desired risk level. The portfolio should be selected and maintained in accordance with the appropriate level of risk. The conventional view of risk-level maintenance requires custom tailoring to the client's needs. Modern portfolio theory, on the other hand, asserts that all clients can hold the same group of common stocks and that the appropriate level of risk is achieved by dampening volatility through the injection of short-term government securities or by increasing volatility through buying on margin.

The tax status of the investor. Returns on investments usually consist of interest or dividends and capital gains. For investors subject to taxation, the proportions of the total return coming from these sources matters because they are taxed at different rates. Clever tax advice can minimize these differences as Miller and Scholes have noted (Chapter 6).[3]

Transaction costs. Possibilities for reducing transaction costs have increased substantially in recent years with the growth of the "third" and "fourth" markets, creation of an automated quotation system for over-the-counter trading, and the use of negotiated rates for trades on the exchanges.

Agreeing with the foregoing list, Black advocates that almost all portfolio managers should be passive.[4] That is, they should: (1) select a diversified portfolio, (2) leverage it through borrowing to a higher degree of risk or dampen it through the purchase of government securities to a lower degree of risk, (3) maintain the appropriate degree of risk, (4) realize tax losses when appropriate, (5) meet the investor's demands for funds,

(6) maintain efficient diversification through periodic shifts in securities, and (7) minimize transaction costs. These tasks are difficult and important, but they are not the tasks conventionally believed to be necessary for the professional portfolio manager. The professional portfolio manager must also stand ready to review the investor's circumstances to make sure that the portfolio's riskiness is appropriate for the client at all times.

INVESTMENT COUNSELING

If markets are efficient, choosing an investment policy will generally have a much greater influence on rates of return than security analysis or conventional portfolio management. Investment counseling deserves more research and resources than it traditionally receives. It is discussed in Chapter 11.

CONCLUSIONS

The accumulating evidence regarding the validity of the random-walk or efficient market hypotheses has changed some conceptions as to the appropriate form of security analysis and the appropriate role of the portfolio manager. The ardent quest for undervalued or overvalued securities by the army of trained security analysts has made it extremely unlikely that more than small and transient margins of superiority can be achieved by any of these analysts. These margins can be profitably exploited only by portfolio managers of financial institutions with large amounts of assets.

Originality, when sound, still has potential for providing rewards. Large financial institutions can seek originality in analysis techniques of conventional information, hoping to improve the speed and accuracy with which public information is organized, analyzed, and interpreted. Other security analysts must develop their originality in other ways. Perhaps it will prove fruitful to seek new, objective data on corporate performance or to view old data in fresh perspectives to get a clearer vision of individual corporations' profitability.

Even though stocks are bought and sold in efficient markets, there remains a need for estimates of contributions which individual securities make to the riskiness of diversified portfolios. This riskiness tends to change slowly so that careful analysis of historical data is still valuable. Knowledge of the relationship between risk and reward is one of the few kinds of knowledge whose value is not diminished seriously by its general dissemination.

The role of the portfolio manager, too, has been changed by increasing conviction that the securities market is efficient. Unless one has a strong feeling, buttressed by hard evidence, that the portfolio manager has superior skill, much is to be said for a strategy of passivity. Under this strategy, the portfolio manager has the following tasks to perform: (1) determination of the appropriate level of risk for the portfolio; (2) achievement of the desired level of risk by constructing a portfolio of well-diversified common stocks, which is either dampened through inclusion of riskless assets or leveraged by purchasing on margin; (3) periodic review of the appropriateness of the level of risk; (4) maintenance of the desired level of risk; (5) management of additions to and deletions from the portfolio to minimize taxes and provide either for additional investment or for the reduction of investment in order to make disbursements; and (6) minimization of transaction costs.

In addition to these functions, the portfolio manager should constantly search for analysts with superior insight. The task is difficult because the superior analyst is rare and because the identification of that superiority is difficult and subject to error. There is also a responsibility to measure performance in order to indentify the causes of inferiority or superiority.

Investment counseling is the selection of an appropriate investment policy. It is an important and neglected subject.

NOTES

1. N. E. Mains, "Risk, the Pricing of Capital Assets, and the Evaluation of Investment Performance: Comment," *Journal of Business* 50 (July 1977), pp. 371–84.

2. Richard A. Brealey, *An Introduction to Risk and Return from Common Stocks* (Cambridge, Mass.: MIT Press, 1968), p. 115.

3. Merton H. Miller and Myron Scholes, "Dividends and Taxes," *Journal of Financial Economics* 6 (December 1978), pp. 333–64.

4. Fischer Black, "Implication of the Random Walk Hypothesis for Portfolio Management," *Financial Analysts Journal* 27 (March–April 1971), pp. 1–7.

6

Dividends and
stock valuation

INTRODUCTION

Basic principles

Few readers will be astounded by the assertion that investments are valuable because of the desirable things which they provide to the investor. This is true whether the investment is in art objects, stamps, wine or in financial assets, such as stocks and bonds. Investments having aesthetic qualities are difficult to value because some of their characteristics are not financial. Fortunately, this book only covers investments in financial assets, so the problem of valuation is somewhat simplified. That is, all of the relevant consequences of investment are financial, and therefore an investment's value is purely monetary. Difficulties arise only when one attempts to identify and estimate the prospective financial consequences of an investment and to determine their impact on the investment's value. The consequences for stocks are changes in the market value and distributions of dividends, interest, and rights. Valuing these items is difficult because of the uncertainty of future events.

In a certain world, all assets would provide the same return which would be equal to the marginal productivity of capital. An asset's value in our uncertain world is the present value of the future cash flows that the asset provides to its owners. The cash flows have two components: (1) periodic payments of such things as dividends and interest and (2) the asset's price when it is sold. The present value is determined by discounting these cash flows at a rate which includes the interest rate on risk-free assets and an additional rate, which is the risk premium on the particular asset.

DIVIDENDS AND EARNINGS

For common stocks, one cash flow is the dividends received, and it would seem that the value of stock is the present value of future dividends (plus money received on the sale of the stock). Nevertheless, much of the academic literature, the popular press, and the professional financial community discuss the importance of earnings per se rather than dividends as the primary determinant of share value. One's skepticism regarding the dominance of dividends might be stimulated by the following observations: Some stocks have never paid a dividend and a larger number of stocks have not paid a dividend in years. These stocks are in successful companies whose owners have, in some instances, enjoyed high rates of return.

Further support for a belief in the primacy of earnings could come from attending almost any meeting of financial analysts or investment committees responsible for managing portfolios. Frequently, usually, or almost always, discussions about prospects for prices of different stocks hinge upon the stocks' earnings prospects. Discussions of dividends are rare, although it is often tacitly recognized that dividends will change when there are large changes in earnings from other than transient causes.

Furthermore, the common stocks of a corporation can be viewed as owning the corporation's assets. It is therefore intuitive to consider owning common stock as analogous to owning any piece of income-producing property. Both the corporation and income-producing property are easily thought of as being valued because of the profit or income which is generated rather than the proportion the owner chooses to transfer to his/her personal account for either consumption or investment in other things.

The dividend and earnings hypotheses reconciled

It seems plausible that dividends (and changes in market value) should determine the value of a common stock, and also plausible is the belief that only earnings matter. A choice between these plausible and superficially inconsistent beliefs is unnecessary because, as Miller and Modigliani[1] have shown in a rightfully famous article, once the underlying assumptions are made explicit and understood, the two hypotheses are equivalent. At least the two approaches would be equivalent to a world of certainty without taxes and without transaction costs. The introduction of these unpleasant realities causes a minor modification in the demonstration of basic equivalence between the two hypotheses.

The reconciliation lies in making explicit the capital expenditure program of the corporation whose stock is being valued. Once one accepts a given program, Miller and Modigliani show the irrelevance of the dividend-payout ratio in valuing shares. In their words, "Values there (i.e., in a rational and perfect economic environment), are determined solely by 'real' considerations—in this case the earning power of the firm's assets and its investment policy—and not by how the fruits of the earning power are 'packaged' for distribution."[2] They mean that the value of a firm is determined solely by its earnings. Dividend policy has no effect.

To see why they say this, let us start with a firm that finances its internal investments with retained earnings and whose dividends are what remains after this investment. If the dividends are increased, the shareholder would be affected in two ways: (1) There would be a benefit from the increased cash receipt; but (2) the shareholder would also suffer, since retained earnings would no longer suffice to finance internal investment, and the deficiency would make it necessary to issue new shares. This would reduce the proportion of the firm owned by existing shareholders. Miller and Modigliani show that the value of the dividend's increase is equal to the reduced value of a share caused by issuing new shares. If the total increase in dividends were $100,000, the firm would have to sell additional shares having a value of $100,000, thus reducing the value of previously outstanding shares by that amount. The result of these two effects would leave existing shareholders in the same position as before the increase in dividends.

The reasoning is symmetrical if dividends were reduced. The reduction in the value of the cash receipt is precisely offset by the increase in value per share caused by the reduction of outstanding shares that would be possible if the firm used its excess retained earnings to buy shares in the open market. It is always assumed, of course, that there are no transaction costs of taxes. In their article, Miller and Modigliani rigorously demonstrate that correct valuation formulas can be derived mathematically from either the stream of earnings or the stream of dividends.

The equivalence arises because once one knows the investment policy of the firm, one knows its earnings. Changes in dividends would have the offsetting effects just described. One might think that if dividends were increased and became large enough to require external financing for investment, the present value of the two streams would be different; earnings would remain the same and dividends would be larger than in the simple case. This is incorrect. The stream of future dividends could not be larger for *existing* shareholders, since the necessary increase in shares that would be required to finance internal investment would prevent dividends per share from being larger. In sum, earnings are all that matter.

There are various ways to become confused in thinking about the preceding propositions, and the literature contains examples of most of them. One mistake is to assume that dividend policy determines the amount available for internal investment, which in turn affects earnings and the value of the firm. Dividend policy might affect internal investment, but it need not and generally should not.

Another mistake is in the calculation of earnings.* The correct calculation includes the cost of capital used internally, whether financed by retained earnings or otherwise. Apparent earnings are greater than real economic earnings, because apparent earnings do not include the cost of equity capital that is employed. Earnings, defined correctly, have the same present value as dividends.

The assertions so far about valuation all apply to a world of certainty without transaction costs or taxes. In a world of uncertainty, the theory of valuation becomes more complicated. Miller and Modigliani demonstrate, however, that even in a world of uncertainty, dividend policy does not affect the value of shares. Their conclusion has been challenged by Gordon,[3] who states that a dollar paid out in dividends is valued more highly in the market than a dollar retained, because the financial consequences of retention by the company are more uncertain than the financial consequences of dividends received. Since an aversion to risk characterizes almost all investors, the higher uncertainty attached to the retained earnings causes them to have less value than an equal number of dollars paid out in dividends, according to Gordon.

Gordon's argument is wrong. The investor can consume the dollar received in dividends, but the investor could also achieve a dollar of consumption if the dividend had not been paid by selling a dollar's worth of stock. Or the investor can abstain from consumption of the dividend and invest it. In order for the dollar paid in dividends to be less risky and valued more highly than the dollar retained by the corporation, one must assume that investment by the dividend recipient would be less risky than internal investment by the firm that paid the dividend. There is no a priori reason to believe in the existence of that superiority, or in the irrationality of the firm. Therefore, there is no reason to believe that earnings paid out will be valued more highly than earnings retained.

Further comments on dividend policy

The Miller-Modigliani paper has been debated for over 20 years, and the proposition that the value of the firm is invariant to dividend policy continues to be challanged.

When their paper was published, the conventional wisdom suggested that firms could increase their market values by increasing dividends. Graham and Dodd, in what was the established industry standard for security analysts, stated: "[T]he considered and continuous verdict of the stock market is overwhelmingly in favour of liberal dividends as opposed to niggardly ones."[4]

---

*Throughout this discussion, earnings refers to economic earnings and not necessarily the earnings reported by the accountant. The reported earnings will differ depending on the bookkeeping procedures used. The relationship of reported earnings to economic earnings is discussed in Chapter 7.

The debate on the Miller-Modigliani proposition was stimulated by early empirical studies that reported a strong association between dividend-payout and price-earnings (P/E) ratios; that is, firms with higher dividend payouts tend to have higher P/E ratios. Unfortunately, this evidence has proven to be unrealiable. Hess provides an excellent summary of the debate in a recent review article.[5] He states that many companies establish target dividend-payout ratios, but they are reluctant to adhere strictly to that target. A constant payout with fluctuating earnings results in fluctuations in dividend payments, and it seems that firms prefer a steady but gradual growth in dividends per share. As such, when earnings are greater than expected, the dividend-payout ratio falls, and if earnings fall, the payout increases.

Coincidentally, when a firm earns higher than expected earnings, its P/E ratio tends to fall. When valuing shares, the market capitalizes the "normalized" or "maintainable" earnings; that is, the annual earnings it expects to be earned on the average in the future. Generally, the unexpected high earnings will not be expected to continue into the future, and the market will not capitalize all the current unexpected high earnings. Consequently, the measured P/E ratio (using the high current earnings number) will fall, as will the dividend-payout ratio. Hence, the observed correlation of P/E ratios and dividend payout is spurious and it is not evidence of a market preference for dividends.

Another serious problem in the earlier work was the failure to allow for differences in risk. Riskier firms tend to pay lower dividends and less risk firms tend to pay higher dividends. Moreover, for a given level of future expected earnings, riskier firms will have lower P/E ratios as these earnings are capitalized at a higher discount rate. The observed correlation of P/E and dividend-payout ratios reflects the markets's perception of firms' risk.

In fairness to the earlier researchers, present methods of measuring a stock's risk (see Chapter 9) were not available. The failure to adequately account for risk, however, reduces the reliability of the early results.

In the second decade after Miller and Modigliani, the debate's focus was altered drastically. The alternative hypothesis now claimed that dividends were penalized in the market. The basis for the new alternative was the relative tax treatment of dividends and capital gains. Miller and Modigliani explicitly assumed taxes away and concluded that earnings retention results in capital gains equal (on a pre-tax basis) to foregone dividends. Capital gains, however, are taxed at a lower marginal tax rate than dividends for most individuals and are only taxed when realized. It was hypothesized that this difference results in investors having an aversion to dividends and that high-dividend paying stocks require a higher pretax return than low-dividend paying stocks.

Perhaps the most obvious weakness in the tax argument against dividends is that it contradicts the behavior of most public corporations. Is it believable that so many corporate managements would forego an opportunity to increase their stockholders wealth by reducing the dividend payments? In an interesting extension of the irrelevance proposition, Miller and Scholes have challenged the tax-effect arguments.[6] They show that, with existing tax laws, individual investors are able to utilize life insurance and similar instruments to borrow so that the personal-tax liability on dividends can be avoided. The implication is that individuals are indifferent between returns of capital gains or of cash dividends. The tax argument is also weakened by the increasing importance of investors such as endowed institutions, pension funds, and retired individuals.

In sum, it appears that the original Miller-Modigliani proposition remains the most robust and accepted viewpoint on dividends. At the empirical level, the arguments over the appropriate methodology have engulfed much of the research effort.[7] However, the consensus is that there is no clear way for a firm to use its dividend policy to influence its share price.

One question remains about the importance of dividend policy. Do changes in dividends convey information which alters investors' expectations of corporate profits? If increases in dividends causes investors to expect future earnings to be greater than they would be based on other information, then increased dividends can be expected to cause higher share prices. Reduced dividends would have the contrary effect. It is the change in expectations, not the dividend policy itself, which would influence the price. Separating the information content of dividends from that of earnings has proven to be a difficult empirical hurdle. In a recent study, Aharony and Swary presented the strongest empirical case.[8] They examined quarterly dividend and earnings announcements for firms when the two announcements were made on different days. When the dividend announcement was made after the earnings release, there was evidence that a change in dividends conveyed information in addition to that reflected in the earnings number.

THE APPROPRIATE RATE OF DISCOUNT

The preceding discussion was designed to show that the value of a firm's shares is the present value of either its stream of dividends or its stream of earnings, adjusted to include the cost of capital employed. The two streams must be equivalent, given the firm's investment policy. A vexing problem still remains: At what rate should these streams be discounted to ascertain their present value?

In theory, the answer is simple. The appropriate rate for each investor in discounting the expected stream of earnings or dividends is the opportunity cost of making the investment, that is, the expected rate of return on alternative assets of similar riskiness. In a world of certainty, such a rate is completely market determined since, in equilibrium, the prices of all corporations' shares would be such that the rate of return on all investments would be equal. This market-determined rate is *the* appropriate discount rate for all investors for all securities. In the real world, the discount rate is more complex, since varying degrees of uncertainty regarding the outcomes of alternative investments create different opportunity costs and discount rates. It is unlikely that the discount rate for two securities chosen at random would be equal. For a particular security, the appropriate rate is market determined in one sense and subjective in another. It is market determined in that the investor should seek to ascertain the expected return in the market on assets of equal risk. The rate is subjective in that the estimation of risk can never be completely objective, nor can the determination of the expected return on other assets of similar risk be completely objective. Risk is the main subject of Chapter 9.

Future returns on any investment are uncertain. A measure of the degree of uncertainty is generally accepted as an estimate of risk. A major tenet of modern investment theory is that it is incorrect to estimate the risk of individual stocks considered in isolation. Since most investors are averse to risk, they choose to hold diversified portfolios. Hence, the riskiness of an individual security should be judged by its effect on the riskiness of such a portfolio.

The importance of the distinction between the two measures of risk is easily illustrated. Consider a security which, on the basis of past performance, is believed to have a very uncertain future when judged in isolation. Perhaps, however, the security has had and is expected to have a pattern of price changes opposite to the whole market. The security's price declined when the market rises and vice versa. The security, though risky in isolation, would contribute to the stability and thereby reduce the riskiness of a diversified portfolio.

The logic and algebra necessary for understanding how the investor can achieve a numerical estimate of an individual security's riskiness is shown clearly in William Sharpe's fine book, *Portfolio Theory and Capital Markets*.[9] These were his conclusions: The proper measure of an individual security's riskiness is its sensitivity to market movements. The appropriate discount rate for future earnings or dividends in determining a stock's present value is the expected rate of return on assets whose riskiness—sensitivity to movements in the market—is similar to that of the security in question.

CONCLUSIONS

This chapter has attempted to demonstrate the following:

1. The value of a stock is equal to the present value of the firm's future earnings.
2. Dividend policy does not affect a stock's value, if one assumes no taxes, no transaction costs, and a fixed internal investment program.
3. Given the foregoing assumptions, the present value of future dividends and future earnings are equal. This may seem impossible, since earn-

ings as ordinarily defined, exceed dividends for almost all firms in almost all years. It is possible if earnings are *correctly* defined. Correct definition requires that ordinary earnings be reduced by the cost of capital that is retained or acquired for internal investment.

4. The present value of earnings (or dividends) depends not only on their amount but also on the discount rate. This rate is the opportunity cost of capital, defined as the expected foregone return on assets of equal riskiness.

5. Risk for an individual security should be estimated by determining its effect on the riskiness of a diversified portfolio. This is equal to the sensitivity of security's return to changes in the return on the whole market. A reasonable rule of thumb is to assume the annual rate of return for average stocks (i.e., those whose changes in rates of return are about the same as for the market). A lower number is appropriate for so-called defensive stocks; a higher number for aggressive stocks.

NOTES

1. Merton H. Miller and Franco Modigliani, "Dividend Policy, Growth, and the Valuation of Shares," *Journal of Business* 34 (October 1961), pp. 411–33.

2. Ibid., p. 414.

3. M. J. Gordon, "Dividends, Earnings, and Stock Prices," *Review of Economics and Statistics* 41, (May 1959), pp. 96–105.

4. B. Graham and D. L. Dodd, *Security Analysis: Principles and Techniques* (New York: McGraw-Hill, 1951).

5. P. Hess, "The Dividend Debate: 20 Years of Discussion," *Issues in Corporate Finance* (New York: Stern, Stewart, Putnam and Mackliss, Ltd., 1983) pp. 141–150.

6. Merton H. Miller and Myron Scholes, "Dividends and Taxes," *Journal of Financial Economics* 6 (December 1978), pp. 333–64.

7. Hess, "The Dividend Debate," pp. 141–50, provides a good discussion of the empirical studies of dividend policy.

8. Joseph Aharony and Itzak Swary, "Quarterly Dividend and Earnings Announcements and Stockholders Returns: An Empirical Analysis," *Journal of Finance* 35, (March 1980), pp. 1–12.

9. William F. Sharpe, *Portfolio Theory and Capital Markets* (New York: McGraw-Hill, 1970), especially Chapter 3.

7

Earnings

INTRODUCTION

Security analysis is popularly thought of as the search for undervalued securities. In light of the convincing evidence on market efficiency, this perception seems misplaced. Indeed, it would be difficult to explain the existence of and persistent demand for the security analysis industry if its service involved only poring over published balance sheets and income statements to find evidence of mispricing. But the coexistence of market efficiency and security analysts is not incongruous.

Recall that market efficiency is defined relative to a set of available information. The purpose of the security analysis function is not to dredge published reports but to generate information on the future earnings of firms that is not yet available. The difference is more than semantics: the emphasis is forward looking, i.e., predicting future earnings and not on the fine-tuning of existing data. Analysis of financial statements is useful only to the extent that it also helps predict future earnings.

The previous chapter's valuation model posits the value of a firm's stock as a function of the firm's expected future earnings (economic, not accounting) and the rate at which those earnings are discounted to a present value return from investing in the stock. If the firm earns more than expected, the firm's stock is worth more, and the stockholders earn higher than the expected rate of return.

The surefire way to investment success is to identify those firms that will earn more than expected. Of course, if short selling is permitted, it is equally valuable to identify firms that will do worse than expected. Security analysts are constantly working to make more informed forecasts of firms' earnings and to incorporate new information in their forecasts earlier than their competition.

As we will see later in this chapter, if there is one number that an investor would wish to know in advance, apart from the future stock price, it is the amount of next year's earnings. Little wonder that earnings forecasting is the central function of security analysis.[1]

We have established that the earnings of a company ultimately determine the value of its stock. It would be fortunate, therefore, if investors could know what those earnings are. Unfortunately, it is almost never easy and sometimes impossible to "know" the earnings of a corporation. The two fundamental sources of this ignorance are:

1. The lack of congruence between accounting principles and economic principles relevant for the determination of earnings.
2. The variety of accounting principles which can be applied.

These comments about accounting stem from chronic discontent rather than from any knowledge about how to improve accounting practices. The first point is discussed well by Treynor in his article on "The Trouble with Earnings":

> The analyst treats earnings as if it were an economic concept. In view of his purpose—attaching economic value to the firm—he can scarcely do otherwise.
>
> The accountant defines it (earnings) as what he gets when he matches costs against revenues, making any necessary allocation of costs to price periods; or as the change in the equity account over the period. These are not economic definitions of earnings but merely descriptions of the motions the accountant goes through to arrive at the earnings number.[2]

It is simple to specify, in principle, what a corporation should report as its income or earnings. Many years ago, economists defined personal income, and an analogy to that definition will serve for the corporation. Income is defined as the change in a person's net worth during a period plus the value of his/her consumption. For a corporation, the analogous definition would be a change in its net worth plus the value of dividends or other distributions to stockholders. This definition is equivalent to saying that a corporation's income is the change in the discounted value of its future earnings plus the value of its dividends and other distributions. Such changes can arise through internal investment by the firm, through changes in the rate at which future earnings are discounted, or through changes in the economic environment, such as taxes, consumer tastes, technology, and so on.

The above definition may seem satisfactory, but there is a circularity problem. Present earnings cannot be satisfactorily explained in terms of a change in the values of future earnings until that change is defined.

Though it is easy to define corporate earnings or income in theory, it is extremely difficult in practice. The primary task of financial analysts is to implement this difficult task. In each year or period, the analyst must ascertain the corporation's change in net worth, or the change in the value of its future earnings. The analyst has the use of numbers produced by accountants. Although these help, they convey an ambiguous message. The analyst is not limited to information provided by accountants; ingenious and competent analysts use many other kinds of information.

Ambiguity in reported income because of numerous accounting options

Investors, and the public in general, often attach great importance to reported earnings per share. This was eloquently stated in a *Forbes* article:

> [T]he annual net earnings figure tends to have a magical significance—not only for the ordinary investor but for security analysts and even for acquisition minded managements. It becomes, in effect, what grades are for the student—a measure of excellence or lack of excellence, of progress or lack of progress.[3]

Historically, accounting has been a flexible art, permitting many opportunities for coping with different situations. While there is obvious justification for this discretion, the result is a fuzziness in data on reported earnings. Although the accounting profession has established standards which delineate acceptable accounting procedures, great diversity remains in the accounting techniques used by different firms. In 1965, Chambers estimated that over 1 million earnings figures could be generated from the same basic data.[4] The diversity of procedures used in preparing firms' financial statements has led many to conclude that the reported numbers are meaningless:

> [I]f earnings reports are differentially distorted by the asset valuation and income calculation rules adopted by different companies—and there is considerable evidence of this—the stock market cannot discriminate between the more and the less efficient companies.[5]

Apparently investors face quite a conundrum: The value of a firm's stock is dependent upon the firm's economic earnings, but the figures reported as earnings bear no easily understood relation to this desired number. Not surprisingly, this reasoning is flawed. One problem is the failure to recognize the importance of nonaccounting information. Accountants may consider their product unique, but they do not have a monopoly in information production. Investors and analysts learn much about a company's performance from press releases, interviews with management, industry production figures, and the like. Furthermore, there is powerful evidence that reported accounting numbers, although ambiguous, convey valuable information.

Stock prices and accounting earnings

The basic premise of this section is that there is a relationship between accounting earnings and stock prices and that accounting earnings are meaningful measures of changes in value. In terms of the valuation model of Chapter 6, accounting earnings are highly correlated with a firm's economic earnings or net cash flows.

This premise is based on evidence provided by Ball and Brown.[6] Their paper is probably the most influential and widely quoted accounting study in the past 20 years, and it rightfully stands as a classic example of research in financial economics.

Accepting both market efficiency and the valuation model (see Chapter 6), Ball and Brown argued that if accounting earnings proxy for economic earnings, there will be a positive relationship between the *unexpected* earnings for a year and the *unexpected* rate of return to the stock. By classifying firms on the basis of the reported accounting earnings being better or worse than expected, the unexpected change in the values of these two classes of firms over that year will be very different. On the other hand, if accounting earnings numbers are meaningless, then the unexpected change in market value will be independent of the reported earnings and no differences will be observed.

Ball and Brown selected a sample of 261 New York Stock Exchange firms with annual earnings reported each year from 1957 through 1965. The crucial element of the research is the classification of firms into good and bad earnings groups. Note that "good" and "bad" are defined relative to the earnings that were expected, and Ball and Brown had to provide a model of each firm's expected earnings in each of the nine years. Their model has subsequently proved accurate and describes annual earnings as being generated by a random-walk process, that is, the best estimate of next year's earnings number is this year's number. A firm is classified as a good-news firm if the actual earnings reported are greater than the previous year. When applied to the earnings data, this model had the desirable feature that the unexpected earnings series (that is, the change from the previous year) is serially uncorrelated. This is important because the unexpected earnings of each firm are uncorrelated through time so that each year's unexpected earnings number is an independent observation; that is, if the firm is classified as good news this year, there is only a 50 percent chance that next year it will be a good news firm again. This also means that any year's change in earnings is independent of the change in earlier years, and on the average, across firms and across time, unexpected earnings are zero.

FIGURE 7-1   Changes in annual earnings and stock returns

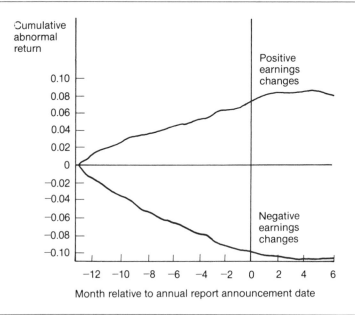

Month relative to annual report announcement date

Source: Ball and Brown, "An Empirical Evaluation of Accounting Income Numbers," Figure 1, p. 163.

To measure the unexpected change in the value of the firm's stock, Ball and Brown used the familiar market model of Chapter 3. They calculated the annual compounded abnormal return to each sample firm over the 12 months before and six months after the announcement of the annual earnings for each firm from 1957 through 1965. Each firm was annually classified as either good news (positive change in earnings) or bad news (negative changes in earnings). Their results are summarized in Figure 7–1 and provide strong evidence that unexpected changes in accounting earnings are highly correlated with unexpected stock price changes. An investor who knew only the sign of the earnings change 12 months prior to its release could earn positive annual abnormal returns (i.e., greater than the risk-adjusted return required by the market) of 8.3 percent by investing long in good news stocks and selling short the bad news stock. There is no dobut that accounting earnings are meaningful.

An interesting aspect of the Ball and Brown results is that more than 85 percent of the total stock price change associated with unexpected earnings occurs before the month of public announcement. They conclude that annual earnirgs numbers are not a timely source of information. Note also that after earnings figures are released, the abnormal returns are randomly distributed around zero, and the market efficiently impounds the information in the earnings number.

FIGURE 7-2   Changes in annual earnings and stock returns: Australian firms

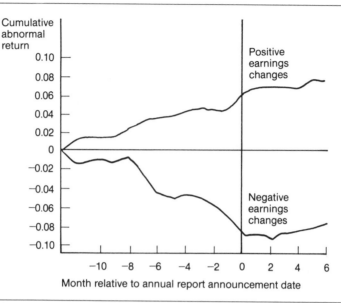

Source: Brown, "The Impact of the Annual Net Profit on the Stock Market," Figure 1, p. 280.

The substantial price adjustment prior to the release of the annual earnings figure suggests investors are using other information sources. One source is the interim accounting report issued each quarter during the year. The effect of these reports is evident in Figure 7-2, which summarizes the results of Brown's replication using Australian data.[7] Note that the price adjustment during the year is slower for the Australian data than for the United States. Australian firms issue only semiannual and not quarterly earnings reports.

The interim reports also explain why Ball and Brown find such a small price effect in the month of the annual earnings announcement. When the interim reports are accounted for separately, it is possible that the information content of accounting reports is substantial.

Foster replicated the Ball and Brown study using quarterly earnings numbers and daily, rather than monthly, stock returns.[8] Again, there is the problem of determining the expected earnings for the firms so as to identify the good-news and bad-news samples. Foster used several models and found that in quarterly earnings, unlike annual earnings, there is a seasonal factor, and this was incorporated into the expectation model. He calculated the abnormal returns to the 69 firms in his sample over the 60 trading days up to and including the announcement of quarterly earnings in *The Wall Street Journal* for each quarter from 1963 through 1974. The results are summarized in Table 7-1. The firms with positive unexpected earnings earn positive abnormal returns over the 60 days (approximately three

TABLE 7-1   Quarterly earnings and stock returns

	CAR positive earnings change group	CAR negative earnings change group	Composite CAR	X^2
All four quarters combined	.0213	−.0326	.0253	130.08
First fiscal quarter	.0267	−.0359	.0300	33.03
Second fiscal quarter	.0156	−.0359	.0229	41.45
Third fiscal quarter	.0312	−.0345	.0323	42.48
Fourth fiscal quarter	.0111	−.0243	.0158	12.80

Source: Foster, "Quarterly Accounting Data," Table 5.

months) and those with negative unexpected earnings earn negative abnormal returns.

Foster later provided further insight into the relationship between the individual quarterly earnings numbers and the aggregate annual figures.[9] Each year, the firms in Foster's sample were classified on the basis of the number of good (+) and bad (−) quarters. The five categories are presented in Table 7-2 with the average annual abnormal returns to each subsample. Those firms with four quarterly earnings of the same sign have the largest unexpected returns. This suggests that the magnitude of unexpected earnings, as well as the sign, is important in valuing firms.

Finally, Foster documents that although the stock market adjusts to the firm's performance over the entire quarter, over 30 percent of the change in stock price occurs when the quarterly earnings number is announced.[10]

The evidence from studies of both annual and quarterly earnings confirms that accounting earnings numbers are meaningful, that is, they are associated with changes in the value of a firm's stock. It is clear, however, that the market does not rely solely on accounting reports when assessing the performance of firms.

Skeptics of market efficiency, however, are not convinced by this evidence. Many commentators believe that the stock market is incapable of economic earnings—and those earnings resulting from changes in account-

TABLE 7-2   Abnormal returns and the severity of unexpected earnings

Category	Percentage annual cumulative abnormal returns
A (+ + + +)	12.9
B(+ + + −)	3.9
C(+ + − −)	− 1.1
D(+ − − −)	− 7.4
E(− − − −)	− 16.2

Source: Foster, *Financial Statement Analysis*, p. 341.

ing procedures that artificially inflate reported earnings. This "functional-fixation" hypothesis posits a mechanical relationship between reported earnings and stock price changes. The market takes the reported number at face value and does not discriminate the source of the earnings change.

Whether or not the market is fooled by changes in accounting techniques is the subject of a study by Ball.[11] Using a sample of 267 firms, which changed the accounting procedures used to calculate annual earnings in the period 1947–1960, Ball tested the hypothesis that the market cannot distinguish real from accounting effects on reported income. The sample included changes in the methods of reporting inventory, depreciation, and other items that affect the reported net income. Using the market model and event time methodology used by Fama *et al.* (see Chapter 3), Ball and Brown, and others, Ball found no significant stock price effect in the month of the accounting change. Furthermore, Ball found no association between the sign of the earnings change for these firms and the sign of the annual abnormal returns. This is the oppositie of Ball and Brown's findings for firms in general. It is strong evidence that the market does not accept the earnings number as magic, and it does not mechanically adjust the stock price according to the observed change in earnings.

PREDICTING EARNINGS

Historical earnings as a predictor of future earnings

Given the evidence that reported accounting earnings produce changes in the value of a firm's stock, much of security analysis is sensibly focused on predicting these numbers. This focus is not simply a response to the evidence provided in Ball and Brown and the other studies considered above.

Traditional financial analysis requires extrapolation of past earnings numbers in the search for the firm's intrinsic value. The presumption is that the changes in earnings are not independent of the past series of changes and that growth rates and so on can be analyzed to accurately predict future earnings.

When the random-walk or efficient-market hypothesis was first discussed in the financial community, there was general incredulity. The disbelief was based upon an initial misconception that a random walk implied a senselessness or irrationality in the marketplace. Once it became clear, however, that a random walk was consistent with a theory of totally rational behavior and an efficient market, acceptance of a random walk in stock prices became much more general. Such randomness would exist even if prices were completely determined by corporate earnings which, in turn, were the result of the interplay of real economic forces with marked temporal patterns, such as seasonal variation, cyclical changes, and secular trends.

This reasoning is consistent with the expectation that a study of changes in the earnings per share of common stocks reveals definite patterns through time. If that is true, a study of these patterns would be valuable in predicting future changes in earnings. (Such prediction would not, on the average, lead to superior rates of return, given the efficiency of the market). Financial analysts have routinely studied historical changes in earnings when formulating views about earnings in future years.

It was with great shock, therefore, that Little's original work, "Higgledy Piggledy Growth," was received in both the academic and financial communities.[12] Little reported on his study of earnings for British firms and found that changes in earnings, like prices, followed a random walk. This meant that successive changes in earnings per share were statistically independent, and the study of the sequence of historical changes in earnings per share was useless in predicting future changes. In other words, historical growth rates in earnings provide no clue to future growth rates.

Little's work was criticized on methodological grounds. The search for such blemishes was almost certainly spurred by general disbelief in the validity of his conclusions. Little responded in good spirit to the criticisms and revised his study with A. C. Rayner. The result was a small book, *Higgledy Piggledy Growth Again*.[13] Little and Rayner expanded the earlier work's coverage and remedied the shortcomings in the methods of analysis, but the conclusions were much the same: changes in earnings for British corporations followed a random walk.

One explanation offered for the apparently bizarre findings was that the quality of British accounting information was so slow that the results reflected events in the accounting world rather than the real world, in which the corporations operated. People believing this felt that the study of American corporate earnings would produce quite different results, since U.S. accounting standards were "higher" and, presumably there was a greater correspondence between reported earnings and "real" or economic earnings. It also seemed plausible that even if short-run changes in earnings were erratic, there might be discernible trends in the long run. Early American studies were carried out by Murphy,[14] Lintner and Glauber,[15] and Brealey,[16] but the watershed article is by Ball and Watts.[17] Using a sample of annual earnings (1947 through 1966) from about 700 firms, they implemented a variety of statistical tests of the data. The results of *all* tests were consistent with annual earnings generated by a random-walk process. These results have been replicated by other researchers, and it is apparent that, for the average firm, annual earnings changes are serially independent.

The Ball and Watts results are for undeflated earnings with no adjustment for inflation. They found slight evidence of a trend term; and later work by Ball, Lev, and Watts confirms that (at least for the period 1958–1967) annual earnings are generated on average by a process of a random walk with drift.[18] Recall from Chapter 3 that this is analogous to tossing a biased coin for which the probability of it landing heads is greater than the probability of tails. One's ability to forecast changes in earnings, however, will not be enhanced by studying changes in historical rates of growth in earnings.

Note that the Ball and Watts results apply to the average firm in a large sample, and it is possible that, for individual firms, earnings processes may differ significantly from a random walk. Watts[19] and later Watts and Leftwich[20] addressed this issue using Box and Jenkins' time-series methodology.[21] After finding a statistical process for each firm's earnings series, they compared predictions from these processes to those of a random walk, and they compared random-walk predictions with drift, over a different period. The overall results again show that the random walk appears to be the best predictor, and it outperforms models incorporating the past series of earnings.

Predictions of security analysts

The persistent finding that earnings changes are best modeled as a random walk poses a serious challenge to security analysts. Such a process is trivial to apply and requires no costly estimation—the best guess of this year's earnings is last year's number. If analysts are to consume resources in their search for better earnings forecasts, they must produce predictions that beat the random walk.

Using data from five financial institutions, Cragg and Malkiel compared the forecasting performance of analysts with time-series predictions for 185 firms.[22] They reported that the analysts slightly outperformed time-series models using the past series of earnings numbers. Since these models are inferior to a random-walk process, the conclusion was not favorable for the analysts.

More recently, Brown and Rozeff have provided a more detailed analysis of this question.[23] They used Value Line investment service forecasts that predict quarterly earnings four times a year for 1,600 firms and replicated their findings using other analyst forecasts published in the *Standard and Poor's Earnings Forecaster.* Comparing the forecast annual earnings (based on the sum of the four quarterly forecasts) with actual reported earnings, Brown and Rozeff found that the analysts produce more small forecast errors and fewer large forecast errors than time-series models, including a random walk and a random walk with drift. The analysts also made better predictions of quarterly earnings than can be generated by the time series.

Although the results are more sympathetic to the analysts, it must be noted that the analysts' forecasts are made two to three weeks after the quarter has begun (after approximately 20 percent of the quarter has elapsed). The analysts are therefore able to incorporate data generated in the current quarter, and it is not surprising that they outperform models that do not have access to that data.

CONCLUSION

Despite the seeming arbitrariness of reported accounting earnings numbers, there is no doubt that these numbers influence changes in the value of a firm's stock. Large investment returns can be had by those with skills to persistently make better predictions of earnings than the market's consensus. It is not surprising that the central focus of security analysis is earnings forecasting.

Interestingly, the evidence shows that elaborate analysis of the historical series of firm's earnings is of little use in the forecasting game. A simple random-walk model, which predicts this year's annual earnings to be the same as last year, is more efficient.

The challenge, then, is for security analysts to find forecasts that outperform the virtually costless random-walk model. There is some evidence that analysts produce more accurate estimates than time series models, but this could simply be a result of analysts' forecasts being made after the quarter has begun.

NOTES

1. A careful and critically thorough analysis of the research involving earnings and other accounting issues is found in Ross Watts and Jerold Zimmerman's book, *Positive Theories of Accounting* (Prentice-Hall, forthcoming 1985).

2. Jack L. Treynor, "The Trouble with Earnings," *Financial Analysts Journal* 28 (September–October 1972), pp. 41–46.

3. "What *Are* Earnings? The Growing Credibility Gap," *Forbes* (May 15, 1967), pp. 28–31, 34, 39, 42, 44.

4. R. J. Chambers, "Financial Information and the Securities Market," *Abacus* 1 (September 1965), pp. 3–30.

5. R. J. Chambers, "Stock Market Prices and Accounting Research," *Abacus* 10 (June 1974), p. 49.

6. Ray Ball and Philip Brown, "An Empirical Evaluation of Accounting Income Numbers," *Journal of Accounting Research* 6 (Autumn 1968), pp. 159–78.

7. Philip Brown, "The Impact of the Annual Net Profit on the Stock Market," *The Australian Accountant* 40 (July 1970), pp. 277–82.

8. George Foster, "Quarterly Accounting Data: Time Series Properties and Predictive-Ability Results," *The Accounting Review* 52 (January 1977), pp. 1–21.

9. George Foster, *Financial Statement Analysis* (Englewood Cliffs, N.J.: Prentice–Hall, 1978), p. 341.

10. Ibid., p. 341.

11. Ray Ball, "Changes in Accounting Techniques and Stock Prices," *Empirical Research in Accounting, Selected Studies, 1972* (suppplement), *Journal of Accounting Research* 10 (Spring 1972), pp. 1–38.

12. Ian M. D. Little, "Higgledy Piggledy Growth," *Oxford University: Institute of Economics and Statistics Bulletin* 24, No. 4 (November 1962).

13. Anthony C. Rayner and Ian M. Little, *Higgledy Piggledy Growth Again* (New York: Augustus M. Kelley, 1966).

14. Joseph E. Murphy, Jr., "Relative Growth in Earnings Per Share–Past and Future" *Financial Analysts Journal* 22 (November–December 1966), pp. 73–76.

15. John Lintner and Robert Glauber, "Higgledy Piggledy Growth in America?" (Paper presented to the Seminar on the Analysis of Security Prices, University of Chicago, May 1967); and "Further Observations on Higgledy Piggledy Growth" (Paper presented to the Seminar on the Analysis of Security Prices, University of Chicago, May 1969).

16. Richard A. Brealey, "The Character of Earnings Changes" (Paper presented to the Seminar on the Analysis of Security Prices, Center for Research in Security Prices, University of Chicago, May 1967).

17. Ray Ball and Ross Watts, "Some Time Series Properties of Accounting Income," *Journal of Finance* 27 (June 1972), pp. 663–82.

18. Ray Ball, Baruch Lev, and Ross Watts, "Income Variation and Balance Sheet Compositions," *Journal of Accounting Research* 14 (Spring 1976), pp. 1–9.

19. Ross Watts, "Information Content of Dividends," (Ph.D. diss., University of Chicago, 1970), Appendix A.

20. Ross Watts and Richard Leftwich, "The Time Series of Annual Accounting Earnings," *Journal of Accounting Research* 15 (Autumn 1977), pp. 253–71.

21. See G. E. P. Box and G. M. Jenkins, *Time-Series Analysis: Forecasting and Control* (San Francisco, Calif.: Holden-Day, 1976).

22. J. G. Cragg and Burton G. Malkiel, "The Consensus and Accuracy of Some Predictions of the Growth of Corporate Earnings," *Journal of Finance* 23 (March 1968), pp. 67–84.

23. L. D. Brown and M. S. Rozeff, "The Superiority of Analysts Forecasts as Measures of Expectations: Evidence from Earnings," *Journal of Finance* 33 (March 1978), pp. 1–16.

8

The theory of portfolio management

INTRODUCTION

So far, this book has covered stock market behavior as a whole and the valuation of individual securities. The final section of the book deals with portfolio management. Perhaps it is necessary at the outset to indicate why this is a separate subject. It might appear that the selection of a portfolio would easily follow from valuing securities.

That this is not true is evident from reflection on investor behavior. Almost all investors choose to hold groups of common stocks rather than the single stock that offers the greatest expected return. This suggests that "attractiveness" does not consist exclusively of expected return. If that were all that mattered, investors would put as much of their resources as possible into the single security offering the greatest expected return.

Since 1952, investors have better understood another dimension of attractiveness and why the rational and professional management of portfolios includes more than the listing of securities by the magnitude of their expected returns. The great 1952 event was the publication of Harry Markowitz's now celebrated article "Portfolio Selection."[1] Markowitz analyzed the implications of the fact that investors, although seeking high expected returns, generally wish to avoid risk. Since there is overwhelming evidence that risk aversion characterizes most investors—especially most large investors—rationality in portfolio management demands that account be taken not only of expected returns for a portfolio but also of the risk that is incurred. Although the expected return on a portfolio is directly related to the expected returns on component securities, it is impossible to deduce a portfolio's riskiness simply by knowing the riskiness of individual securities. The riskiness of portfolios depends not only on the attributes of individual securities, but also on the interrelationships among securities. It is primarily for this reason that portfolio management is a separate subject.

Another reason for treating portfolio management separately is that it depends upon the preferences of individual investors. It is possible to estimate expected returns for individual securities without regard to any investor, but is is impossible to construct an optimum portfolio for an investor without taking personal preferences into account. The output of security analysts is essential for portfolio management, or at least portfolio managers make use of security analysts' output, but this output must be analyzed with reference to the tastes and financial circumstances of individual investors when building portfolios. Although security analysis can be impersonal, portfolio management cannot.

The next section of this chapter discusses Markowitz's portfolio theory, the basis of all scientific portfolio management. The last section discusses the subject of a portfolio optimality for the individual investor.

THE MARKOWITZ CONTRIBUTION

The portfolio theory developed by Markowitz can be summarized as follows:

1. The two relevant characteristics of a portfolio are expected return and riskiness.
2. Rational investors will choose to hold efficient portfolios, which maximize expected return for a given degree of risk or alternately and equivalently minimize risk for a given expected return.
3. It is theoretically possible to identify efficient portfolios by analyzing information for each security on its expected return, the variation in that return, and the relationships between the return for each security and that for every other security.
4. There is a specified, manageable computer program which utilizes inputs from security analysts, in the form of three kinds of information about each security, to specify a set of efficient portfolios. The program indicates the proportion of an investor's fund which should be allocated to each security to achieve efficiency; that is, the maximization of return for a given degree of risk of the minimization of risk for a given expected return.

Efficient portfolios

The notion of efficient portfolios is illustrated in Figure 8–1. The vertical axis measures the expected return on a portfolio; its associated risk is mea-

FIGURE 8-1   Hypothetical efficient frontier

Expected return

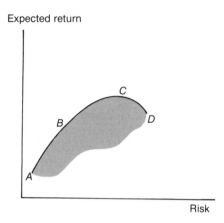

Risk

sured along the horizontal axis. The shaded area represents all possible portfolios that can be obtained from a given set of securities. The portfolios lying on curve ABC are efficient because they offer a maximum return for a given level of risk and minimum risk for a given level of return. The portfolio at point D is on the boundary of the feasible set, but is not efficient, because the portfolio on curve ABC offering the same expected return is less risky. Similar statements can be made for all portfolios within the shaded area. The Markowitz analysis assumes that any rational investor will prefer efficient portfolios to all other portfolios. The choice of a particular efficient portfolio depends on the investor's preference or utility function, a subject discussed later in this chapter.

Portfolios and securities

Let us examine a portfolio's relationship to its component securities. First, what is the relationship between the return on a portfolio and the returns on component securities? The return on a portfolio is the weighted average of returns on its component securities, the weight of each security being the fraction of the portfolio's total value which is invested in it. The following example illustrates this: Assume that a total of $100 is invested in three securities. The proportions, X_i, invested in each are given in the second column of Table 8-1. The third column indicates the rates of return, R_i. The sum of the products of these two columns is the portfolio's rate of return R_p. In this case, the portfolio's rate of return is $(0.5)(0.10) + (0.3)(0.20) + (0.2)(0.05) = 0.120$, or 12 percent. Symbolically:

TABLE 8-1 The calculation of the rate of return on a portfolio

Security (i)	Proportion invested (X$_i$)	Rate of return (R$_i$)	X$_i$R$_i$
1	0.5	0.10	0.050
2	0.3	0.20	0.060
3	0.2	0.05	0.010
Total	1.0		0.120

$$R_p = X_1R_1 + X_2R_2 + X_3R_3 = \sum_{i=1}^{3} X_iR_i$$

A complication arises because portfolio managers are concerned with future outcomes. If the rates of return on individual securities could be known with certainty, the portfolio's rate of return could be predicted accurately and rates on all securities would be equal. Since the future is uncertain, portfolio managers must base their selections on forecasts of future outcomes. Suppose, in Table 8-2, an analyst made the following forecast for a specific security.

The forecast of 8 percent is the analyst's "best" estimate, but she cannot be certain. She may be able to state her feelings about the security more precisely so that a picture like that in Figure 8–2 can be drawn. This "probability distribution" represents the probabilities that the security will provide specified rates of return over some designated future period. The probabilities must sum to one.

In the example, there is a 0.05 probability that the return will be 5 percent or 12 percent, and a 0.25 probability that it will be 8 percent. The mean of the distribution, or the "expected" rate of return, is simply the weighted average of the possible returns, with the weights equal to the probabilities. The expected return on a portfolio can now be stated as the weighted sum of the expected returns on the individual securities. Again, the weights are the proportions invested in each security.

Unfortunately, the relationships between estimates of risk for individual securities and estimates of risk for portfolios are not so simple. For now, the measure of risk we will use is variability as measured by the variance. This is defined as the weighted sum of the squared deviations of a variable around its expected value where the weights are the probabilities that the

TABLE 8-2 Forecast of rate of return

Rate of return	Likelihood
8%	Very likely.
5	Possible, but not likely.
12	Possible, but not likely.

FIGURE 8-2   Analyst's forecast of possible rates of return for security A*

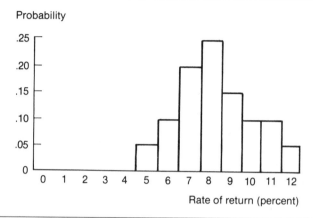

*In figure 8-2, the numbers on the horizontal axis represent the midpoints of class intervals. For example, "5" means at least "4.5" and less than "5.5."

deviations will occur. It provides a measure of the distribution's spread or dispersion.

The square root of the variance is the standard deviation. Its meaning is straightforward for normal (bell-shaped) distributions. The chances that an outcome will be in the range of the expected value (E) plus or minus one standard deviation (σ), are about two out of three. The chances that it will be between $(E + 2\sigma)$ and $(E - 2\sigma)$ are approximately 95 out of 100. (These statements do not hold for non-normal distributions, but the standard deviation is still a useful measure of deviation from expected value). In computations, the variance is more convenient to use than the standard deviation, but the results are usually stated in terms of the latter.* Portfolios that are efficient in the mean-variance plane are efficient in the mean-standard deviation plane, and vice versa.

Although a portfolio's expected rate of return is simply a weighted average of the expected rates on the component assets of the portfolios, a portfolio's variance is not simply a weighted average of the variances of component assets. The variance of each asset matters, but it is also necessary to know the relationships among changes in the rates of return on component assets, as illustrated by the following examples. (All of these examples refer to portfolios of only two assets, but the principles apply equally to portfolios of more than two assets.) It will be assumed that the securities in the portfolios pay no dividends or interest so that changes in prices completely

---

*The arithmetic is such that the standard deviation per dollar of investment does not change with the amount invested, while the variance per dollar invested increases with the amount invested.

FIGURE 8-3   Percentage changes in prices of securities *i* and *j* (with a correlation of 1.0)

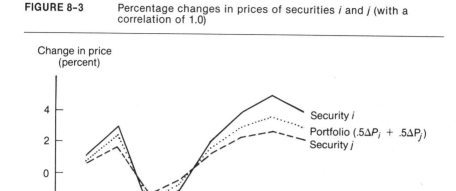

determine the rates of return. Therefore, the charts refer to changes in prices through time.

In the first example (Figure 8–3), the two assets move together in perfect lockstep. Although the amplitudes of the price movements are different, the price changes are perfectly correlated. This means that one can specify with perfect accuracy the price change in either security with knowledge of the price change in one of the securities. In this example, the correlation is positive; when security *i* rises or falls 1 percent, security *j* inevitability rises or falls by one half of 1 percent. If one assumes equal initial investments in each security, the portfolio, as a whole, rises or falls three fourths of 1 percent. Using the customary formula for computing the variance, one discovers that this portfolio's variance is 3.1 percent; the variance for security *i* is 5.5 percent; and the variance for security *j* is 1.4 percent.

In the next example (Figure 8–4), the securities again move in perfect lockstep, but in opposite directions. When security *i* rises 1 percent, security *j* falls one half of 1 percent, and vice versa. If equal amounts were initially invested in each security, the portfolio's value would rise or fall by only one fourth of 1 percent as compared with three fourths of 1 percent in the preceding example. The variances for security *i* security j, and the whole portfolio are 5.5 percent, 1.4 percent, and 0.3 percent, respectively.*

---

*In this example, if the variances for the two securities were equal, changes in the price of security *i* would be exactly offset by changes in the price of security *j*, and the variance of the portfolio would be zero.

FIGURE 8-4 Percentage changes in prices of securities *i* and *j* (with a correlation of − 1.0)

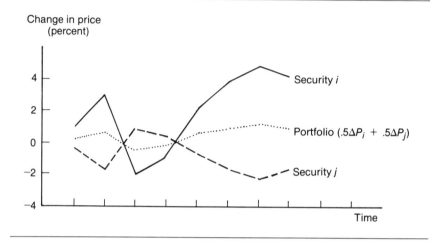

The third example (Figure 8–5) is more realistic in that the securities move together to some degree but not in perfect lockstep. This is true of most listed securities. When stocks rise and fall in perfect lockstep, diversification does not reduce the variance of the portfolio, since movements of individual securities are never offsetting. When the movements are contrary, the offsetting is maximized, as is the effect of diversification on the reduction in variance. When the lockstep is not perfect, that is, when the correlation is between + 1 and − 1, the movements in individual securities are partially offsetting. This makes diversification useful in reducing risk as measured by the variance in return on the portfolio.

At this point, it seems necessary to reveal the formula for computing a portfolio's variance from knowledge of the movements of its component assets. For simplicity, we present the formula for two securities, *i* and *j*.* The variance of the portfolio, σ_p^2, is given by the following equation:†

$$\sigma_p^2 = X_i^2\sigma_i^2 + X_j^2\sigma_j^2 + 2X_iX_j\text{cov}_{ij}$$

x_i = The proportion invested in security *i*.
x_j = The proportion invested in security *j*.
σ_i^2 = The variance of the rate of return on security *i*.

---

*The formula is readily extended to the *n* security case;

$$\sigma_p^2 = \sum_{i=1}^{n} \sum_{j=1}^{n} X_iX_j\text{cov}_{ij},$$

†With cov$_{ij}$, the covariance of security with itself ($i = i$, $j = i$) is equal to its variance, σ_i^2.

FIGURE 8-5   Percentage changes in prices of securities *i* and *j* (with positive correlation less than 1.0)

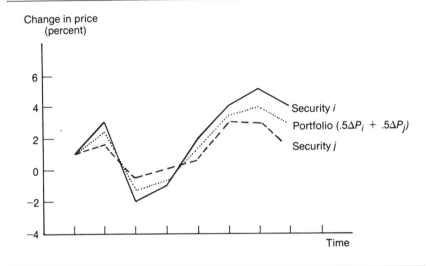

σ_j^2 = The variance of the rate of return of security *j*.
cov_{ij} = The covariance between the rates of return of *i* and *j*.

An explanation and proof that the variance of the portfolio can be calculated in this way can be found in either Sharpe[2] or Markowitz.[3]

An understanding of this formula is worthwhile. Although it refers to a portfolio of only two securities, it has great generality, since groups of securities can be considered as a single security in analyzing the problems of portfolio management. For example, if one is interested in understanding what the addition of a security does to the variance of an existing portfolio, one can think of the existing portfolio as a single security. The simple formula then has great expository power.

Most of the terms of the equation are clear and familiar, but the final term contains the covariance between securities *i* and *j*. As the word suggests, the covariance is a measure of the extent to which two securities move together. The term also has a very precise mathematical meaning, which is illustrated in Figure 8–6. The first diagram indicates the relationship between the rates of return for *i* and *j* at four different periods. It is possible to draw a line which indicates the *average* relationships for these four times. This line has been drawn in such a way that the squared vertical distances of the points from the line are minimized, and the line is appropriately named a least-squares regression line.

It is also possible to measure the squared deviations of the points around the mean or average rate of return of security *j*. This is illustrated in the second chart in Figure 8–6. The total variance in the rate of return of security *j*

FIGURE 8-6   Relationship between rates of return of securities *i* and *j*

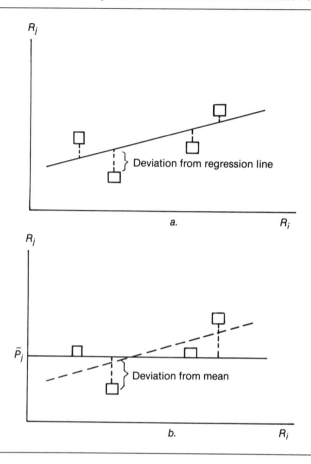

a.

b.

(the average of the squared deviations from the mean) is thus composed of two parts: (1) that attributable to deviations from the regression line; and (2) that attributable to variations in the rate of return for security *i* or to the forces that caused them. The extent to which prices of the two securities move together is measured by the following formula:

$$\rho = \sqrt{1 - \frac{\sigma_{j.i}^2}{\sigma_j^2}}$$

where $\sigma_{j.i}^2$ equals the variance of the rate of return of security *j*, *after* allowing for the relationship to the rate of return of security *i*, or that part of the total variance attributable to the deviations from the regression line, and σ_j^2 equals the total variance of the rate of return for security *j* or deviations about its mean. As the formula indicates, if the deviations around the regression line, $\sigma_{j.i}^2$, are equal to the deviations around the mean, the expression's value or correlation is zero.

In other words, knowledge of the variation in the rate of return for security i does not help to predict the variation in the rate of return for security j. If, on the other hand, all of the points lie precisely on the regression line, the correlation would be $+1$. The expression defines the familiar correlation coefficient, which has a value between 0 and $+1$ when the two variables generally move in the same direction, and a value between 0 and -1 when they generally move in opposite directions.

The covariance between i and j is a first cousin to the correlation between i and j, which is the correlation coefficient multiplied by the standard deviation of i and by the standard deviation of j.* In other words, the covariance between i and j equals the correlation between i and j times the standard deviation of i times the standard deviation of j. Using conventional symbols, the relationship is:

$$\text{cov}_{ij} = \rho_{ij}\sigma_i\sigma_j$$

To see how different values of the covariance or correlation affects a portfolio's variance, consider the following examples. Assume that two assets (single securities or portfolios) have the same rates of return and variances and that equal amounts are invested in each asset. If the rates of return are 5 percent and the variances are 2 percent, the expected return on the portfolio is 5 percent. The formula for the variance tells us that:

$$\sigma_p^2 = X_i^2\sigma_i^2 + X_j^2\sigma_j^2 + 2X_iX_j\rho_{ij}\sigma_i\sigma_j$$

$$= (.25)(.02) + (.25)(.02) + (.5)\rho_{ij}(\sqrt{.02})(\sqrt{.02})$$

$$= .01 + .01\rho_{ij}$$

This illustrates the importance of securities interrelationships. If there is no correlation ($\rho = 0.0$), the variance of the portfolio is 1 percent, or less than that of a portfolio fully invested in only one of the securities. If the correlation is perfect and positive ($\rho = 1$), the portfolio's variance is 2 percent, the same as that of a single security. If the correlation is perfect and negative ($\rho = -1$), the portfolio's variance is zero. If there is a perfect correlation, the expression for the variance can be factored, and in this special case the standard deviation of the portfolio is linearly related to the amounts invested in each security.† If the correlation is not perfect, the standard devi-

---

*It is difficult to have an intuitive feeling about the absolute value of the covariance since its size depends not only on how closely i and j covary but also on the amplitude of the fluctuations in i and j. The correlation coefficient is the covariance standardized by dividing it by the product of the standard deviations of i and j.

†For example, if the correlation between i and j is perfect and postitive, $\rho_{ij} = +1$; the variance of the portfolio is:

$$\sigma_p^2 = X_i^2\sigma_i^2 + X_j^2\sigma_j^2 + 2X_iX_j\sigma_i\sigma_j = (X_i\sigma_i + X_j\sigma_j)^2$$

and the standard deviation is:

$$\sigma_p = X_i\sigma_i + X_j\sigma_j.$$

FIGURE 8-7   Expected return and risk of portfolios

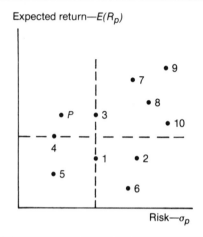

ation of a portfolio is not a linear function of the amounts invested in each asset.

Since investors like to avoid risk, and since negative correlation or covariance between a security and a portfolio reduces the variance of the portfolio, negatively correlated securities, if they exist, would be highly valued. On the other hand, securities that are highly correlated with a portfolio do not contribute much to the kind of risk reduction that is the purpose of diversification. In an intermediate position are securities with low positive covariance in relation to other securities in the portfolio.* In subsequent chapters, there will be an expanded discussion about measurement of riskiness for individual securities and the relationship of such risk to rates of return.

The efficient frontier

The attractiveness of a portfolio depends upon both expected return and riskiness. Risk, as measured by the variance in rates of return on a portfolio, depends upon the variances of the individual securities and the covariances of each security with every other security. Now, it is possible to understand an efficient portfolio more fully. The following diagram (Figure 8-7) indicates the risk and rates of return for 10 portfolios, each consisting of a single different security. Clearly, portfolio 3 is preferred to portfolio 1. It offers a

---

*A portfolio of two securities will have a standard deviation smaller than that of either security alone if the correlation is less than the ratio of the smaller standard deviation to the larger. See William E. Sharpe, *Portfolio Theory and Capital Markets*. (New York: McGraw Hill, 1970), p.48.

FIGURE 8-8   The feasible set and efficient frontier

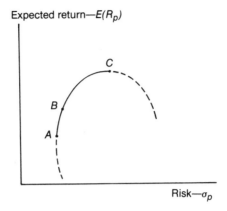

higher return for the same risk. Similarly, portfolio 1 is preferred to portfolio 2, since it offers a lower risk for the same rate of return. If the securities are not perfectly correlated—and here, they are not—portfolios made up of combinations of these securities can have smaller variances for given returns or larger returns for given variances than the single-security portfolios. Portfolios having such characteristics would be in the region above and left of the portfolio consisting of single securities. For example, portfolio P might represent a combination of portfolios 3 and 4.

For any given group of securities, the feasible set of portfolios consists of all single-security portfolios and all their possible combinations. Those portfolios which are efficient will plot along the upper border of the feasible set. This border is called the efficient frontier of portfolios of risky assets and is represented by the curve ABC in Figure 8–8.

The efficient frontier will be concave from below. That is, all points on the border between, say, A and B in Figure 8–8 will lie on or above a straight line connecting the two points. To see why, consider Figure 8–9. Portfolios that are combinations of A and B will have values of $E(R_p)$ and σ_p, which plot along or above the dotted line AB. If the returns on A and B are perfectly correlated, combinations will lie on line AB, since for any combination, both the return and the standard deviation will be a linear function of the amount invested in A or B. If the returns on A and B are not perfectly correlated , combinations will plot above the line AB because the variances (and standard deviations) will be smaller when the correlation is imperfect, and combinations will therefore be upward and to the left of the line connecting A and B. In either case, the combinations would be preferred to portfolios on the convex curve, APB , and the latter cannot be part of the efficient frontier.

FIGURE 8-9   The efficient frontier—possible and impossible

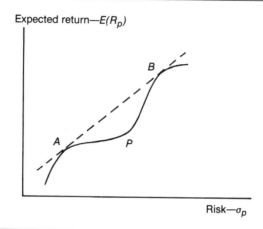

Although the efficient frontier can be linear in the $E(R_p)$, σ_p plane, it will never be linear in the $E(R_p)$, σ_p^2 plane. The $E(R_p)$, σ_p^2 border will always have more curvature.* This is illustrated in Figure 8–10. The efficient frontier is linear between A and B, when σ_p is the unit on the horizontal axis, whereas the efficient frontier is concave throughout if σ_p^2 is the unit.

The essential contribution of Markowitz's analysis is the result that investors will hold only efficient portfolios and that the portfolios of risky assets selected will lie on the efficient frontier. The investor's portfolio decision is to identify the efficient frontier and to select the efficient portfolio that is optimal. Estimating the efficient frontier, however, is not easy.

To define Markowitz's efficient set of portfolios, it is necessary to know each security's expected return and variance and its covariance with every other security. Security analysts play an important role in this process. In most securities firms, analysts specialize by industry and follow a small number of stocks. It seems reasonable to expect the analysts to provide estimates of the expected return and variance of return on the stocks they follow. On the other hand, it seems unlikely that analysts can directly estimate the correlation structure among stocks. For example, if 20 analysts are responsible for providing portfolio inputs on 1,000 stocks, each analyst would be responsible for providing almost 25,000 covariances. The volume of work would be intolerable, and it is quite difficult to have an intuitive feeling about the magnitude of a covariance.

---

*The efficient set will be the same in the mean-standard deviation and mean-variance planes.

FIGURE 8-10 Expected return related to σ_p and σ_p^2

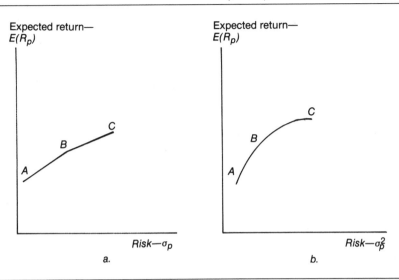

Because of this practical difficulty, the Markowitz portfolio model was exclusively of academic interest until William Sharpe suggested a simplification.[4] Since almost all securities are significantly correlated with the whole market, Sharpe suggested abandoning the covariance of each security with each other security and substituting information on the relationship of each security to the market. In his terms, it is possible to consider the return for each security as represented by the following equation:

$$R_i = \alpha_i + \beta_i I + \epsilon_i$$

where
R_i is the return on security i.
α_i and β_i are parameters.
ϵ_i is a random variable with an expected value of zero.
I is the return of some index, typically a common stock price index.

The return on any stock depends on some constant (α) plus some coefficient (β) times the return of a comprehensive stock index (say, the S&P 500), plus a random component.

The essence of Sharpe's simplification is that the covariance of return between securities can be estimated using the beta or slope coefficient from the single index model as follows:

$$\text{cov}_{ij} = \beta_i \beta_j \sigma_i^2.$$

Now, for N stocks, instead of requiring $N(N-1)/2$ covariances, we can use N beta estimates and the variance on the market index. For our list of 1,000 securities, Sharpe's simplification reduces the estimates that the analysts must produce from 501,500 to 3,002.*

As Markowitz's work and Sharpe's work became more accepted in the late 1960s and early 1970s, controversies quickly arose over the method of estimating betas. An estimate of future betas is required, and not surprisingly the initial approach used estimates calculated from past data. However, studies by Blume showed that although historical betas on large portfolios provided accurate predictions of future betas, this was not true for individual securities.[5] One problem is that historical betas are estimates from a sample of data and are subject to sampling error. Since the average beta across all stocks (weighted by market values) is 1.0, in any period the estimated betas of high-beta stocks (those greater than 1.0) will tend to have positive sampling errors, and the low-beta stocks will tend to have negative sampling errors. Because the error in any individual estimate is random, some of the high-beta stocks will have smaller betas in a subsequent period, and as a whole, the average beta of the high-beta group will be subsequently lower. Similarly, the stocks with low betas in the earlier period will have, on the average, higher subsequent betas.

Different approaches to estimating the beta have been suggested, including adjustments to historical betas to correct for sampling error. Investors and portfolio managers can now purchase such beta estimates from a variety of firms that compete in the "better beta business."

Those wishing to hold more or less risky portfolios chose a sufficiently diversified portfolio with a high or low beta. Those who believe they have superior skills at estimating stock specific expected returns and variances can use the betas purchased to produce their estimated efficient frontier.

Lending and borrowing

A natural extension of the Markowitz analysis was to consider the problem of building portfolios which included riskless assets and portfolios purchased in part with borrowed funds, as well as portfolios of risky assets paid with the investor's equity.

Recall that the efficient frontier for portfolios made up of many risky assets is typically concave from below in the plane whose axes are risk (as measured by the standard deviation) and expected return. For any given period, there are assets whose rates of return can be predicted with virtual certainty—except for times of nuclear holocausts, natural disasters, and revolution. Most investors have confidence that they can accurately predict the rate of return on federal government securities for any period which is

---

*The number of estimates necessary for the Markowitz model with N stocks is $N(N+3)/2$; the Sharpe simplification requires $3N+2$.

FIGURE 8-11   The efficient frontier with lending

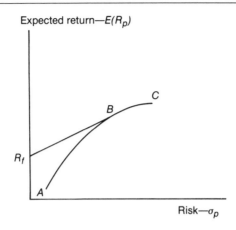

equal to their maturity. For example, Treasury bills maturing in one year have a precisely predictable rate of return for one year.*

The introduction of riskless assets into portfolios has interesting consequences. In the following diagrams, the return on a risk-free asset is designated by R_f on the vertical axis. Sharpe[6] and Tobin[7] stated that if this alternative exists, it is possible to select portfolios at any given point on line $R_f B$ defined by the return on the riskless asset and the point of tangency with the efficient frontier of portfolios with risky assets (Figure 8–11.) This follows from the discussion of asset combinations.

As stated above, the rate of return on a portfolio of any two assets, A and B, is always a linear function of the amounts invested in the assets. The formula for the variance of such a portfolio is as follows:

$$\sigma_p^2 = X_i^2 + X_j^2\sigma_j^2 + 2X_iX_j\rho_{ij}\sigma_i\sigma_j$$

If the riskless asset is represented by i, and the portfolio of risky assets is represented at the point of tangency by j, it is easy to see that only the equation's second term has a positive value. The first term's value is zero because the return on the riskless asset has zero variance. The third term has a value of zero because the return on the riskless asset has a standard deviation of zero. It is also true that the variance of the portfolio of risky assets is a given parameter. Thus, the variance of the combined portfolio depends exclu-

---

*For government securities with periodic interest payments, the prediction of the rate of return to maturity is somewhat less certain, since the rates that will exist when interest payments have to be reinvested cannot be known with certainty.

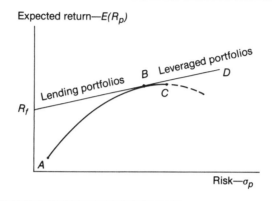

FIGURE 8-12   The efficient frontier with lending and borrowing

sively on the proportion invested in risky assets or, equivalently, the proportion invested in the risk-free asset:

$$\sigma_p^2 = X_j^2 \sigma_j^2;$$

then,

$$\sigma_p = X_j \sigma_j$$

In other words, portfolio risk measured by the standard deviation is linearly related to the proportion invested in j (or i). Investing entirely in the risk-free asset is possible, investing entirely in the risky assets at the point of tangency is possible; and achieving portfolios at any point on a straight line between these points is also possible. Portfolios on this line are preferred to portfolios on curve AB, consisting solely of risky assets, since the former provide more return for given risk.

Sharpe further showed that one can hold efficient portfolios on line $R_f B$ beyond the point of tangency if borrowing is allowed.[8] If it is assumed that one can borrow to buy financial assets at a rate similar to what the investor receives on the risk-free assets, the efficient portfolios beyond the point of tangency lie on a linear extrapolation of the line to the point of tangency (Figure 8–12). Any point on line $R_f BD$ is now attainable by combining the portfolio of risky assets at point B with the riskless asset, or by levering portfolio B by borrowing and investing the funds in B . Portfolios on $R_f BD$ are preferred to portfolios between A and B and between B and C, since they offer greater return for a given level of risk or less risk for a given level of return. The efficient frontier is now entirely linear. $R_f BD$ is Sharpe's capital market line. It relates the expected return on an efficient portfolio to its risk as measured by the standard deviation.

FIGURE 8-13   The capital market line

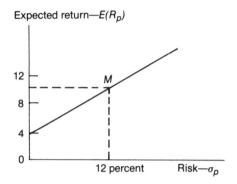

In Figure 8–12, there is only one portfolio of *risky* assets that is optimal, and it is the same for all investors. Since only one portfolio of risky assets is optimal, it must be the market portfolio. That is, it includes all assets in proportion to their market value. We can now describe the capital market line mathematically in terms of the risk-free rate of interest and the return on the market portfolio. The equation is:

$$E(R_p) = R_f + \frac{[E(R_M) - R_f]}{\sigma M}\sigma_p$$

This says the expected return on an efficient portfolio is a linear function of its risk as measured by the standard deviation. The slope of the line is the price of risk. It is the additional expected return for each additional unit of risk.

In Figure 8–13, the pure rate of interest is 4 percent. The expected return on portfolio M is 10 percent, and its standard deviation is 12 percent. An investor who chooses this portfolio earns a reward of 6 percent (10 percent minus 4 percent) for bearing a risk correponding to a standard deviaton of 12 percent. The slope of the line (0.06/0.12) is 0.5. In other words, each additional unit of risk is rewarded with an additonal half unit of expected return.

In Sharpe's model, individual preferences will determine only the amount of borrowing or lending. The fact that this choice is independent of the optimal combination of risky assets is called the "separation theorem.[9]

Two qualifications should be noted. If only lending is allowed, the separation theorem will not hold. For example, in Figure 8–14, the efficient set of portfolios is not limited to those on line R_fM. It also includes portfolios of risky assets between M and C. A particular investor might prefer one of the latter to portfolios on R_fM. In other words, there is no single optimum combination of risky assets.

FIGURE 8-14   The efficient frontier with no borrowing

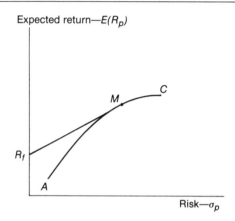

The second qualification is that the efficient frontier for portfolios of risky assets can have linear segments. If the frontier is linear at the point of tangency, once again there is more than one optimum portfolio of risky assets. This is illustrated in Figure 8–15. Portfolios B and C, and all those on the line between them, are efficient portfolios of risky assets. Their returns are perfectly correlated.

FIGURE 8-15   The efficient frontier with a linear segment

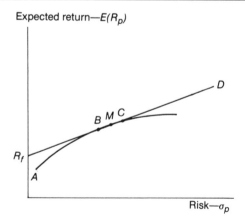

UTILITY, RISK AVERSION, AND OPTIMALITY

Markowitz provided the world with a way of analyzing data on each security so as to specify all portfolios which were optimum or "efficient" in that no other portfolio could be superior in both dimensions. Specification of an efficient portfolio means indicating the proportion of the investor's assets that should be allocated to each security in the portfolio. Rational investors who are risk averse would choose to hold one of the efficient portfolios. Each investor faces a problem in deciding which of the efficient portfolios is optimum for him or her.

So far, this chapter has been based on the assumption that most investors like high rates of return but dislike risk. The definition of efficient portfolios follows this idea. Given predictions about individual securities and their interrelationships, the efficient set is the same for all investors. Since investor preferences for return vis-à-vis risk are likely to differ, we now need to discuss how an investor chooses an optimum portfolio from all the efficient portfolios. Optimization implies that something is maximized. The fact that almost all investors diversify indicates that they do not seek to maximize expected gain, rate of return, or wealth. The underlying principle that guides their behavior is the maximization of expected utility. Utility will be maximized when a given combination of expected return (or wealth) and risk is preferred to all other combinations.

Now, we must relate ideas about efficient portfolios and utility functions. A utility function is the relationship between wealth and utility. Since money has diminishing marginal utility, the relationship looks like Figure 8–16. That is, utility increases at a decreasing rate as wealth increases. Each additional (marginal) unit of wealth provides less of an incre-

FIGURE 8-16   The utility of wealth

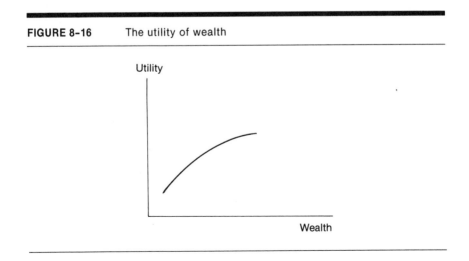

Utility

Wealth

FIGURE 8-17   Hypothetical example of the relationship between preferences for expected return and risk

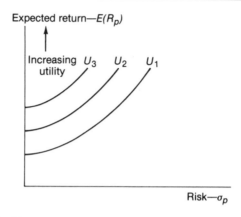

ment in utility that the preceding unit. Thus, the curve is concave from below. It would be convenient if portfolios that are efficient in terms of their means and variances are portfolios that maximized the expected utility of the investor. If that were true, all the individual things about portfolio management that seem plausible would be consistent with each other.

In beginning to reconcile utility theory and efficient portfolios, it is unfortunately necessary to characterize the relationship between wealth and utility more explicitly. All that has been said so far is that the curve representing this relationship is concave from below. A concave curve can be described by several methematical functions. It is not unusual to describe a curve by using quadratic equation, such as the following:

$$U(R_p) = a + bR_p - cR_p^2$$

where

U is the utility of a portfolio.

R_p is the rate of return on a portfolio.

a, b, and c are constants (b and c being positive) whose values will depend upon investor preference.

If the utility function is represented by the foregoing equation, expected utility depends only on the mean and variance of the probability distribution for future returns.[10] In other words, for investors whose utility functions are quadratic, the mean-variance approach to portfolio selection is valid. A portfolio that is efficient in terms of the mean and variance will be one which maximizes expected utility.

Since investors like to increase their expected wealth and like to avoid risk or uncertainty, it is possible to imagine different combinations of expected gain and risk that are valued equally by an investor. That is, an investor will be willing to assume greater risk if she/he achieves greater expected wealth. The combinations of expected gain and risk that are valued equally lie on a so-called indifference curve, which has the shape indicated in Figure 8–17.

Each investor has an infinitely large family of indifference curves. Each curve represents a set of expected returns and risks that are equally valued, and each investor will seek to invest so that he acquires the greatest expected utility. In Figure 8–17, the investor would prefer indifference curve U_3 to U_2, U_2 to U_1, and so forth.

The individual investor is now conceptually prepared to select the optimum portfolio from the efficient set of portfolios. The optimum portfolio (the one which maximizes expected utility) is the one at the point of tangency between the efficient frontier and an indifferent curve. In Figure 8–18, the investor can do no better than choose the portfolio at point A on the efficient frontier, since no other portfolio is on as high an indifference curve.

This happy reconciliaton between utility theory and portfolio theory has a few theoretical blemishes. Some have stated that a utility function or relationship that is quadratic is one that eventually will have utility declining as wealth increases. This is unsatisfactory, since one thing economists know for sure is that people always prefer more money to less money. There are two escapes from this difficulty. One is to forget about what happens eventually and assume that the relevant range of wealth is one in which utility

FIGURE 8-18   The optimal portfolio with lending or borrowing

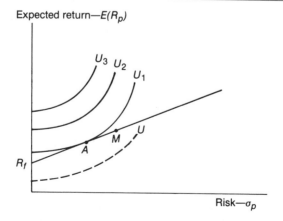

Expected return—$E(R_p)$

U_3 U_2 U_1

U

M

A

R_f

Risk—σ_p

FIGURE 8-19   The utility of wealth

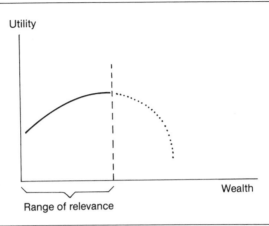

continues to rise.[11] This is illustrated in Figure 8–19. Another escape is to say that concavity does not necessarily imply that the relationship is quadratic and that other equations can preserve the concavity without ever implying a maximum value from which utility will decline as wealth increases. The difficulty with these other curves if that efficiency, in terms of the mean and variance of a portfolio, does not necessarily imply maximization of expected utility. Markowitz has shown, however, that many utility functions are reasonably approximated by the quadratic.[12]

Of course, if the distribution of security returns is normal or is described by other distributions that can be fully explained in terms of mean and variance only, then the choice of optimal portfolio follows the analysis above.

Fama has shown that monthly returns to stocks on the New York Stock Exchange are approximately normal and normality can be reasonably invoked as a working assumption in the portfolio decision.[13] So long as investors prefer more portfolio return, but are averse to the standard deviaton of portfolio return, the fundamental results of Markowitz's theory are implied.

CONCLUSIONS

One is not excused from reaching tentative conclusions simply because the theoretical development of a field is still rudimentary. A conclusion that is consistent with many real-world observations and that is satisfying theoretically is the one with which we started: namely, that portfolios, which are efficient in terms of their means and variances, necessarily maximize expected utility, even if things other than the mean and variance of the distributions of returns affect the expected utility of investors. Even if the investor is concerned about the magnitude of the expected loss, the maximum expected loss, the probability of a loss, or other distribution attributes, portfolios selected according to those criteria will be similar to portfolios selected according to their means and variances.

This chapter has been abstract and general. It has indicated the great contribution of Harry Markowitz in defining the efficient set of portfolios for risk-averse investors. These are the portfolios that maximize expected return for given risk or that minimize risk for given expected return. We have discussed how expected returns and risks for individual securities contribute to the expected returns and risk of portfolios. There has also been discussion of utility theory in an effort to show that maximizing expected utility is consistent with risk aversion, and it allows the individual investor to choose an optimum portfolio from the efficient set in light of personal resources, needs, and tastes.

NOTES

1. Harry M. Markowitz, "Portfolio Selection," *Journal of Finance* 7 (March 1952), pp. 77–91.

2. William E. Sharpe, *Portfolio Theory and Capital Markets* (New York: McGraw-Hill, 1970), pp. 37–44.

3. Harry M. Markowitz, *Portfolio Selection: Efficient Diversification of Investments*, Cowles Foundation, Monograph no. 16 (New York: John Wiley & Sons, 1959), pp. 72–101.

4. William F. Sharpe, "A Simplified Model for Portfolio Analysis," *Management Science* (January 1963), pp. 277–93.

5. M.E. Blume, "On the Assessment of Risk," *Journal of Finance* 30 (June 1975), pp. 785–96.

6. Sharpe, "A Simplified Model for Portfolio Analysis," pp. 277–93.

7. James Tobin, "Liquidity Preference as Behavior Towards Risk," *Review of Economic Studies* 6 (February 1958), pp. 65–86.

8. Sharpe, "A Simplified Model for Portfolio Analysis," pp. 277–93.

9. Tobin, "Liquidity Preferences," pp. 65–86.

10. The proof of this assertion is in Sharpe, *Portfolio Theory*, pp. 196–201.

11. Markowitz, *Portfolio Selection*, pp. 288–89.

12. *Ibid.*, pp. 282–86.

13. Eugene F. Fama, *Foundation of Finance* (New York: Basic Books, 1976), chap. 2.

9

Capital market
equilibrium theory and
evidence on the risk-return
trade-off

INTRODUCTION

The determination of prices of financial assets

In a famous article entitled "Capital Asset Prices: A Theory of Market Equilibrium under Conditions of Risk,"[1] Sharpe considered the relationship between portfolio theory and the determination of prices for financial assets. Portfolio theory is normative in that it tells how investors should behave. It tells nothing about how prices of individual assets adjust to reflect differences in risk. Capital market theory is positive. It describes the market relationships that will result in equilibrium if investors behave according to portfolio theory. These relationships provide a clue to the relevant measures of risk for portfolios and for individual assets.

The assumptions

Sharpe's simplifying assumptions are: risk aversion, identical time horizons and expectations for all investors with respect to each financial asset, identical borrowing and lending rates, no taxes or transaction costs, and rational investors seeking to hold portfolios efficient in the Markowitz sense. To some readers, the assumptions underlying Sharpe's model for determining asset prices may seem so restrictive or even absurd that the model appears unworthy of serious consideration. At the very least, however, the

132

model is useful for understanding some forces which affect asset prices; at most, the lack of reality in the assumptions will have far less practical importance than most persons might believe. After discussing the model, we will look at the assumptions in more detail.

In the preceding chapter, we discussed Sharpe's capital market line, which relates to the expected return on an efficient portfolio to the risk-free rate and the return on the market. The equation is as follows:

$$E(R_p) = R_f + \frac{[E(R_M) - R_f]}{\sigma_M} \sigma_p$$

where

$E(R_p)$ is the expected portfolio return.
R_f is the risk-free return.
$E(R_M)$ is the expected market return.
σ_p is the standard deviation in portfolio returns.
σ_M is the standard deviation on the market.

Since this holds only for *efficient* portfolios, it does not describe the relationship between the rates of return on individual assets (or inefficient portfolios) and their standard deviations.

Sharpe's capital asset pricing model states that the expected return on *any* asset (or portfolio) is related to the riskless rate and the market return as follows:

$$E(R_i) = R_f + [E(R_M) - R_f]\beta_i$$

where

$E(R_i)$ is the expected return on the asset (or portfolio).
R_f is the return on a riskless asset.
$E(R_M)$ is the expected return on the market.
β_i (the beta coefficient) is the measure of the asset's sensitivity of return to market movements.

This relationship is similar to, but not the same as, the capital market line, which holds only for efficient portfolios. Here, risk is measured by beta rather than by the standard deviation. For efficient portfolios, the two relationships are equivalent. By definition, the riskiness of efficient portfolios is determined exclusively by market movements and their returns are linearly related to both the standard deviation and the beta.

The capital asset pricing model or equation is represented in Figure 9–1.

If the risk-free rate is 4 percent, the expected return on the market is 10 percent, and B_i is 0.5 , then the expected return on i would be:

$$E(R_i) = .04 + 0.5(.10 - 0.4)$$
$$= .04 + 0.5(.06)$$
$$= .07$$

FIGURE 9-1 The capital asset pricing model (relationship between expected return and risk for *any* asset or portfolio)

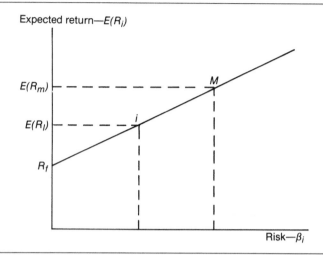

The risk premium for asset i is equal to β_i (its beta coefficient) times the risk premium on the market. In this example, since $\beta_i = .05$, the risk premium on asset i is .03, and the total return is this premium plus the rate on the riskless asset, or 0.7.

The above equation and figure deal with the *expected* return on an asset. The relationship between the actual risk premium on an asset (the actual return minus the riskless rate of return) and returns on the market can be estimated by a regression equation derived from the expectations equation. It is as follows:

$$R_i - R_f = a_i + b_i(R_M - R_f) + c_i$$

where

R_i is the actual return on asset i.
R_f is the riskless rate of return.
a_i is a constant.
b_i is the sensitivity of i to the market.
R_M is the return on market.
c_i is a term representing variability in R_i not associated with variation in R_M.

If actual returns were exactly as "expected," the value of a_i and c_i would be zero, and R_i would be completely explained by R_M, R_f, and b_i. Even if random disturbances caused departures from expectations in any single period, on the average, a_i and c_i would be equal to zero.

The Sharpe model presents a simple and intuitively appealing picture of financial markets. All investors hold efficient portfolios, and all such portfolios move in perfect lockstep with the market. Portfolios differ only in their market sensitivity. Prices of all risky assets adjust so that their returns are appropriate, in terms of the model, to their riskiness. This riskiness is measured by a simple statistic, beta, which indicates the sensitivity of the asset to market movements.

If there should be a momentary disequilibrium such that the price of an asset were "too high," causing expected returns to be "too low," investors would sell the asset, and its price would return to the equilibrium level. The converse would be true for assets whose prices were "too low" and whose expected returns were consequently "too high."

The realism of the model

The attractions of a religion based upon faith in Sharpe's model are obvious. There is an understandable predispositon to be a believer. Yet one is naturally moved by the lack of realistic assumptions to see whether their apparent absurdity is as great as it seems at first glance. Another approach is to ignore the realism of the assumptions and to see whether predictions based on the model are confirmed by experience. Fortunately, it is generally understood that the value of a model lies in its predictive power, and the model cannot be judged by reference to the realism of its underlying assumptions. This point has been expressed with great clarity and persuasiveness by Milton Friedman in a famous essay:

> [T]he relevant question to ask about the "assumptions" of a theory is not whether they are descriptively "realistic," for they never are, but whether they are sufficiently good approximations for the purpose in hand. And this question can be answered only by seeing whether the theory works, which means whether it yields sufficiently accurate predictions.[2]

Risk-free borrowing and lending

Perhaps the most contentious aspect of the equilibrium analysis deriving the capital market line is the reliance on risk-free borrowing and lending. Since Treasury bills offer opportunities for investors wishing to lend at a nominal risk-free rate of return, the issue is really the borrowing opportunities. It is clear that no investor can borrow at the Treasury bill rate. The effect of introducing a differential borrowing rate is easily portrayed graphically (Figure 9-2). R_l is the lending rate and R_b is the borrowing rate. Efficient portfolios lie on the line segments $R_l A$ and BD or on the curve AB. With lending or borrowing, the optimal portfolio for an individual investor is no longer necessarily the market portfolio. The market portfolio lies on the efficient frontier between points A and B and some investors will select portfolios along that curve.

FIGURE 9-2   The relationship between expected return and risk with different lending and borrowing rates

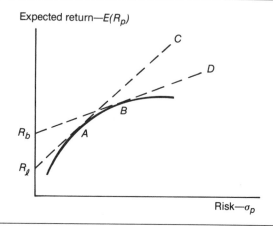

Fortunately, the introduction of different lending and borrowing rates has only a minor effect on the model of asset prices that describes the equilibrium in this market. Black has shown that the model becomes:

$$E(R_i) = E(R_z) + [E(R_m) - E(R_z)]\beta_i$$

where $E(R_z)$ is the expected return on a portfolio with zero beta.

The equation is identical to the earlier Sharpe model except for the substitution of $E(R_z)$ for R_f.[3] The basic relationship still holds, and differences in expected returns across stocks and portfolios are due only to differences in betas.

Efficient portfolios

Sharpe's capital market line describes the relationship between risk and rate of return for efficient portfolios. All are perfectly correlated with the market and, as a consequence, the market is the only source of variation (or risk) for all of them. Either the beta coefficient or the standard deviations is a practical, theoretically satisfying measure of risk.

Most portfolios are not efficient and, consequently, they are not perfectly correlated with the market. Thus, part of the variation in returns on such portfolios is not attributable to market variation. Whereas the beta coefficient is sufficient to indicate the relative volatility (riskiness) of efficient portfolios, it may not be sufficient to indicate the relative variability (riskiness) of inefficient portfolios.

The total variability of inefficient portfolios or of a single asset is greater than that indicated by the beta coefficient. Thus the question arises as to the appropriate measure of their risk. The standard answer of modern financial theory is that the proper measure of *total* risk for a single asset is a measure of its total variability. However, the measure of risk which determines an asset's risk *premium* is its contribution to the variability of a diversified portfolio. The answer is based on the premise that most investors dislike risk and therefore hold diversified portfolios. An asset's contribution to the riskiness of a portfolio—its systematic risk—is measured by the familiar beta coefficient, since a portfolio's beta coefficient is simply a weighted average of the coefficient of its component securities, each individual coefficient being weighted by the value of its security as a percent of the portfolio's total value.

In other words, the risk premium that an asset commands depends upon only that part of its variability which is associated with general market movements and not upon its independent variability. We are led to the startling conclusion that there is no risk premium for an asset if its rate of return has no correlation with rates of return on the market as a whole. The relationship between the beta coefficient of an asset and its correlation with the market is as follows:

$$\beta_{iM} = \frac{\rho_{iM}\sigma_i\sigma_M}{\sigma_M^2}$$

where

β_{iM} is the beta coefficient of asset i.
ρ_{iM} is the correlation coefficient between asset i and the market.
σ_i is the standard deviation of i.
σ_M^2 is the variance of the market.

The equation makes it clear why the beta coefficient would be zero if there were no correlation between asset i and the market. Thus, even if returns on asset i were extremely variable, its beta coefficient would be zero, and asset i would not increase the variability or riskiness of a diversified portfolio. Modern portfolio theory would say that such an asset would not provide a risk premium.

Single assets are inefficient portfolios. What is true for single assets is true for other inefficient portfolios. The total risk (variability) is greater than that caused by movements in the market. Thus, beta is not a good measure of total risk, but beta is the proper measure of that part of total risk that will produce a risk premium. Beta measures the systematic risk or volatility—the risk that cannot be eliminated by diversification. The remaining variability or unsystematic risk can be eliminated by diversification.

Risk and return: the evidence

In the early aftermath of the publication of Sharpe's work on the price of risk, a new industry was created to manufacture and distribute beta coefficients. This coefficient was simple; it measured the sensitivity of the return of an asset or portfolio to changes in returns on the market. Furthermore, it was *the* measure of risk and was in itself sufficient to explain differences in returns among securities and portfolios.

Surprisingly, the results of modern portfolio theory and capital asset pricing models were resisted by many people committed to traditional investment theory. Although the trade-off between risk and return was well founded, many rejected the notion of beta as the appropriate measure of risk. As always, these arguments can only be settled at the empirical level and we now consider the evidence on the risk/return trade-off in the market.

Beta as a measure of risk

The primary implication of the previous chapter's capital market equilibrium analysis is that portfolios or stocks with higher betas will earn higher returns. If beta is not the appropriate measure of risk, then investment strategies that concentrate on stocks of different betas will not produce differential performance.

Sharpe and Cooper provide a relatively straightforward test of this proposition.[4] Each year from 1931 through 1967, betas for all New York Stock Exchange stocks were calculated using monthly returns over the previous five years. Each year the stocks were ranked by beta, divided into deciles, and equally weighted portfolios were formed using the stocks in each decile. At year-end the portfolios were rebalanced to again form equally weighted portfolios of decreasing beta values.

Note that the investment strategies used by Sharpe and Cooper could have been adopted by investors and require rebalancing transactions only once a year. Investors wanting to follow a high beta risk strategy would divide their funds each year among those stocks in the highest beta decile. The results from following such strategies are in Table 9–1.

Although not perfect, there is a strong relationship between the average return and the portfolio beta. Investors following the high-beta strategies would have earned higher average returns than investors following the low-beta strategies.

The evidence of Sharpe and Cooper is relatively easily interpreted and shows that, on the average, actual market returns are a positive function of beta as predicted by the equilibrium asset pricing models of this chapter. Evidence of this type was a powerful lure and explains the rapid and widespread acceptance of the tenets of modern capital market theory.

Additional risk measures

The results of Sharpe and Cooper confirm that security returns are a function of beta, but they do not allow us to conclude that the capital asset

TABLE 9-1 Average returns to investment strategies of investing in portfolios of different betas

Strategy	Portfolio beta	Percentage average annual return
10	1.42	22.67
9	1.18	20.45
8	1.14	20.26
7	1.24	21.77
6	1.06	18.49
5	0.98	19.12
4	1.00	18.88
3	0.76	14.99
2	0.65	14.63
1	0.58	11.58

Source: Sharpe and Cooper, "Risk-Return Classes of New York Stock Exchange Common Stocks, 1931–1967," p. 52.

pricing model is strictly valid. It is argued that other measures of risk are equally important and that beta is not the only risk that is compensated in the market.

This conjecture was studied by Fama and MacBeth.[5] Responding to both academic and practitioner arguments, they tested whether the relationship between risk and return is linear as predicted by the capital asset pricing models and whether the firm-specific variance of a stock's return, (the unsystematic risk) has any impact on return. Fama and MacBeth tested the following model, which is a modification of Black's asset-pricing model:

$$E(R_i) = E(R_z) + [E(R_m) - E(R_z)]\beta_i + C\beta_i^2 + d\sigma_{ei}$$

The first two terms on the right side of the equation are the basic components of the Black model; the third term is beta squared, and it is a measure of nonlinearity; the final term is a measure of the unsystematic risk. To test the model, Fama and MacBeth estimated the coefficients of the following regression equation:

$$R_i = \gamma_1 + \gamma_2\beta_i + \gamma_3\beta_i^2 + \gamma_4\sigma_{ei} + \eta_i$$

The basic capital asset pricing model predicts γ_3 and γ_4 will not be significantly different from zero, and γ_2 will be nonzero.

Fama and MacBeth's procedures involved detailed efforts to avoid selection bias and measurement errors. Based on beta rankings of stocks, 20 portfolios were formed each year, and the average beta, beta squared, and unsystematic risk to each portfolio were calculated. The above regression was estimated each year across the 20 portfolios and the coefficients γ_1 through γ_4 were produced. By averaging these yearly estimates of the coefficients, Fama and MacBeth were able to test whether the actual returns from 1935 through 1968 were a function of the beta, beta squared, and unsystematic risk. Their results are summarized in Table 9–2.

TABLE 9-2 Results of Fama and MacBeth test of the capital asset pricing model

Coefficient	Average	t statistic
$\gamma 1$	.0020	0.55
$\gamma 2$	.0114	1.85
$\gamma 3$	−.0026	−0.86
$\gamma 4$	.0516	1.11

Source: E. Fama, *Foundations of Finance* (New York: Basic Books, 1976), p. 364.

The only coefficient that is statistically nonzero is γ_2, and the results again confirm that returns are a positive function of beta. Moreover, there is no evidence that unsystematic risk or nonlinear factors are rewarded in the market.

Fama and MacBeth's analysis was a test of beta against specified alternative risk measures, that is, beta squared and unsystematic, stock-specific risk. While their results reject these alternative specifications, it is possible that other risk specificatons may be rewarded along with beta. This is the context in which Gibbons tested the capital asset pricing model.[6] He noted the basic model can be reformulated as:

$$E(R_i) = R_f(1 - \beta_i) + \beta_i E(R_m)$$

This formulation is similar to the market model (see Chapter 7), but the α_i or intercept term is now constrained to be equal to $R_f(1 - \beta_i)$. Gibbons tested this constraint. Note that this test does not specify any alternative risk measures , but it provides a test of the basic capital asset pricing model.

After careful econometric analysis, Gibbons rejected the hypothesis that the intercept terms satisfy the constraint imposed by the capital asset pricing model. The implication is that something besides beta is priced in the market.

In sum, the accumulated evidence suggests that beta is an important determinant of the returns to stocks. However, the capital asset pricing models of Sharpe and Black are not complete descriptons of the asset-pricing process.

Extension of the CAPM

The finding that the basic capital asset pricing omits variables that are used in pricing assets stimulated the search for these variables. At a theoretical level Ross has developed an asset pricing model that allows for a set of factors and that is consistent with capital market equilibrium.[7]

In Ross's Arbitrage Pricing Model, the expected return on a stock is a function of several independent factors. Each factor is priced in the market and a particular stock's expected return depends upon the expected factor returns and that stock's sensitivity to each of the factors. Intuitively the Arbitrage Pricing Model is akin to the market model of Chapter 3 with several factors instead of just the market return. Different stocks can have different sensitivities to the factors and competition in the market ensures that each stock is priced to reflect this sensitivity.

Unfortunately, the theoretical model does not specify what the factors are and research into their identity is at a relatively early stage. Preliminary statistical investigation suggests that there are only a few factors that empirically seem to matter. Given the evidence in Chapter 3 it is not surprising that these initial results find that the most significant factor, although unknown, is highly correlated with the return on the market portfolio. Of course, given that the stock market is one of the leading indicators of the economy's predicted or expected health, it is likely that the market return itself reflects other more direct macroeconomic variables affecting investment returns. Whether these variables can be identified and whether they explain more of the variability in stock returns than a simple one factor market model, is still to be decided.

Another line of theoretical research has been to modify the basic model to allow for specified deviations from the underlying assumptions. Merton has derived an asset-pricing model that allows for changes in the risk-free rate over time.[8] If this return is stochastic, investors are exposed to another kind of risk apart from systematic or beta risk. If the risk-free rate changes , the investment opportunity set faced by investors shifts, and investors will pay to hedge against these shifts.

Alternatively it has been proposed that the different tax treatment of dividends and capital gains alters the basic model. Brennan develops a capital asset pricing model that is still a function of beta, but the expected return depends upon dividend yield and systematic risk.[9] As explained in Chapter 6, Miller and Scholes present convincing evidence that, in general, there is no dividend yield effect and that the Brennan model can be rejected.[10].

Perhaps the most intriguing development in the study of asset pricing is at the empirical level. A number of studies have documented that portfolios based on stocks with different market values have performed differentially, even after adjusting for beta. In terms of the Fama and MacBeth analysis, these studies find that in a model that incorporates beta and a relative size measure, S_i,

$$R_i = \gamma_1 + \gamma_2 \beta_i + \gamma_3 S_i + \mu_i$$

the estimates of the γ_2 and γ_3 coefficients are statistically different from zero. Smaller firms tend to outperform larger firms even after adjusting for systematic risk.

From an economic perspective, this result makes little sense. If size were a variable determining equilibrium returns, there would be an incentive for larger firms to split into smaller units and become more valuable. This is over simplified, however, and size is used in place of missing factors. Although the factors are unknown, they still affect small firms differently.

Interestingly, Keim reports that the size effect has a distinct seasonal element, and small-firm stocks do particularly well in January. [11] An explanation for this is that the season reflects tax effects induced by the end of the financial year. Miller and Scholes found no dividend yield effect in general, but it is possible that the differential tax treatment of dividends and capital gains is obvious only in January.

What does it all mean?

The search for a valid description of how stocks are priced is an intriguing example of scientific progress. Sharpe's original capital asset pricing model provides a powerful, yet simple, quantatative measure of risk, and there is little doubt that beta is an important determinant of stock returns. As more refined methodology and data have been utilized, the incompleteness of the basic model has been exposed.

This has stimulated development of asset-pricing models that might provide more complete descriptions. Concurrently, empirical regularities in the stock return data are being investigated. We are slowly learning more about the complex process that generates stock prices.

CONCLUSIONS

Markowitz's original work on portfolio theory has been extended in two important ways. Sharpe and Tobin indicated the consequences of including riskless assets in the population of assets among which an investor's funds were to be allocated. The inclusion of the riskless asset changes the set of opportunities available to the investor, permitting the creation of portfolios superior to those consisting soley of risky assets with respect to both risk and rate of return.

The second major extension of Markowitz's work is the development of the capital asset pricing model. It explains how the prices of financial assets are determined in a world of rational, risk-averse investors following Markowitz's prescribed portfolio analysis.

Adam Smith, and undoubtedly his forebears, understood that risk was related to rates of return. People do not like risk, and if they expect to incur it, they expect to be paid. This payment is called the risk premium or price of risk.

Prior to Sharpe's article, "Capital Asset Prices: A Theory of Market Equilibrium under Conditions of Risk," discussions of risk and its relation to return were theoretically casual or exercises in brute empiricism.

Sharpe's article finally provided a theoretically satisfying definition of risk and gave focus to most subsequent serious work and controversy. He stated that rational risk-averse investors in an efficient market would hold efficient portfolios (in Markowitz's sense of the term), and that, therefore, the proper measure of risk was the contribution of an asset to the riskiness of an efficient portfolio. That measure is the beta coefficient. The cult of beta and the beta industry quickly flowered. The empirical evidence accumulated since Sharpe's article has shown that beta is an important determinant of returns. However, the simple capital asset pricing model is apparently not a complete description of the asset-pricing process. Some specified alternative forms have been suggested, and the search continues at both a theoretical and empirical level.

Beta, however, remains a valuable concept, and the capital asset pricing model remains one of the most powerful developments in modern finance.

NOTES

1. William F. Sharpe, "Capital Asset Prices: A Theory of Market Equilibrium under Conditions of Risk," *Journal of Finance* 19 (September 1964), pp. 425–42.

2. Milton Friedman, "The Methodology of Positive Economics," *Essays in Positive Economics* (Chicago: The University of Chicago Press, 1953).

3. Fisher Black, "Capital Market Equilibrium with Restricted Borrowing," *Journal of Business* 45 (July 1972), pp. 444–54.

4. William E. Sharpe and Guy M. Cooper, "Risk-Return Classes of New York Stock Exchange Common Stocks, 1931–1967,"*Financial Analysts Journal* 28 (March–April 1972), pp. 46–54.

5. Eugene F. Fama and James D. MacBeth, "Risk, Return and Equilibrium: Empirical Tests," *Journal of Political Economy* 71 (May–June 1973), pp. 607–36.

6. Michael R. Gibbons, "Multivariate Tests of Financial Models: A New Approach," *Journal of Financial Economics* 10 (March 1982.), pp. 3–28.

7. Stephen Ross, "The Arbitrage Theory of Capital Asset Pricing," *Journal of Economic Theory* 8 (December 1976), pp. 343–62.

8. Robert C. Merton, "An Intertemporal Capital Asset Pricing Model," *Econometrica* 41 (September 1973), pp. 867–87.

9. Michael J. Brennan, "Taxes, Market Valuation and Corporate Financial Policy," *National Tax Journal* 23, (1970), pp. 417–27.

10. Merton H. Miller and Myron Scholes, "Dividends and Taxes," *Journal of Financial Economics* 6 (December 1978), pp. 333–64 ; and "Dividends and Taxes: Empirical Evidence," *Journal of Political Economy* 90 (December 1982), pp. 1118–41.

11. Donald B. Keim, "Size-Related Anomalies and Stock Return Seasonability: Further Empirical Evidence," *Journal of Financial Economics* 12 (June 1983), pp. 13–32.

10

Options

INTRODUCTION[1]

The year 1973 was a landmark in the history of U.S. capital markets. In April of 1973, the Chicago Board Options Exchange (CBOE) opened and began trading call options on stocks. Options had been traded over the counter before 1973, but transaction costs were high, secondary trading was limited, the contracts were not standardized, and prices were not published. The formation of the CBOE eliminated many of these problems, and listed options have become a popular investment avenue.

The growth of the listed options market has been exceptional. On the CBOE, the annual dollar volume of contracts written (based on the prices paid for the options) has risen from $1.6 billion in 1974 to more than $39 billion in 1983. A seat on the CBOE sold for $17,000 in 1973 and for more than $200,000 in 1983.[2] In 1984, over 1 million contracts were traded on a single day.

Despite this enormous growth, the options market remains a mystery to most people. This lack of understanding results partially from ignorance of the investment attributes of options, and it also reflects the confusion created by the peculiar market vocabulary that has developed. Security traders are renowned for their jargon, and the options market is no exception. Unsophisticated investors have some inkling of bulls and bears, but they are

144

usually bewildered by strips, straps, and straddles and inhibited by naked positions, spread positions, and covered calls.

In this chapter, we provide an introduction to the investment attributes of options, together with some analysis of characteristics affecting their pricing. Definitions of terms are provided in the glossary, and the chapter also includes a brief discussion of market procedures.

Definitions and market procedures

The two basic instruments traded in the options market are calls and puts. A call option entitles the holder to buy 100 shares of an underlying stock at a stated price on or before a fixed expiration date.* A put option is the right to sell 100 shares. An option writer sells the option to an option buyer for a price called the option premium. The price, at which the shares can be bought or sold, is called the striking or exercise price.

A major advantage of exchange-listed options is the standardization of contract terms. Each underlying stock has options that expire on a cycle of three specified months approximately three months apart. The most common cycle is January, April, July, and October, but some stocks use other cycles. In all cases, maturity is restricted to nine months or less. When an old contract expires, two new, nine-month options are introduced on the underlying stock. The striking prices of these contracts are whole numbers ending in 5 or 0, and they are set to bracket the current stock price in $5 or $10 intervals. As the underlying stock price moves substantially, options with new striking prices are introduced. The standardization of option contracts reduces the variety of contracts to be evaluated by traders in the secondary market, and the consequent depth of the organized secondary market is an added advantage of listed options.

After the contract is initiated and the premium has been paid, the writer and buyer have no direct relationship. Each has a contract only with the Options Clearing Corporation (OCC), which effectively guarantees the performance of the contract. The OCC becomes the writer of each contract as far as the purchaser is concerned, and the OCC becomes the purchaser of each contract as far as the writer is concerned. Either party to the initial contract can close out his/her position by writing or buying another contract and thereby reversing the original transaction. If a buyer chooses to exercise an option, the OCC randomly selects a writer who has not closed out that position.

Listed options are not adjusted for regular cash dividends, but they are adjusted for stock splits and stock dividends. The number of shares that can be bought or sold and the exercise price are modified when these latter events occur.

---

*Options that can be exercised at any time before the expiration date are called *American options*, and those that can be exercised only at maturity are called *European options*.

Having initiated an opening transaction by either buying or writing an option, the investor has three alternative actions to take on the expiration date. Suppose investor A has purchased a call option on IBM stock with an exercise price of $125, and investor B has purchased a put option on Xerox stock with an exercise price of $60.

If the IBM stock price at the expiration date is less than the exercise price of $125, there is no point in exercizing the call, since it is cheaper to buy the stock in the market. The rational investor will let the call expire. The loss to the buyer, and the profit to the writer of the option, is the premium at which the initial transaction was priced. If, on the other hand, the IBM stock price at expiration is greater than $125, investor A will exercise the call. The difference between the exercise price and the stock price can be realized by selling the stock in the market.

If the Xerox stock price at the expiration date is greater than $60, investor B will let the put expire, since more can be earned by selling the stock in the market. Whenever the stock price at expiration is less than the exercise price, investor B will exercise the put and earn the difference as a return on the investment in the put option.

When the price of a stock makes the exercise of an option worthless, the option is said to be *out-of-the-money*. When it is worthwhile to exercise the option, it is said to be *in-the-money*. When the stock price is close to the exercise price the option is said to be *at-the-money*.

Investment strategies using options

The principal result of any option transaction is to alter the risk characteristics of investors' portfolio positions. The net effect is a reallocation of risk and reward between the buyer and writer. Since there is a buyer for every writer, option investment is a zero sum game (ignoring transaction costs) and profits to call (put) writers in total must be at the expense of call (put) buyers in total. Options, however, provide a significant expansion of the patterns of portfolio returns available to investors.

While the actual uses of options in investments are many and varied, it is beyond our scope to describe them all. An analysis of some of the more general types of strategies, however, will illustrate the peculiar investment characteristics of options.

The simplest strategy is to hold a naked or uncovered position in options. Here, the investor buys or sells calls or puts without holding the underlying stock. The payoff to this strategy is presented in Figure 10–1 and compared with the profits made from investing in the underlying stock itself. Note that selling the stock short involves selling stock that is not owned. In essence, the investor borrows the stock and sells it. To close the short position, the stock is repurchased and returned to the lender. If the stock price falls between the sale and repurchase, the investor profits. A short position in a call or put is equivalent to writing the option.

FIGURE 10-1

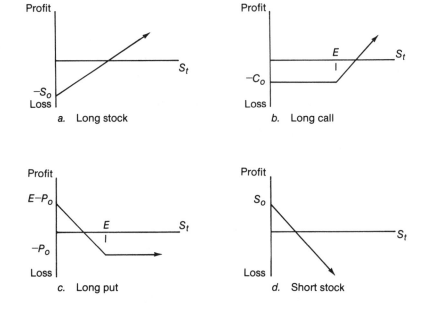

a. Long stock

b. Long call

c. Long put

d. Short stock

e. Short call

f. Short put

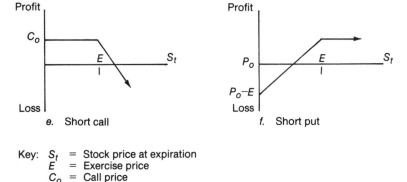

Key: S_t = Stock price at expiration
E = Exercise price
C_o = Call price
P_o = Put price

As shown in Figure 10–1, naked positions in options (relative to holding the stock) enable the investor to limit the profit or loss that is earned when the expiration stock price is favorable or unfavorable. The net profit or loss depends on the premium at which the option was initially traded. The attractive characteristics of options become evident when options are combined with other securities to produce patterns of returns for a portfolio of investments.

Options enable investors to limit their portfolio risk by insuring against unfavorable changes in the prices of stocks held. In effect, options can be effectively used as investment insurance.[3]

A put option with exercise price equal to the current stock price insures the investor against any declines in the stock's value over the life of the option. When the exercise price is less than the current stock price, the put becomes equivalent to an insurance policy with a deductible. Unlike other insurance contracts, however, the investor can buy the insurance (the put) without owning the asset insured (the stock).

Although the similarity is not as obvious, call options are also akin to insurance policies. To see this, consider the following investment strategy: (1) Buy one share of a nondividend-paying stock, (2) borrow money in the form of a discount loan with the face value of $E repayable in T months time, and (3) buy a put option on the stock with exercise price $E and expiring in T months.

At expiration, when the stock price is S_T, the investment will have a value of either zero or $$(S_T - E)$. If $S_T < E$, the put is exercised, and the stock exchanged for $E, which is just enough to repay the loan. If $S_T > E$, the stock is sold for S_T, and after repaying the loan, the balance is $$(S_T - E)$.

These payoffs are identical to those from an investment strategy of buying a call on the same stock with exercise price $E and expiring in T months. It follows that a call option is functionally equivalent to a long position in stock leveraged by a term loan, plus a put as an insurance policy against stock price declines. Although the leverage component of call options is usually emphasized, the insurance component differentiates call option strategies from stock strategies, such as buying on margin.

Besides holding options as stand-alone investments, investors take advantage of the insurance component to hedge positions in stocks by buying or writing options on those stocks. The idea is to protect the portfolio against unfavorable stock price outcomes. One hedge strategy is the covered call, wherein calls are written against shares of the underlying stock held in the portfolio. The position is fully covered, since the call obligation is guaranteed by holding the stock. The profit from a covered call held to expiration is shown in Figure 10–2(a). All unfavorable stock outcomes are hedged or improved by the amount received as the call premium, but the profits from all favorable stock price outcomes are restricted to a constant hedge profit. By varying the exercise price relative to the initial stock price, however, the hedged properties of the covered call can be altered to allow the investor to garner more or less of the favorable stock price outcomes. Similarly, the hedge position payoffs will become closer to long-stock investment payoffs when fewer calls are written against a fixed number of shares.

Figures 10–1(f) and 10–2(a) show that the payoffs to a covered call virtually replicate those to a written put. Likewise, a hedge involving a long position in both stock and a put on that stock replicates the payoff to a pur-

FIGURE 10-2

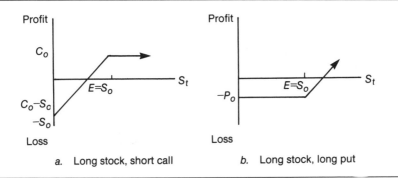

a. Long stock, short call   b. Long stock, long put

chased call. This relationship between puts and calls is known as the put-call parity, and it can be used by traders to relate prices of puts and calls on the same stock. Puts were not traded on the CBOE until January 1977, and the put-call parity enabled brokers to fabricate a put using calls and positions in the underlying stock.

The relationship between options can be used to analyze any hedge strategy. For example, the covered call is functionally equivalent to lending money and issuing insurance to the buyer.* Similarly, a strategy of buying calls and investing in fixed income securities is functionally equivalent to taking a long position in the stock with insurance against stock price declines.

Some investors use options for speculation, and others use the leverage component of calls to trade on nonpublic information. Still others use options to buy or sell insurance. Like others in the insurance business, however, buyers and sellers of options expect that the price set is actuarily fair and that neither can expect to earn an above-normal rate of return at the expense of the other.

Apart from hedging and buying leverage, other strategies are used in the options market. For example, there are many forms of *spreading*, wherein the investor simultaneously buys and sells options on the same stock. The options can be at different expiration dates with the same exercise price ("horizontal spreads") or at different exercise prices with the same expiration dates ("vertical spreads"). Other combinations involve buying or selling both puts and calls on a stock; that is, a straddle. In effect, all these investment strategies are initiated on a belief that the options are mispriced.

---

*Writing a call is simply a short sale of a call option and is equivalent to: (1) selling the stock short, (2) lending money on a term basis, and (3) insuring the buyer against declines in the stock below the exercise price. With a covered call, the long stock position offsets the implicit short sale of the stock (1), and the position is then functionally equivalent to (2) and (3).

If options and their underlying stocks are correctly priced, such strategies will not, on the average, earn abnormal investment returns.

The pricing of options

The analysis of various option positions shows that at expiration date an option's value depends only upon the stock price and the exercise price at the expiration date. If the stock price at expiration is below the exercise price, the price of a call is zero, and the price of a put is the difference between the exercise and stock prices. When the stock price at expiration is above the exercise price, the put is worthless, and the call has a market value equal to the difference. However, the value of an option prior to expiration is a function of other variables.

The search for the correct ingredients for pricing stock options has been as arduous as the search for the correct model of stock prices. Just as the development of the Capital Asset Pricing Model was a landmark achievement, there was an equally significant development in option pricing. In 1973, Fischer Black and Myron Scholes[4] presented what has since been called the first completely satisfactory equilibrium option pricing model.[5] Together with some important extensions provided by Robert Merton, this trailblazing article has been a watershed for much recent research in finance.[6]

For those with limited math background, the derivation of the Black-Scholes model is complex. Indeed, the final form of the model is somewhat forbidding, although it is provided here in a footnote.[7] The Black-Scholes model, however, allows us to explain the determinants of the value of an option prior to expiration:

Current price of underlying stock. The greater the stock price relative to the exercise price, the greater the value of a call option and the smaller the value of a put.

Exercise price. Increasing the exercise price decreases the payoff to a call option and hence reduces its price, but it has the opposite effect on puts.

Volatility of stock returns. The greater the total variability of stock returns (including marketwide influences), the greater the price movements of the stock. These are offsetting effects for the owner of the stock but not for owners of options on the stock. Increasing the volatility increases the magnitude of favorable outcomes, and for a given exercise price, increases the option's price.

Time to maturity. The longer the time to maturity, the greater the likelihood of favorable outcomes for both puts and calls. In effect, the longer maturity allows more time for the stock price to experience wide fluctuations. Also, the longer the time to maturity, the smaller the present value of the exercise price. Since the call buyer pays this amount and the put buyer receives it, the increasing maturity increases call values and decreases put values.

Interest rates. The higher the interest rate, the lower the present value of the exercise price the call buyer has contracted to pay in the event of exercise. Therefore, the greater the interest rate, the greater the call price, and this effect is accentuated by a greater probability of exercise.

Anticipated dividends. The holders of listed options do not receive the rights to any cash dividends. Moreover, on an ex-dividend date, when holders of stock are no longer entitled to the dividend that has previously been declared, the price of the underlying stock will fall by approximately the amount of the cash dividend. Reductions in the stock price relative to the exercise price reduce the value of a call option by making it less likely that the option will be exercised. On the other hand, a put option on a dividend-paying stock is more valuable than a put option on a nondividend-paying stock.

The above factors have a primary impact on prices of options. However, institutional rules such as tax laws, margin requirements, and transactions costs can also affect the values of options. As always, however, prices are set by the marginal investor, and the impact of these secondary factors is unclear.

An important by-product of the Black-Scholes pricing model is the intuition it provides in valuing other complex securities. For example, the equity of a leveraged firm can be viewed as a call option purchased from the bondholders. The exercise price is the set of payments promised to the bondholders. Bankruptcy, where the bondholders retain all of the firm's assets, is effectively also nonexercizing of the option by the stockholders. When the firm's value is greater than the claims of the bondholders, the equity is "in the money." The notion that the claims on the firm can be viewed as options enables us to analyze the effects of major changes in investment or financing policy. For example, a merger that results in an increased variance of the firm's cashflows will benefit stockholders at the expense of the bondholders.

This analysis can be extended to other financial instruments. Some firms issue warrants that allow the holders to buy new shares at a specified price within a given period. Warrants are call options written by the corporation. Similarly, many firms issue bonds with call provisions that allow the firm to buy back the bond at specified call prices during the bond's life. This is equivalent to the firm selling a straight bond (noncallable) simultaneously with a purchase of a call option written by the bond purchasers. The firm pays the premium on the call by taking a lower price than would be paid for a bond without the call provision. A convertible bond is a bond which carries a call option providing that the holder can convert the bond into equity. The firm writes the call and receives the premium in the form of a higher price than would be paid for bonds without the conversion provision.

Recently, firms have begun to issue bonds with put provisions entitling the bond holder to sell the bond back to the issuer at a specified price.

CONCLUDING REMARKS

Since the creation of the Chicago Board Options Exchange in April 1973, the options market has played an increased role in the U.S. capital markets. This shows an increasing awareness of the options market by investors. As with the stock market, interested investors are inundated with advice on strategies for winning. The proliferation of folklore prompted Fischer Black to write "Fact and Fantasy in the Use of Options," in which he stated that "for every fact about options, there is a fantasy—a reason given for trading or not trading in options that doesn't make sense when examined carefully."[8]

Indeed, many of the investment strategies promoted in the options market rely on some contracts being mispriced. Undoubtedly, as in the stock market, the important role of many traders is to arbitrage situations of mispricing, thus ensuring that prices faced by investors are, on the average, unbiased. As such, much option trading can be considered active investment strategy.

Options do, however, provide opportunities for the sale and purchase of investment insurance. They enable investors to repackage the risk-return profile of their portfolios in ways not available with stocks and bonds. Interestingly, the most popular trading is in the recently developed options on the stock indexes. These contracts were first offered at the CBOE in March 1983, and they are based on a basket of stocks that proxy for the whole market. All transactions are settled in cash. For investors with diversified portfolios who track the stock index, the options allow the investor to insure against most unfavorable outcomes to the portfolio. By buying at-the-money puts, the investor is shielded from portfolio losses (in excess of the premium paid) due to marketwide factors.

Besides the expanded use of options by investors, there has been remarkable progress in research around the options market. The ground breaking paper by Black and Scholes has elevated the option pricing model to the highest plateau in modern finance. Not only has it become the industry standard for pricing in the market, it has also generated substantial research extending both its theoretical contribution and its applications. It has provided a powerful vehicle for analyzing many complex issues in corporate finance, and it has reshaped our thinking in such areas as capital structure, dividend policy, and mergers and acquisitions.

NOTES

1. The variety of investment strategies involving options is great, and it is beyond our scope to provide a detailed description. Furthermore, the technical level of analysis required to rigorously discuss option pricing requires a level of math skill beyond that required in the rest of this book. For a more detailed and technically thorough presentation, see Robert A. Jarrow and Andrew Rudd, *Options Pricing* (Homewood, Ill.: Richard D. Irwin, 1983).

2. These figures were provided by the Chicago Board Options Exchange.

3. The insurance component of options is described in Robert C. Merton, Myron S. Scholes, and Mathew L. Gladstein, "The Returns and Risk of Alternative Call Option Portfolio Investment Strategies," *Journal of Business* 51 (April 1978), pp. 183–242.

4. Fischer Black and Myron Scholes, "The Pricing of Options and Corporate Liabilities," *Journal of Political Economy*, 3 (May–June 1973), pp. 637–54.

5. See John C. Cox, Stephen A. Ross, and Mark Rubinstein, "Option Pricing: A Simplified Approach," *Journal of Financial Economics*, 7 (September 1979) pp. 229–63.

6. Robert C. Merton, "The Theory of Rational Option Pricing," *Bell Journal of Economics and Management Science*, 4 (Spring 1973), pp. 141–83.

7. The Black-Scholes option pricing model is:

$$C = SN(d + 1/2\,\sigma\sqrt{T}) - Ee^{rT}N(d - 1/2\,\sigma\sqrt{T})$$

where

$$d = \frac{1}{\rho\sqrt{T}}\ (\ln\tfrac{S}{E} + rT)$$

C = Market price "premium" of a European call option.
S = Market price of the underlying stock.
E = Exercise "striking" price.
T = Time to maturity.
r = Riskless interest rate.
σ = Standard deviation of the *ex ante* rate of return on the stock.
N( ) = Cumulative standardized normal probability distribution.

8. Fischer Black, "Fact and Fantasy in the Use of Options," *Financial Analysts Journal*, 31 (July–August 1975), pp. 36–41, 61–72.

11

Evaluating portfolio performance

INTRODUCTION

In Chapter 1, we saw that institutional investors are controlling a large and increasing share of investment. With the growth of mutual funds and pension plans, it is not surprising that a strong interest has developed in objective and rational measurements of the relative skill that financial agents employ for their clients.

One of the first major efforts to specify a system of objective measurements was implemented by a group of academic authors for the Bank Administration Institute (BAI) in 1968.[1] Since then, the performance of professional investment managers has been persistently scrutinized.

Essentially, performance evaluation is concerned with the measurement and comparison of the return earned on one portfolio with that earned on others. It is important that the comparison portfolios or benchmarks are appropriate. In particular, the benchmark must be of comparable risk. In this chapter, we discuss both the risk and return elements that are appropriate in evaluating investment performance.

Rate of return

The correct definition of rate of return should be based upon changes in the market value of assets held and the value of dividends, interest, and

154

TABLE 11-1   Example of calculation of the internal rate of return

Year	Cash flows (year-end)	Present value (discounted at 10 percent)
0	− $ 87.53	− $87.53
1	+ 5.00	+ 4.545
2	+ 5.00	+ 4.130
3	+ 105.00	+ 78.855
		$\Sigma = 0$

other payments received. In some contexts, it may be necessary to distinguish between dollars as interest and dividends and dollars as capital gains. Clearly, it is returns after taxes that matter to the investor. When taxes vary for different kinds of dollars, returns from the various sources must be segregated to allow accurate computation of relevant taxes. Also, trustees of personal trusts must deal evenhandedly with lifetime beneficiaries and remaindermen. Lifetime beneficiaries receive income (dividends, interest, and so forth), and remaindermen receive principal. Trustees must choose investments that reasonably divide the total return between the conflicting claims of the two classes of beneficiaries.

Despite the fact that some investors must account for taxes and others have to distinguish between some kinds of dollars and others, the following discussion refers to investors who pay no taxes and who make no such distinctions. This group certainly includes the managers of private, noninsured pension funds and also includes many endowed institutions. The problem of including investors subject to taxes in this discussion is not difficult. The obvious adjustments are to measure returns after taxes and to be sure that comparisons among portfolios are limited to portfolios whose owners or beneficiaries are in similar tax brackets.

Remembering that the discussion relates to tax-exempt investors, the gentle reader can now proceed to consider the problem of measuring returns. One prominent candidate for such measurement is the internal rate of return. This is the rate of return that is calculated to find the yield to maturity of a bond. It is the rate of discounting of the cash flows associated with an investment, which makes their algebraic sum equal to zero. An example makes this clear (Table 11–1).

If a $100 bond paying 5 percent at the end of each year is purchased for $87.53 and sold at the end of three years for $100, the cash flows are as presented in Table 11–1.

The 10 percent discount rate makes the algebraic sum of the cash flows equal to zero and is the internal rate of return. It measures the performance of the initial investment and assumes that any additions to the original investment earn the same rate of return.

The internal rate of return is an interesting and useful number. It tells the rate at which a fund's assets are growing because of returns on investments. All prudent fund managers and investors will want to know the internal rate of return on their investments.

Nevertheless, the internal rate of return is not ideal for evaluating the relative skill with which different portfolios are managed. Its blemish is that it is affected by factors outside the fund manager's control. To use a number for evaluating the fund manager when the number is affected by outside factors is a mistake. The factor affecting the internal rate of return, which the fund manager typically does not control, is the time at which new funds are received for investment and the time at which funds must be disbursed to the owners or beneficiary.

For example, consider two hypothetical fund managers of two portfolios on January 1, 1980. The two fund managers had identical judgments about investments, and the portfolio managed by each had the same percentage distribution of funds among particular assets. On January 2, the first fund manager received a large amount of money from the trustor or the individual investor for investment; the second fund manager did not. The first fund manager distributed the new capital among existing assets to preserve the same percentage distribution. For six months, the market rose very rapidly, which provided large, positive returns for both portfolios. On July 2, the first fund manager had to make a large payment from the fund, and the second fund manager received a large check for investment. After the disbursal and the new investment, both fund managers continued to have identical judgments and portfolios with identical distributions of funds among particular assets. The market then fell rapidly for six months. For 1980, the first fund manager's portfolio had a higher internal rate of return than the second fund manager's portfolio, despite the fact that at every moment each had identical judgments and exhibited identical skills. It is that shortcoming of the internal rate of return which must be eliminated.

There has been some misunderstanding in the financial community about the use of the word *time* or *timing* in discussing this subject. The fund manager can control shifts between common stocks and cash or fixed-dollar assets in an effort to judge the timing of general market movements, and any measure of the fund manager's skill should reflect skill in making such judgments. The fund manager, however, does not control the time at which funds are received or at which they must be disbursed, and the measure should not reflect this timing.

There is an easy way to measure the rate of return that is insensitive to the timing of receipts and disbursals. In the BAI report, this measure is called the "time-weighted rate of return." Although the name may be confusing, the principle is not. The time-weighted rate of return is logically equivalent to the rate of return on mutual fund shares that are bought and redeemed at net asset value per share. The investor who purchases shares in a mutual fund can measure the rate of return on his/her investment by knowing the price paid, the value of payments received, and the shares' price at the end of the period in question. The investor does not need to

FIGURE 11-1 Changes in value of a fund with net investment and disinvestment

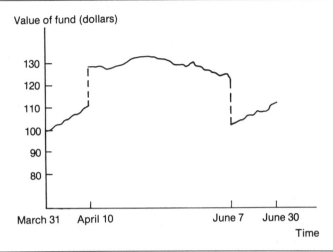

Value of fund (dollars)

Source: Lorie et al., *Measuring Investment Performance of Pension Funds,* p. 75.

know the time or amount of new investments in the fund by other investors who bought shares, or the time or amount of disbursals from the fund to shareowners who redeemed their shares. The individual investor's rate of return is totally insensitive to those injections of capital into the fund or withdrawals of capital from the fund.

It is the same with the time-weighted rate of return for portfolios other than mutual funds. The time-weighted rate of return calculation is illustrated in Figure 11-1 and Table 11-2.

Fluctuations in the value of a hypothetical fund are shown in Figure 11-1, and the fund values and cash flows are summarized in Table 11-2. The market value of the fund increased from $100 on March 31 to $110 on April 10. There were no contributions or withdrawals during the period. On April 10, there was a $15 contribution, raising the fund value to $125. On June 7, the $125 fund was worth $120, and there was a withdrawal of $25.

TABLE 11-2 Summary of fund values and cash flows

	March 31	April 10	June 7	June 30
Value of fund before contribution	$100	$110	$120	$105
Net contribution	0	15	− 25	0
Value of fund after contribution	100	125	95	105

Source: Lorie et al., *Measuring Investment Performance of Pension Funds,* p. 76.

No further contributions or withdrawals were made through June 30, when the value of the fund was $105. The time-weighted rate of return for the period March 31 to June 30 is a weighted average of the internal rates of return for each of the three subperiods.*

It can be costly to calculate the time-weighted rate of return precisely. The internal rate of return requires only that one know the value of the portfolio at the end and the time and amount of all flows into and from the fund. To calculate the time-weighted rate of return, one also needs to know the market value of the fund at the time of each cash flow. Determining that market value for hundreds or thousands of different funds many times a week or month could be quite burdensome. However, there are methods that produce close approximations without requiring such detailed data.[2]

Risk

It should not be surprising that performance must take account of both the rate of return on assets and the risk that the investor has been subjected to. It is undesirable for all investors to subject themselves to the same degree of risk, and, therefore, not all investors should expect the same rate of return. The elderly widow whose primary objective is the protection of her assets from loss cannot expect as high a return as the more adventuresome young physician whose primary objective is to maximize the value of her holdings 25 years in the future. If one knew only the rates of return on the widow's and the physician's respective portfolios, one could not judge the skill of their investment advisers.

It's desirable to measure risk for another reason. In judging the significance of any observed difference in the rates of return on two portfolios, it is desirable to distinguish between differences that can be attributed to random fluctuations in returns on each portfolio and differences that could only be attributed to differences portfolio of managers' skills. This is an old and ordinary problem in statistical inference, and all of the usual principles apply in this context. The distinction between random and other differences can be made only if the variability in each series is known. Any observed difference for any period between rates on two different portfolios is more reasonably attributable to differences in skill, if rates on each portfolio have been rather constant than if rates have been extremely variable. Since estimates of risk are typically based on variability in rates of return, measurements of risk are useful in distinguishing between random and other differences in rates. They are also useful for evaluating rates in terms of assumed risks.

---

*In terms of an annual rate of interest compounded continuously, it can be calculated as follows:

$$i = (\frac{365}{91})\ln[(\frac{110}{100})(\frac{120}{110} + 15)(\frac{105}{120} - 25)]$$

The term 365/91 converts the quarterly rate to an annual rate.

Some of the difficulties of measuring risk have been discussed in earlier chapters, and we saw that an investment's total risk or variance can be dichotomized into unsystematic (diversifiable) and systematic (nondiversifiable) risk. If all investors held perfectly diversified portfolios, systematic risk (as measured by beta) is equivalent to total risk (as measured by standard deviation), and there is no diversifiable risk.

We must recognize, however, that some investors do not hold efficiently diversified portfolios. If a portfolio is imperfectly diversified, not all variations in rates of return will be accounted for by market movements. Some measure of total variability is therefore justified.

The evaluation of portfolio performance in terms of total dispersion measures both the manager's ability to pick winners and the manager's ability to diversify efficiently. In contrast, if risk is measured by market sensitivity alone, performance evaluation depends only on the manager's ability to choose investments with higher rates of return than others with similar levels of systematic risk.

Combining measurements of rate of return and risk

Since two criteria are necessary for evaluating portfolio performance, the difficult problem of combining these criteria warrants discussion. Consider the four portfolios whose risks and returns for a given period are represented in the following diagram (Figure 11-2).

It is clear that portfolio C is superior to portfolio B, in that C provides more return for the same risk. It is not immediately clear whether D is superior or inferior to any of the other portfolios; the same can be said for port-

---

FIGURE 11-2   The relationship between risk and return for four hypothetical portfolios

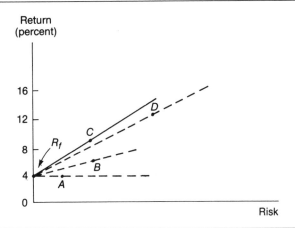

folio A. Although D provides more return, it also provides more risk; A provides less risk and less return. Whether the additional return for D is adequate compensation for the additional risk, and whether the reduced risk for A is worth the foregone return are questions with complicated answers.

The standard answer is to talk about the amount of return per unit of risk and to judge a portfolio that provides the most return per unit of risk as superior. The reasoning behind that answer is simple. In Figure 11–2, assume that the risk-free rate of return is 4 percent. If that is true, portfolio C is superior to all other portfolios, using the criterion of return per unit of risk. This can be seen by drawing rays from the risk-free rate of return through the points representing each portfolio. The ray passing through portfolio C has the greatest slope, and this is just a geometric reflection of the fact that the additional return per unit of risk is greatest for that portfolio. Portfolio C is considered best because it would allow, by appropriate combinations of it with the risk-free asset or by buying on margin, the achievement of a rate of return superior to that for any other portfolio, with the same degree of risk. For example, by combining portfolio C with the risk-free asset, one could move the portfolio down the ray passing through portfolio C to a point directly above portfolio A, thus achieving a greater return than on portfolio A for the same degree of risk. Similarly, by buying portfolio C on margin, one could move the portfolio up the ray that passes through portfolio C to a point directly above portfolio D, thus achieving a rate of return superior to that on portfolio D for equivalent risk. In this sense, portfolio C is the "best" portfolio of the four.

Though this is, in some ways, a satisfying conclusion, there are some difficulties. For example, a particular investor may not be allowed to buy on margin and may therefore be unable to move along the ray passing through portfolio C in order to achieve a higher return from that portfolio. Given that limitation, the investor might prefer portfolio D to portfolio C, even though the skill with which C is managed is somewhat superior to that with which D is managed.

Another difficulty has to do with the proper measurement of the additional return per unit of risk. There is general agreement that a portfolio's rate of return should be expressed as a risk premium by subtracting the risk-free rate of interest from the rate of return. To determine the rate of return per unit of risk, this risk premium should be divided either by a measure of total variability, such as the standard deviation or mean-absolute deviation, or by a measure of volatility or sensitivity to the market such as the beta coefficient. The choices between these two measures of risk can be better made if the relationship between them is understood. The beta coefficient is related to the standard deviation algebraically:

$$\beta_{im} = \frac{\rho_{im}\sigma_i}{\sigma_m}$$

FIGURE 11-3 The relationship between historical rates of return on funds and rates of return on the market

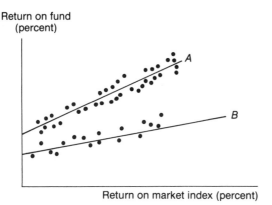

Return on fund
(percent)

Return on market index (percent)

This equation shows the importance of something discussed earlier.* If all portfolios were "efficient," all would be perfectly correlated with the market, and the beta coefficient of each would be the ratio of the individual portfolio's standard deviation to the market's standard deviation. Since the standard deviation for the market would be constant across portfolios, portfolio rankings according to the standard deviation would be identical to rankings according to the beta coefficient. Unfortunately, not all portfolios are perfectly correlated with the market, so rankings according to one risk measure can differ from rankings according to another.

In studies of mutual funds, Treynor has used an index based on volatility to rank funds.[3] His method is easily illustrated. In figure 11-3, the returns on two funds are plotted against a market index.

The circles represent the returns on fund *A*, and the dots represent the returns on fund *B*. Each point represents the return for a year. The two regression lines fitted to these points are Treynor's "characteristic" lines. The volatility of the fund is given by the slope of the characteristic line. If the fund *B* line were parallel to and below the fund *A* line, fund *B* would be inferior, since it would provide a lower return for the same volatility. In Figure 11-3 all we can deduce so far is that fund *A* is more volatile. To rank funds, Treynor draws a horizontal line through the risk-free rate of interest. This is illustrated in Figure 11-4. Since the intersection (*X*) of this line with the characteristic line for fund *A* is to the left of that (*Y*) for fund *B*, fund *A* is superior.

Treynor shows this mathematically, but it is also obvious geometrically, since a ray rotated through *X* until it is parallel to the characteristic line for fund *B* could be achieved by combining fund *A* with the riskless asset.

*See Chapter 8.

FIGURE 11-4 A diagrammatic illustration of the Treynor index for ranking funds

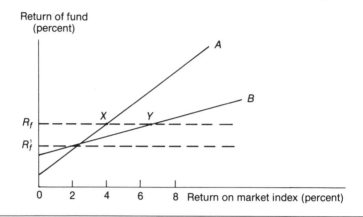

The horizontal distance to the point of intersection—R_fX for fund A and R_fY for fund B—is the Treynor index of fund performance. It is read off the horizontal axis as a percentage; the smaller the percentage the better the relative performance. The index indicates the rate of return on the market index required to make the fund's expected return equal to the risk-free rate of return. In the example above, it is 4 percent for fund A and 6 percent for fund B. It is in this sense that fund A is superior. It is important to recognize, however, that a fund's rankings will depend upon the level of the risk-free rate of interest. In Figure 11–4, if the riskless asset earned a return of R_f^1 instead of R_f, fund B would be superior according to the Treynor measure.

Sharpe's method is similar, but he uses the standard deviation to compute the reward-to-variability ratio as a means of ranking funds.[4] For example, in Figure 11–5, each point represents the average return on a fund for some period, and the standard deviation of returns for subperiods.

Since the slope of the line from R_f, the risk-free rate of interest, to point A is the steepest, fund A has the highest ranking. This is Sharpe's reward-to-variability ratio:

$$\frac{R_a - R_f}{\sigma_a}$$

The Treynor index is equivalent to:

$$\frac{R_a - R_f}{\beta_a}$$

and is, therefore, a reward-to-volatility ratio.

FIGURE 11-5   The relationship between the average return on funds and risk (σ)

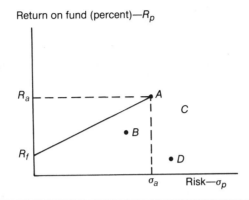

Recently Roll has stated that performance measures utilizing beta risk are questionable.[5] Unfortunately, beta is an ambiguous risk measure, and different betas are estimated when different market indexes are used. The true market index, which is the theoretical underpinning of the capital asset pricing model, includes all assets in the economy in proportion to their total market values. In practice, the indexes used are only proxies for the market portfolio (see Chapter 3). For instance, these indexes ignore assets of unlisted firms and omit human capital (arguably one of the most significant asset classes). According to Roll, it is likely that the indexes used to proxy for the true market portfolio are not mean-variance efficient. Performance measures based on these indexes are subject to persistent benchmark error. The fact that beta does not totally explain the variations in returns across securities is evidence of this benchmark error. It is possible that for a given portfolio the measured return is greater than that expected from the CAPM benchmark, yet the portfolio has performed poorly. If the benchmark used had been replaced by a mean-variance efficient portfolio, measured beta would have been different, and the poor performance would have been recognized.

Roll's message is important: When evaluating performance, it is crucial to carefully consider the appropriateness of the benchmark used for comparison.

MEASURING DIFFERENT PARTS OF THE PORTFOLIO

We have discussed measurements of risk and return for the whole portfolio in evaluating the skill with which it has been managed. One might ask whether or not it is also necessary to measure the risk and return separately for the different classes of assets in the portfolio. Is it necessary, for example, to measure the risk and return on the equity portion, bonds, convertible securities, and so forth?

One of Markowitz's maxims, which should be highly valued, is that investors should think of themselves as choosing portfolios rather than securities, so that the performance of investors should be judged by the total portfolio rather than one or more securities. Although it is fairly standard practice to measure the risk and return for different kinds of assets, the purpose should be diagnosis rather than the overall evaluation of portfolio management. Such separate measurements can cast light on the reasons for superior or inferior performance.

The basic objection to reliance on measurements for separate classes of securities is that they fail to account for relationships and interactions among classes of securities. Just as it is foolish to attempt to measure the risk and return on an individual asset apart from its relationships to the rest of the portfolio, it is foolish to measure the risk and return for individual groups of assets apart from their relationships to the other parts of the portfolio. In fact, one of the clear lessons of portfolio theory is the impossibility of finding a meaningful measurement of an individual asset's riskiness—or gorup of assets—apart from the other assets in an investor's portfolio. Viewed in isolation, such securities might seem very risky with the expectation of a large risk premium. Viewed with the rest of a portfolio, such securities would correctly be judged as risk reducing, and they would have a very small or even negative risk premium.

Diagnosing the causes of performance

Some investors undoubtedly will be satisfied with a simple evaluation of the skill their trustee or investment adviser has used in managing a portfolio. If the evaluation is favorable, the investor can relax and congratulate him or herself on a wise choice. If the evaluation is unfavorable, the investor can seek a new trustee or new adviser. The investor may not want to understand the causes for the adviser's success or failure.

Most large investors and especially most large trustors of employee pension plans are not content with a mere summary evaluation, and they wish to understand the causes. Such an understanding may be just as helpful in achieving better performance as a switch to another adviser or trustee who is believed to have greater investment ability. In fact, if evidence concerning the likelihood that superior performance in any one period will be followed by superior performance in a subsequent period is taken seriously, understanding the causes of investment performance will do more to improve it than switching trustees or advisers.

Conventional discussions of investments usually identify two major decisions. The first is selecting particular assets in each asset class, and the second is deciding the allocation of funds between asset classes, primarily between stocks and bonds.

The fund manager's performance is affected by the ability to select stocks that perform above expectations. In a large portfolio of many assets, some stocks will perform better than expected and others worse than expected in any one period. Diversification offsets the effects of such random fluctuations, but consistent superior stock selection will be reflected in a higher return-to-risk measure.

The second decision is often referred to as the *timing* problem. Successful coping with the timing problem results in extensive switches from equities to short-term debt instruments just prior to large, general declines in the prices of common stocks, and it results in a reverse movement of funds just prior to large, general advances.

Although there is little evidence to support the belief that actual investors consistently play the timing game successfully, many investors continue to try, and perhaps some consistently succeed. Skill in making the timing judgment can be extremely rewarding.

The persistent finding in studies of mutual funds is that very few managers appear to have special information regarding the formation of expectations for market portfolio returns.

Other factors that affect investment performance are transactions costs, management fees, and levels of diversification. These factors must be considered, and it is unrealistic to assume these factors are zero when comparing performance to a benchmark portfolio.

REACHING A CONCLUSION

The purpose of evaluating a portfolio manager is almost always to find a conclusion about his or her superiority or inferiority. Clearly, the measurements of performance, period by period, are the raw materials for this ultimate judgment, but they do not automatically lead to that judgment. The problem exists because performance in any period is affected by both the skill of the portfolio manager and random influences. Just as in acceptance sampling, one typically does not reject a supplier because of one deficient batch or unit, so an investor should not reject or discard an adviser because of poor performance in any single period. Neither should the investor be quick to distribute gold stars or enlarged responsibilities on the basis of superior performance in any one period.

There is an interesting question as to when an investor is justified in reaching the conclusion that a trustee or adviser is truly superior or inferior. There is no completely satisfactory answer to that question, but the judgment can be reached sooner and with greater confidence if the margins of superiority or inferiority are large and stable than if they are small and erratic. The principles of sequential sampling, which have proved so useful in acceptance sampling for mass-produced items in industry, might also be applied here.

NOTES

1. James H. Lorie et al., *Measuring the Investment Performance of Pension Funds for the Purpose of Interfund Comparison* (Park Ridge, Ill.: Bank Administration Institute, 1968).
2. See ibid., pp. 21–26.
3. Jack L. Treynor, "How to Rate Management of Investment Funds," *Harvard Business Review* 43, (January–February 1965), pp. 63–75.
4. William F. Sharpe, "Mutual Fund Performance," *Security Prices: A Supplement, Journal of Business* 39 (January 1966), pp. 119–38.
5. Richard Roll, "Performance Evaluation and Benchmark Errors," *Journal of Portfolio Management* 6 (Summer 1980) pp. 5–12.

12

A note on
investment counseling

INTRODUCTION

There are many fine investment counseling firms, and their staffs are honorable, conscientious, and sophisticated. Yet, most of their resources are devoted to security analysis and portfolio management rather than investment counseling. Investment counseling is advising an investor regarding investment policy. Portfolio management is the execution of policy. Security analysis provides some of the information traditionally considered necessary for portfolio management.

Those who are convinced by the evidence regarding the efficiency of markets will believe that the most important investment decision—the one with the greatest impact on results—is the choice of policy with respect to risk. Rates of return for mutual funds, for example, vary consistently and substantially—almost entirely because of differences in risk. There is little evidence that the managers of any mutual fund consistently display superior judgment in picking assets of a given degree of risk.

If all of these statements are valid, investment counseling becomes important—almost certainly more important than security analysis or even portfolio management.

THE PREFERENCES AND RESOURCES OF INVESTORS

Many trustees and investment counselors make only rudimentary efforts to analyze the cash flow requirements, risk preferences, resources, and tastes of their clients—whether they be individuals, corporate trustors of pension funds, endowed institutions, or others. In view of the importance of investment policy, the lack of any systematic, sophisticated analysis of the investor's relevant circumstances is unfortunate.

For example, actuaries for large corporations typically provide estimates of employees' characteristics for only a year or two into the future, although longer-term estimates are sometimes provided. Such data can be the raw material for estimating the liabilities of the corporate pension fund. Of course, there is uncertainty regarding the size of the work force, its composition by age and job classification, its retirement benefits, and so forth, but actuaries can and should provide both probability distributions of these variables and a summary probability distribution of the fund's liabilities.

When such information is combined with rates of return distributions resulting from different investment strategies, it is possible to simulate the fund's operation, indicating the likely annual range of requirements for corporate contributions and other items of interest to the trustor. Based on such simulations, the trustor and trustee have the raw material for a rational choice of investment policy.

A declining firm with a relatively old work force almost certainly should choose a different policy than a rapidly growing firm with a relatively young work force. The former has great demand for liquidity and a relatively short horizon, indicating the desirability of a portfolio of relatively low risk. The latter company has virtually no possibility of liquidity demands in the near term, is therefore relatively immune to the impact of near-term fluctuations in the value of its pension fund, and can (should?) bear relatively high risk with the associated relatively high expected return. Management science is allowing actuaries to play a more useful role in helping trustees and trustors choose an investment policy more rationally.

Similar techniques can be applied to other classes of investors. Universities, for example, have to choose expenditure and investment policies. Simulation permits trustees to see the probable effects of different combinations of such policies on annual expenditures from endowments and annual changes in their market value. Simulations do not prevent pleasant or unpleasant surprises, nor do they automatically produce wise decisions regarding the relative importance of near-term and more remote demands. Simulations provide the raw material for a decision-making process that will likely be superior to the common, short-term, and formless "intuition."

The first example of such simulations, to our knowledge, was undertaken at the University of Rochester. A hypothetical example derived from their work shows the probable range of annual expenditures from endowment and the probable range of year-end values of endowments from a policy of

FIGURE 12-1   Expenditure profile of a hypothetical endowment assuming annual expenditures equal to 5 percent of the market value of the endowment at the beginning of each year

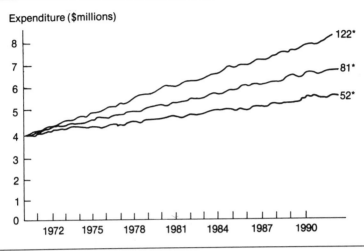

*Ending portfolio value.
The lower line represents the 20th percentile of the 100 simulated values for each year; the middle and top lines represent the 50th (median) and 80th percentiles.

spending 5 percent of the year-end value and assuming that the distribution of rates of return on the portfolio during the next 40 years would be the same as during the preceding 40 years. The assumed mean of the returns is 8.8 percent, and the standard deviation is 10.8 percent (Figure 12–1).

The firm of O'Brien Associates, Inc. has done serious work on a system for understanding the interrelationships between actuarial assumptions and returns based on market simulations. The hypothetical example shown in Figures 12–2 and 12–3 is taken from their work.

Other actuarial assumptions about returns on the market would produce different results. Those analyses and simulations provide a more rational basis for choosing an investment policy than the casual intuitive process.

Individuals also require better investment counseling than they often receive. The problem is especially difficult for small investors, but even large investors typically manage their portfolios or have them managed with only unsystematic regard for their current and prospective requirements, resources, and tastes. Portfolios should change in response to changes in earned income, lifestyle, number of dependents, and attitudes toward risk. Marriages, divorces, children, grandchildren, and many other factors should determine investment policy. Yet, they seldom are systematically taken into account. Yet, in efficient markets, investment counseling is the most important investment function, and the available tools of scientific investment have been used insufficiently in performing that function.

FIGURE 12-2   Assumptions used in example simulation

---

1. Work force projection model
  Work force growth = 1 percent per annum.
  Salary scale growth = 3½ percent per annum.
  Male/female hiring ratio = 1:3.
2. Actuarial liability computation
  Discount rate = 3½ percent per annum.
3. Investment portfolio projection model
  Capital market assumptions
  Mean equity market return = 9½ percent per annum.
  Standard deviation of equity market return = 16 percent per annum.
  Riskless rate of return = 4½ percent per annum.
  Investment policy parameters
  Portfolio diversification = 95 percent.
  Turnover = 20 percent per annum.
  Dividend yield = 3.0 percent per annum.
  Relative equity exposure (β) range = 0.0–1.2.
  Mean independent return (α) = 0.0 percent per annum.

THE SPECIFICATION OF INVESTMENT POLICY

Investment counselors and trustees do not ignore the choice of investment policy. In fact, they typically produce a written policy statement for reference. Current practice deserves criticism not only because of the casual, intuitive process by which policy is chosen, but also because of the ambiguity and vagueness of its expression. These deficiencies are often so pronounced that the policy neither provides meaningful guidance to the portfolio manager nor the effective means for controlling and evaluating the manager's performance.

Many trust departments and investment counseling firms rely on three criteria to give operational meaning to policy statements:

1. A list of securities eligible for purchase—the so-called buy list.
2. A diversification requirement, usually specifying the maximum percentage of a portfolio that can be invested in the securities of a single company and the maximum percentage that can be invested in a single industry.
3. A maximum percentage that can be invested in equities.

These three criteria are designed to restrict investments to undervalued securities, to control risk through diversification and a maximum commitment to equities, and to deal with the timing problem by changing the maximum permissible commitment to equities. Although there is remarkably little evidence that buy lists outperform other securities of similar risk, the three criteria provide some control over portfolio managers.

Yet, the control is crude and inexact. Portfolios are constructed from the same buy list, with the same percentage in equities and full compliance with the criteria for diversification, but they have quite different charac-

FIGURE 12-3 Impact of investment policy on annual pension plan cost

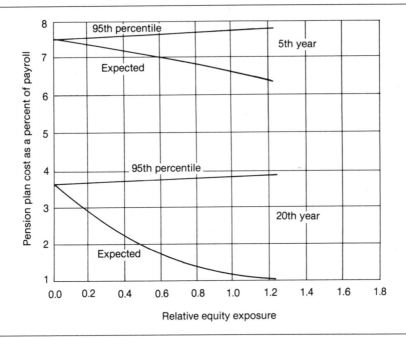

Relative equity exposure

teristics. Trust departments and investment counseling firms that predict a bear market can seek to effect portfolio modifications through changes in buy lists and reductions in maximum permissible levels of investment in equities. The control mechanism will fail, however, if portfolio managers, not sharing the pessimism of their policymakers, shift to equities more sensitive to market movements than those previously held. Reducing the proportion of a portfolio in equities from 80 percent to 60 percent will not make the portfolio less vulnerable to a market decline, if the equities held have substantially higher beta coefficients than those formerly held.

A more precise prescription of policy could be achieved through the use of beta coefficients and correlation coefficients. The prescription of a beta coefficient would perform two functions. It would control the relative riskiness of all portfolios and would permit a controlled adjustment in absolute levels of systematic risk in response to convictions of policymakers regarding future, major market movements. The prescription of a correlation coefficient would control diversification, and thus the proportions of total risk that would be unsystematic—that is, caused by something other than movements in the market. A buy list can also be used, but its value should be frequently tested.

Since the use of beta and correlation coefficients provides a precise prescription of investment policy, it is easy both to audit portfolio managers' degree of compliance and to evaluate their performance in light of the precisely stated, theoretically relevant constraints on their choice of investments. Thus, the institution employing the portfolio managers can discharge its inescapable responsibility of having a policy for each portfolio, knowing whether the policy is being followed, and evaluating the performance of those who execute policy.

The use of beta and correlation coefficients permit prescient policy-makers to see that portfolio managers proportionately reduce the vulnerability of their portfolios to a coming sharp decline in the market. The institution employing these managers could avoid embarrassing or even absurd ignorance of the degree to which their portfolio managers were adapting to the anticipated decline.

The value of the beta coefficient in measuring the sensitivity of a diversified portfolio to market movements has been discussed at length. The use of the correlation coefficient in prescribing and controlling policy has only been mentioned briefly. The correlation between the return on a portfolio and the return on a comprehensive market index measures the extent to which the portfolio return is determined by the market. A correlation coefficient of 0.9, for example, would mean that 81 percent (0.9^2) of the portfolio's change in value was due to a systematic change; 19 percent would be unsystematic and attributable to the lack of complete or efficient diversification.

Very high correlations would be appropriate for portfolios for which low risk was appropriate or for portfolios whose managers had not demonstrated the ability to discriminate between undervalued and overvalued stocks. In efficient markets, there is no expected reward for bearing unsystematic risk. Portfolio managers should not, therefore, be permitted to incur such risk unless there is evidence that they possess that very rare quality, the ability consistently to make superior judgments about investments.

CONCLUSION

The relatively high degree of efficiency in American security markets makes investment counseling the most important of the investment functions. That is, the choice of an investment policy is likely to have a greater influence on results than either security analysis or portfolio management. Yet, investment counseling is typically treated casually, despite the availability of theories and techniques that could make it more precise and rational.

Glossary

Abnormal performance index (API).   An abnormal performance index measures the behavior of stock prices not explained by their normal relationships to general market movements. The normal relationship of the return on a security to the return on the market is described by the market model:

$$R_i = a_i + \beta_i R_M + e_i$$

where R_i is the return on the security, R_M is the return on the market, a_i and β_i are parameters, and e_i is a random variable with an expected value of zero. Abnormal behavior will result in values of e_i different from zero and nonrandom.

Abnormal return.   The abnormal return for a security is the price change which accrues to it from a particular event rather than via marketwide influences. The Capital asset pricing model (CAPM) can be used to generate abnormal returns by replacing expected returns with realized returns. The residual is the abnormal return (that is, nonzero and nonrandom). Cumulative abnormal return (CAR) is the sum of the individual abnormal returns over a set period.

Accounting earnings.   Accounting earnings represent the change in recorded book values between two time periods. The application of accounting rules and principles may yield results that are consistent over

173

periods but do not capture other events of significance (such as inflation). The concept of economic value seeks to capture all relevant factors which affect a firm's value. The market's estimate of this value is reflected in the market capitalization of the corporation, or more simply, in the price of its stock. Economic earnings represent the change in economic value adjusted for any dividend payments. More specifically, economic earnings from a particular asset are given by the total revenue earned less all real operating costs associated with the asset (but not interest payments as they are related to financing—a separate issue) and less economic depreciation (that is, the fall in *market* value of the asset as it is consumed over time). In short, the earnings are given by the change in the real command over goods and services in a given period.

Alpha (α_i). Alpha is the constant term in the equation relating the risk premium on an asset to the risk premium on the market. Its *expected* value is zero, but its actual value may differ from zero. It is this possibility that explains investors' efforts to identify under- or over-valued securities; that is, those with nonzero alphas.

Beta coefficient (β). The beta coefficient measures sensitivity of rates of return on a portfolio or on a particular security to general market movements. If the beta is 1.0, a 1 percent increase in the return on the market will result, on average, in a 1 percent increase in the return on the particular portfolio or asset. If beta is less than 1.0, the portfolio or asset is considered to be less risky than the market. Beta is the regression coefficient for the rate of return on the market in the market model equation,

$$R_i = \alpha_i + \beta_i R_M + e_i.$$

An estimate of the beta coefficient of a portfolio is a weighted average of the betas of the portfolio's component assets.

Beta factor (R_z). In Sharpe's capital asset pricing model, the expected risk premium on an asset depends on the expected risk premium on the market multiplied by the asset's beta coefficient.

In a more elaborate model (attributable to Black, Jensen, and Scholes), the expected return on an asset depends also on the expected return on a portfolio not correlated with the market (R_z) multiplied by $(1 - \beta)$. This second factor is called the beta factor.

Call option. A contract that entitles the owner to buy, at his/her discretion, a number of shares in an underlying security at a stated price, called the striking or exercise price, on or before a fixed date of expiration. Call options increase in value as the price of the underlying security increases.

Capital asset pricing model (CAPM). The capital asset pricing model describes the way prices of individual assets are determined in markets where information is freely available and reflected instantaneously in asset prices—that is, efficient markets.

Prices are determined in such a way that risk premiums are proportional to systematic risk, which is measured by the beta coefficient.

Capital market line. The capital market line in the Sharpe model is the ray from the risk-free rate of return (R_f) that is tangent to the efficient frontier of risky assets. It describes the relationship between expected rates of return on efficient portfolios and risk as measured by σ_p. All efficient portfolios lie on this line if lending and borrowing are permissible at the (same) risk-free rate.

The mathematical relationship is

$$E(R_p) = R_f + \left[\frac{E(R_M) - R_f}{\sigma_M} \right] \sigma_p.$$

The slope of the line,

$$\left[\frac{E(R_M) - R_f}{\sigma_M} \right],$$

is the reward per unit of risk.

Characteristic line. A characteristic line relates the return on an asset or portfolio to the return on a market index. The slope, β, measures volatility, or sensitivity to market movements.

Coefficient of variation $\left[\frac{\sigma_x}{\bar{x}} \right].$ The coefficient of variation is the standard deviation divided by the mean, or

$$\sqrt{\frac{\Sigma(x_i - \bar{x})^2}{N}} \Big/ \bar{x}$$

It is a measure of the *relative* spread of a distribution about its mean. Coefficients of variation can be compared, since they are relative measures.

For example, if the standard deviation of a distribution of rates of return were 2 percent, and the mean were 5 percent, the coefficient of variation would be 0.02/0.05 or 0.4 percent.

Compounding. Compounding is the arithmetic process of finding the final value of an investment or series of investments when compound interest is applied. That is, interest is earned on the interest as well as on the initial principal.

Continuous compounding. The annual rate of return compounded continuously is the natural logarithm $(\log_e)$ of the ratio of the investment's value at year-end to the value at the beginning of the year.

For example, if the wealth ratio were 1.1, its natural logarithm would be 0.09531. The annual rate of return compounded continuously would be 9.531 percent. This is easily converted to an annual rate of return compounded annually using the formula $e^x - 1$, where x is the annual rate compounded continuously.

If the period is other than one year, the annual rate compounded continuously can be found by dividing the logarithm of the wealth ratio by the number of years in the period.

Correlation coefficient $(_p)$. A simple correlation coefficient is a measure of the degree to which two variables move together. If the relationship is causal, it can be interpreted as a measure of the degree to which knowing the value of one variable helps to predict the value of the other.

The coefficient is the square root of 1 minus the unexplained variance of one variable, given its relationship to the other, divided by its total variance. Symbolically, for the variables, x_i and x_j

$$\rho_{ij} = \sqrt{1 - \frac{s_{i \cdot j}^2}{s_i^2}}$$

The square of the correlation coefficient is the coefficient of determination. It measures the percentage of the total variance of i explained by its relationship to j.

Covariance (Cov_{ij}). Covariance is a measure of the degree to which two variables move together. A positive value means that on average, they move in the same direction. The covariance is related to, but not the same as, the correlation coefficient. It is difficult to attach any significance to the absolute magnitude of the covariance.

Symbolically, the covariance between two variables, x_i and x_j, is

$$\frac{\Sigma(x_i - x)(x_i - x_j)}{N}$$

The covariance is also equal to $\rho_{ij}\sigma_i\sigma_j$, so its magnitude depends not only on the correlation, but also the standard deviations of the two variables. Stated alternatively, the correlation coefficient is the covariance standardized by dividing it by the product of σ_i and σ_j.

Covered position. When stock in an underlying security is held, a writer can sell an option and cover his risk by having stock on hand in case that delivery is demanded.

Deviation, Residual $(x_i - x)$ or (e_i). A deviation is the amount by which a particular value differs from some other value such as the average, or mean. Deviations can also be related to values, such as normal trend values, or to theoretical values one would expect based on an historical relationship among the variables. This type of deviation is usually called a residual. Deviations from the mean are used to compute the variance and standard deviation of a distribution. A deviation from an expected value, given the existence of a relationship with one or more other variables, is the error term in a regression equation. In the two variable case, $y = a + bx + e_i$, e_i is a residual, which is a random variable with a mean of zero.

Diminishing marginal utility of wealth. Marginal utility is the amount of additional satisfaction associated with an additional amount of something such as money or wealth. If successive increments in satisfaction decline as the level of wealth increases, there is diminishing marginal utility. This implies risk aversion, because, at a given level of wealth, the gain in utility associated with some increment in wealth is less than the loss in utility associated with a decrement of the same amount of wealth.

Dispersion. Dispersion is the spread of a distribution about its average, or mean value. The greater the spread, the greater the variability. It can be measured either absolutely or relatively. Common absolute measures are the standard deviation, the variance, and the semi-interquartile range. The most common measure of relative dispersion is the coefficient of variation (the standard deviation divided by the mean).

Diversification. Diversification is the spreading of investments over more than one company or industry to reduce the uncertainty of future returns caused by unsystematic risk.

Economic earnings. See Accounting earnings.

Efficient frontier. The efficient frontier is the locus of all efficient portfolios. If neither lending nor borrowing is allowed, it is that part of the boundary of the feasible set that includes only efficient portfolios of risky assets. If lending and borrowing are permissible, the efficient frontier is the ray drawn from the risk-free rate to the point of tangency on the efficient frontier of risky assets. This line is called the capital market line.

Efficient market. An efficient market is one in which prices always fully reflect all available, relevant information. Adjustment to new information is virtually instantaneous.

Efficient portfolio. An efficient portfolio is one that is fully diversified. For any given rate of return, no other portfolio has less risk, and for a given level of risk, no other portfolio provides superior returns. All efficient portfolios are perfectly correlated with a general market index, except portfolios with beta coefficients above 1.0 and which do not achieve that relatively high risk by leveraging an efficient portfolio. Such portfolios lie on the curved frontier of portfolios consisting exclusively of risky assets.

Expected rate of return. The expected rate of return on an asset or portfolio is the weighted arithmetic average of all possible outcomes, where the weights are the probabilities that each outcome will occur. It is the expected value or mean of a probability distribution. For example, the expected return on a portfolio, $E(R_p)$, is the weighted average of all possible returns, R_i, each weighted by its probability. Mathematically, $E(R_p) = \Sigma p_i R_i$.

Feasible set. The feasible or attainable set includes all individual securities and all combinations (portfolios) of two or more of these securities available to the investor within the limits of available capital.

Filter rules. A filter rule is a simple mechanical rule for deciding to buy or sell assets. An x percent filter rule for investing states that if the price of a security rises at least x percent, buy and hold the security until its price falls by x percent from a subsequent high. The security should then be sold or sold short until the price rises by x percent from a subsequent low.

For example, if the filter is 5 percent and the price of Security A rises from a low of 100 to 105, the security should be purchased. If the price rises to 110 and then declines to 104½, the stock should be sold or sold short. This position should be maintained until the price rises by 5 percent above a subsequent low. The filter need not be the same percentage for buy and sell signals.

Gini's coefficient of variation. Gini's coefficient of variation is the mean difference between all possible pairs of observations divided by the mean. Symbolically, it is:

$$\sum_{i=1}^{N} \sum_{j=1}^{N} \frac{(x_i - x_j)}{N} / \bar{x},$$

where $i \neq j$.

Geometric mean (M_g). The geometric mean is the nth root of the product of n observations. It is the correct measure to use when averaging annual rates of return, compounded annually, over time.

In calculating the average of rates of return, it is necessary to take the geometric mean of wealth ratios in order to allow for negative rates. The average rate of return is then the geometric mean minus one. For example, if the annual rates of return for two years were 10 percent and 8 percent, the average annual rate of return would be

$$\sqrt[2]{.1 \times 1.08} - 1$$

or .0899. If the annual rates for two years were 100 percent and -50 percent, the average annual rate of return would be

$$\sqrt[2]{2.0 \times 0.5} - 1 = 0.0.$$

Indifference curve. An indifference curve represents combinations of, say, risk and return, that are equally valued.

For risk averters, indifference curves are convex from below when return is measured on the vertical axis and risk on the horizontal axis. The shape varies with the risk-return preferences of the individual.

Internal rate of return. The internal rate of return is analogous to the familiar yield to maturity on a bond.

The internal rate of return is the rate of discount which makes the net present value of an investment equal to zero. In the case of a bond, if

$$P_o - \sum_{t=1}^{N} \frac{I_i}{(1+i)^t} + \frac{P_N}{(1+i)^N} + 0,$$

where P_o is the initial price, P_N is the terminal price, I_t is the interest in year t, i is the internal rate of return.

Intrinsic value. The intrinsic value of an asset is the value that asset "ought" to have as judged by an investor. Discrepancies between current value and intrinsic value are often the basis for decisions to buy or sell the asset.

Investment performance index (IPI). An investment performance index differs from a price index in that it includes cash dividends and other distributions to shareholders.

Least-squares regression line. A least-squares regression line minimizes the sum of the squares of the vertical deviations of observations from a line drawn through them.

For example, if a regression line is fitted to points representing pairs of values of x_i and x_j, the equation is

$$x_i = a + bx_j$$

The squared vertical distances of the actual values of x_i from the theoretical values, given its relationship to x_j are minimized. The mean values of x_i and x_j will always be a point on the regression line.

Market model. The market model describes the relationship between the rates of return on individual securities or portfolios and the rates of return on the market.

For example, for a particular security i, the relationship can be written as follows:

$$R_i = a_i + \beta_i R_M + e_i$$

where R_i is the rate of return on i, R_M is the rate of return on the market, a_i and β_i (beta) are parameters, and e_i is a random variable with an expected value of zero.

The model is useful for isolating "abnormal" stock-price behavior from that due to the influence of several market conditions.

Market portfolio. The market portfolio includes all risky assets in proportion to their market value. In the capital asset pricing model, it is the optimum portfolio of risky assets for all investors. Graphically, it is located at the point of tangency of a ray drawn from the risk-free rate of return to the efficient frontier of risky assets.

Mean absolute deviation. The mean absolute deviation is the average of the absolute values (the signs are disregarded) of the deviations of a group of observations from their expected value. Symbolically it is

$$\frac{\Sigma|x_i - \bar{x}|}{N}.$$

Median. The median of a distribution is the value that divides the number of observations in half. If the distribution is normal, the mean and the median will coincide. If the distribution is not normal and has positive skewness, the mean will exceed the median. If the skewness is negative, the mean will be below the median.

Multiple correlation. Multiple correlation is a measure of the relationship between one variable (the dependent variable) and two or more other variables (the independent variables) simultaneously. It is an extension of simple correlation to include more than one independent variable.

Naked writing. When a call is written without owning the underlying stock, the writer is exposed to potentially unlimited risk. This is also termed *uncovered writing*, and it is constrained by the margin requirements of the Options Clearing Corporation.

Nominal return. The nominal return on an asset is the rate of return in monetary terms, that is, unadjusted for any change in the price level. The nominal return is contrasted with the real return, which is adjusted for changes in the price level.

"Normalized" earnings. "Normalized" earnings are the earnings one would expect in a "normal" or mid-cyclical year. There is no general agreement about the best way to normalize earnings, but it is common to use a moving average for three, four, five, or more years. Normalized earnings are sometimes called "steady-state" earnings.

Present value or worth. The present value of a payment or payments is the actual value discounted at an appropriate rate of interest. The discounting reflects the productivity of capital and the risk premium. For example, the present value of a share of stock, $V\sigma$, is the stream of future earnings discounted to perpetuity, or,

$$\sum_{t=1}^{\infty} \frac{E_t}{(1+i)^t}$$

where E_t are the earnings in period t and i is the rate of discount.

Probability distribution. A probability distribution is a distribution of possible outcomes with an indication of the subjective or objective probability of each occurring.

Put option. A contract that entitles the owner to sell, at his/her discretion, a number of shares in an underlying security, at a stated price, on or before a fixed expiration date. Put options increase in value as the price of the underlying security decreases.

Random selection. Random selection is similar to picking stocks by throwing darts at a stock listing.

Technically, random selection means that each element in the relevant population has a known and positive probability of selection. For example, if an index were based on 10 randomly selected stocks from a population (list) of 1,000, the stocks could be selected with equal probabilities or, say, with probabilities proportional to the market value of the outstanding shares of each of the 1,000 firms.

Random walk. A random walk implies that there is no discernible pattern of travel. The size and direction of the next step cannot be predicted from the size and direction of the last or even from all the previous steps. If one wanted to find a random walker, the best place to look would be the starting point.

Random walk is a term used in mathematics and statistics to describe a process in which successive changes are statistically independent. The serial correlation is zero. The changes are a random variable with an expected value of zero.

Regression analysis. Regression or correlation analysis is a statistical technique for estimating the relationship between one variable (dependent variable) and one or more other variables (independent variables).

The estimated relationship, usually a least-squares regression equation, is often used to predict the value of the dependent variable, given the values of the independent variable or variables.

Regression coefficient. A regression coefficient indicates the responsiveness of one variable to changes in another. If the relationship between two variables is described by a straight line, the regression coefficient is the slope of the line.

The regression coefficient between rates of return on an asset and rates of return on the market is called the beta coefficient.

Reward-to-variability ratio. The reward-to-variability ratio is the risk premium on an asset per unit of risk as measured by the variability or standard deviation. Sharpe used this measure to rank mutual funds.

Risk aversion. Risk aversion means riskiness matters and is disliked. A risk averter will hold a portfolio of more than one stock in order to reduce risk for a given expected return.

Technically, the utility function of a risk averter will depend on rate of return *and* risk and will not be linear. This implies diminishing marginal utility of wealth.

A risk-averse investor will incur additional risk only if he or she *expects* a higher rate of return.

Risk-free rate of return (R_f). The risk-free rate of return is the return on an asset that is virtually riskless. For example, Treasury bills maturing in one year have a precisely predictable nominal rate of return for one year. The risk premium on an asset is the rate of return in excess of the risk-free rate. The risk-free rate is normally used in portfolio theory to represent the rate for lending or borrowing.

Risk neutrality. Risk neutrality means risk doesn't matter. A risk-neutral investor cares only about rate of return and would hold a portfolio of one asset—the one with the highest expected rate of return. Risk neutrality implies constant marginal utility of wealth. The utility function for such an investor is linear. It is represented by the equation

$$U = a + bE(R)$$

where U is the utility of the return on an asset and $E(R)$ is the expected return on the asset.

Risk premium $(R_i - R_f)$. The risk premium on an asset is the actual return minus the riskless rate of return. In Sharpe's capital asset pricing model, the risk premium for any asset is proportional to its beta—the measure of sensitivity to general market movements.

If R_i is the rate of return on an asset, and R_f is the riskless rate, $R_i - R_f$ is the risk premium.

Runs. A run is a sequence of changes in the value of a variable, all having the same sign. The number of runs in a sequence of changes is the number of reversals in sign plus one.

For example, if price changes are classified as zero, positive, or negative, a sequence of $+ + - + + 0 - -$ would include five runs.

Sampling. Sampling is the process of selecting a subset of a population. It may or may not be random. The usefulness of a sample depends upon its representativeness, or the degree to which one can make inferences about the excluded population on the basis of the sample.

Semistandard deviation. The semistandard deviation is analogous to the standard deviation, but only the observations below the mean are included. The deviations, $(x_i - x)$, are all negative. The measure is relevant if one is interested only in downside or adverse risk.

Separation theorem. The separation theorem states that the choice of an optimum portfolio is independent of, or separate from, the optimal combination of *risky* assets. The latter is the same for all investors if lending and borrowing are allowed. Individual needs determine only the amount of borrowing or lending.

Serial correlation (ρ). Serial correlation is measured by the simple correlation coefficient between two variables, one being the successive value of the other. Serial correlation can also be measured with lags. For example, a change in the price of a stock can be serially correlated with the change before the last one as well as with the last one. Serial correlation measures the degree to which what happens next is related to what happened previously.

Short selling. Selling a security that is not owned, but purchasing it at a later time for delivery. The sale would be made in anticipation of a fall in the share price.

Skewness. Skewness is a measure of the asymmetry of a distribution. A normal distribution is symmetrical and has no skewness. If there are more observations to the left of the mean, the skewness is positive; if there are more observations to the right, the skewness is negative.

Spread position. A spread is created by selling and purchasing call or put options in the same underlying stock. The two basic variants are: (1) buying and selling options with different expiration dates and (2) buying and selling with the same expiration date but at different striking prices.

Standard deviation. The standard deviation is a commonly used measure of dispersion. It is the square root of the variance. It is based on deviations of observations from the mean and is therefore in the same units as the observations. A measure of relative dispersion is the standard deviation divided by the mean (the coefficient of variation). This is often useful in comparing distributions that differ substantially in the magnitude of the numbers.

The formula for the standard deviation, σ, is

$$\sqrt{\frac{\Sigma(x_i - \bar{x})^2}{N}}$$

For a probability distribution,

$$\sigma = \sqrt{\Sigma P_i[x_i - E(x)]^2}$$

Statistical independence. If two variables are statistically independent, the correlation between them is not significantly different from zero. That is, the changes in the two variables are unrelated. Knowledge of the changes in one is of no value in predicting the other.

For example, the weak form of the efficient market hypothesis asserts the statistical independence of successive price changes. Current prices reflect and impound the implications of the historical sequence of prices so that a knowledge of that sequence is of no value in forming expectations about future price changes.

Stock dividend. The issuing to existing stockholders, new scrip in lieu of or in conjunction with cash dividends. The issued capital is increased by accounting entries, which transfer funds from retained earnings to issued capital.

Stock splits. Subdividing outstanding stock units, without changing the issued equity.

Straddle. Combining an equal number of put and call options on an underlying security, at the same striking price and expiration date.

Striking price (exercise price). The price per share at which the holder of an option may buy or sell the underlying security when the contract is exercised.

Systematic risk. Systematic risk is the volatility of rates of return on stocks or portfolios associated with changes in rates of return on the whole market. It can be estimated statistically from the market model. The percentage of systematic total variability is given by the coefficient of determination, and the degree of responsiveness to market movements is measured by beta.

Time-weighted rate of return. The time-weighted rate of return is a weighted average of the internal rates of return for subperiods dated by the contribution or withdrawal of funds from a portfolio. To calculate it, one needs to know the portfolio's value during each cash inflow or outflow and the dates when these occur. Rates of return on mutual fund shares are time-weighted rates of return.

Treynor index. The Treynor index of fund performance is the reward per unit of risk as measured by volatility or beta. It indicates the rate of return on the market index required to make the expected rate of return on a fund equal to the risk-free rate.

Unsystematic risk. Unsystematic risk is the variability not explained by general market movements. It is avoidable through diversification. Only inefficient portfolios have unsystematic risk.

Utility function. A utility function describes the relationship for an individual between various amounts of something such as wealth and the satisfaction it provides.

If one's preferences are known, his/her utility functions can often be approximated by precise mathematical equations. The signs and values of its derivatives indicate the direction and magnitude of changes in utility associated with changes in the amount of the good possessed.

Variance (σ^2). The variance of a distribution is a measure of variability based on squared deviations of individual observations from the mean value of the distribution. Its square root, the standard deviation, is a commonly used measure of dispersion.

The formula for the variance is,

$$\sigma^2 = \frac{\Sigma(x_i - x)^2}{N}$$

If the distribution is of future outcomes that not certain, the variance is a weighted average of the squared deviations and the weights are the probabilities of occurrence. That is,

$$\sigma^2 = \Sigma P_i[x_i - E(x)]^2$$

Volatility. Volatility is that part of total variability due to sensitivity to market changes. It is systematic and unavoidable risk. It is measured by the beta coefficient. Efficient portfolios have no additional risk, and volatility is the only source of variability in rates of return.

Wealth Ratio $\left(\dfrac{W_t}{W_o}\right)$ A wealth ratio is the terminal value of an investment divided by its initial value. It is used in calculating rates of return.

The wealth ratio is expressed as W_t/W_o where W_t refers to the terminal value and W_o to the initial value. The annual rate of return compounded continuously is

$$\log_e \frac{\left(\dfrac{W_t}{W_o}\right)}{n},$$

where n is the number of years in the period. The annual rate of return compounded annually is $e^x - 1$, where x is the annual rate compounded continuously.

Weighting. Weighting is the specification of the relative importance for each item in a group. For example, stocks included in indexes may be weighted equally or according to value.

Writer. The seller of an option.

Yield to maturity. The actual return from a fixed coupon investment allowing for: the purchase price (may be above or below par), the stream of interest payments, and the redemption value. The yield to maturity is the internal rate of return of the cash flow such that the present value equals the current market price of the bond, or conversely, the net present value equals zero.

Index

A

Abnormal performance index (API), 173
Abnormal return, 64, 68, 71, 100–103, 173
Acceptance sampling, 165
Accounting earnings, 173–74
  relationship between stock prices and, 99–103
Accounting principles
  and ambiguity in reported income, 98–99
  and determination of earnings, 97
Actuarial liability computation, 170
Actuaries, role of, in choosing investment policies, 168
Aharony, Joseph, 93
Albin, P. S., 30
Alexander, Sidney S., 60
Alpha, 174
American options, 145 n
American Stock Exchange (ASE)
  share volume of, 8
American Stock Exchange Price Level Index, 41, 44, 49–50
Anticipated dividends, 151
Arbitrage game, 72
Arithmetic mean, 15, 30, 44–46

Asset-pricing model, 139, 140–42
Assets, determining prices of financial, 132
AT&T, 48
At-the-money option, 146
Australia, annual earnings and stock returns in, 101
Averaging, methods of, 44–46

B

Bachelier, Louis, 56–57
Ball, Ray, 99, 101, 103–5
Bank Administration Institute (BAI), 154, 156
Bankruptcy, 151
Bear market, 171
Becker Securities Funds Evaluation Service, 75
Benchmark, and evaluation of portfolio performance, 33, 38, 154, 163
Beta, 121–22, 135
Beta coefficient, 38–40, 136–37, 160–61, 171–72, 174
Beta factor, 174
Black, Fischer, 85, 136, 139, 150, 152
Black-Scholes pricing model, 151

Blue chip stocks, 47
Blume, Marshall, 21, 52, 54, 60, 63, 123
Bond investments, rate of return on, 13–14
Boness, A. James, 63
Borrowing, 122–26, 135–36
Box, G. E. P., 105
Brealey, Richard A., 104
Brennan, Michael J., 141
Brokerage industry, effect of deregulation on, 11–12
Brokerage rates
  fixing of, 9–11
  sanctioning of fixed, 9
Brown, L. D., 105
Brown, Philip, 99, 101
Brownian motion, 57
Business cycle, relationship of stock prices to, 2, 4–5

C

Call option, 145, 148, 151, 174
  Short sell of, 149 n
Calls, 145
Capital asset pricing model (CAPM), 74, 133–34, 138–40, 150, 173, 174–75
  extension of, 140–42
  realism of, 135
Capital funds, allocation of, 1
Capital gains, taxation of, 92
Capital market equilibrium theory, 141–42
  assumptions of, 132–35
  beta, 138
  determining prices of financial assets, 132
  efficient portfolios, 136–37
  extension of capital asset pricing model, 140–42
  measurement of risk, 138–40
  realism of, 135
  risk and return, 137–38
  risk-free borrowing and lending, 135–36
Capital market line, 125, 133, 135–36, 175
Capital markets, and transference of risk, 1–2
Cash flows, components of, 88–89
Center for Research in Security Prices (CRSP), 14, 51, 65
  U.S. Government Bond File, 17
Chambers, R. J., 98
Characteristic line, 175
Chicago Board Options Exchange (CBOE), 144, 149, 152
Coefficient of determination, 38–39
Coefficient of variation, 175
Cohn, Richard A., 29
Commissions, effect of, on rates of return, 28–31
Common stocks
  rate of return on, 14, 16–19
  risk premiums and inflation-adjusted returns on, 26–27

Common stocks—*Cont.*
  variability in rates of return on, 20–21, 23
Compounding, 14, 175
Compustat financial statement data base, 65
Computers, use of, to calculate rate of return, 14
Consumer price index (CPI)
  and investment returns, 16–21, 23
  measurement of inflation, 17
Continuous compounding, 14, 158 n, 175–76
Convertible bond, 151
Cooper, Guy M., 138
Cootner, Paul, 46
Corporate bonds, long-term
  risk premiums and inflation-adjusted returns on 26–27
  variability in returns, 20–21, 23
  year-end cumulative wealth indexes for, 18–19
  year-by-year returns on, 16–17
Corporate equity securities, market value of, 7–8
Corporate mergers, 70–71, 151
Corporate securities, discount rate for, 6
Corporations, financing of assets, 1
Correlation coefficient, 60–61, 117, 171–72, 176
Covariance of security, 114–15, 176
Covered position, 176
Cowles, Alfred III, 41, 51, 57
Cox, John C., 150 n
Cragg, J. G., 105
Crockett, Jean, 52, 54
CRSP; *see* Center for Research in Security Prices
Cumulative abnormal return (CAR), 173
Currency, assets in, 8
Cyclical pattern, 2

D

Dann, L., 30, 69
Debt instruments, assets in, 8
Degree of investor uncertainty, 5
Demand deposits, assets in, 8
Deregulation, effect of, on brokerage industry, 11–12
Deviation, residual, 176
Dimensional Fund Advisors of Chicago, 30
Diminishing marginal utility of wealth, 177
Discount brokerage firms, emergence of, 12
Discount rate
  in real world, 94
  in world of certainty, 93–94
Dispersion, 23, 177
Diversification, 84–85, 165, 170, 177
  effect of, on variability of stock returns, 23
Dividend-payout ratio, 92
Dividends, and earnings, 89–93

Dodd, D. L., 91
Dodd, Peter, 72
Dow Jones Averages, 43–44, 60
Dow Jones Industrial Average (DJI), 33, 41–42, 46–48, 74
Dryzcimski, Eugene F., 67
Durand, David, 14 n

E

Earnings, 96–98
  ambiguity in reported income, 98–99
  and dividends, 89–93
  historical, as predictor of future, 103–5
  predictions of security analysts, 105
  stock prices and accounting, 99–103
Economic earnings, 91 n, 174, 177; *see also* Earnings
Economies of scale, of security analysis and portfolio management, 82–83
Economy, effect of national, on stock market, 1–12
Efficient frontier, 118–22, 177
Efficient market, 55, 177
Efficient market hypothesis, 55–56, 103
  history of, 56–57
  implications of, 80–87
  quests for theory of, 63–65
  semistrong form 56
    tests of, 65–73
  strong form, 56
    tests of, 73–77
  weak form, 56
    early tests of, 57–63
Efficient portfolio, 109–10, 133, 136–137, 161, 177
Equal-weighted indexes, 43
Equal weighted portfolio strategy, 28, 30
Equilibrium analysis, 135–36
European options, 145 n
Event time methodology, 103
Exercise price, 150, 183
Expected level of earnings, 5
Expected rate of return, 111, 177
Explorer Fund of the Vanguard Group, 42
Exxon, market value of common stock, 9

F

Fama, Eugene F., 25, 34–35, 40 n, 44 n, 55, 57, 60, 61 n, 62 n, 63, 65–69, 103, 130, 139–41
Feasible set, 177
Filter rules, 178
Filter technique, 60, 63
Financial intermediaries, use of, by individual investors, 9
Financial markets, functions of, 1
Fischer, Irving, 6, 41
Fischer, Lawrence, 14–15, 23, 24 n, 29, 34, 44 n, 46, 51, 65–69, 103

Foster, George, 101–2
French, Kenneth, 25 n
Friedman, Benjamin, 1
Friedman, Milton, 6, 135
Friend, Irwin, 52, 54, 73, 75
Functional-fixation hypothesis, 103
Futures, stock index, 52–53

G

Geometric mean, 15, 30, 44–46, 178
Gibbons, Michael R., 140
Gini's coefficient of variation, 178
"Give up" system, 11
Gladstein, Mathew L., 148
Glauber, Robert, 104
Good news firm, 99
Gordon, M. J., 91
Government bonds
  and inflation, 25–27
  risk premium and inflation-adjusted returns on, 26–27
  variability in returns, 20–21, 23
  year-by-year returns on, 16–17
  year-end cumulative wealth indexes, 18–19
Graham, B., 91
Granger, Clive W. J., 57
Great Britain, earnings in, 104
Grier, P. C., 30

H

Hedging, 53, 141, 148–49
Hess, P., 92
Hickman, W. Braddock, 14 n
Homa, K. E., 7
Horizontal spread, 149
Host International, Inc., 35–38
Hostile tender offers, 70–71

I

Ibbotson, Roger G., 14–15, 29, 17 n, 19 n, 21 n, 27 n
Index of leading economic indicators, stock price index as component of, 2
Index funds, 85
Indifference curve, 129, 178
Industrial production, relationship to stock prices, 2–3
Inflation, effects of, on rates of return, 24–27, 29
Inside information, 76–77
Insider trading, 76
Insurance companies, investments of, 1
In-the-money option, 146
Interest rates, 151
Internal rate of return, 155–56, 178–79
International Business Machine (IBM), market value of common stock, 9
Intrinsic value, 179
Investment committees, 84

Investment counseling, 86, 167
    preferences and resources of investors,
      168–70
    specification of investment policy, 170–72
Investment Management Services, 65 n
Investment-performance index (IPI), 51–52,
    179
Investment portfolio projection model, 170
Investment strategies, and use of options,
    146–50
Investments, reasons for value of, 88

J

Jaffe, J., 76
Jaffee, D. M., 7 n
Jarrow, Robert A., 144
Jenkins, G. M., 105
Jensen, Michael, 34, 44 n, 55, 65–68, 75, 103
Johannseon, Richard I., Jr., 17

K

Kaplan, R., 34
Keim, Donald B., 141
Kendall, Maurice G., 57
Kessel, Reuben A., 25 n
King, Benjamin F., 21, 40
Kraus, Alan, 69

L

Least-squares regression line, 179
Leftwich, Richard, 105
Lending, 122–26, 135–36
Lev, Baruch, 104
Leverage, buying of, 149
Liebowitz, Martin L., 17
Life insurance and pension reserves, 8
Lintner, John, 74, 104
Little, Iam M. D., 104
Lorie, James H., 14–15, 23, 29, 154 n, 24 n

M

MacBeth, James D., 139, 140–41
Maccaulay, Frederick R., 14 n
Macroconsistency, 43
Mains, N. E., 82
Malkiel, Burton, G., 105
Management science, 168
Market efficiency, 55, 96
Market efficiency model, 99
Market moel, 35-41, 100, 103, 140, 179
Market portfolio, 179
Markowitz, Harry, 108–9, 115, 120–22, 127,
    130–31, 133, 142, 164
Mayers, D., 30, 69
Mean-absolute deviation, 160, 179
Mean-variance approach, to portfolio
    selection, 128
Median, 180
Mendelbrot, Benoit, 56, 63

Merrill Lynch, Pierce, Fenner & Smith,
    Inc., 65 n
Merton, Robert, 140, 148, 150
Miller, Merton H., 85, 89–93, 141
Milne, Robert D., 47 n, 48 n
Modern portfolio theory, 38, 85
Modigliani, Franco, 29, 89–93
Money supply, growth rate of, 6–7
Moore, Arnold B., 57, 60, 63
Moore, Geoffrey H., 2 n
Morgenstern, Oskar, 57
Multiple correlation, 180
Murphy, Joseph E., Jr., 104
Mutual funds
    diversification of, 85
    professional management of, 73–76, 167
    rate or returns of, 167
    specialization of, by industry, 42
    Treynor index of performance, 161–62

N

Naked writing, 146–47, 180
NASDAQ Composite Index, 51
NASDAQ market, share volume of, 8
National Association of Security Dealers
    Automated Quotation service, 8
New York Stock Exchange (NYSE)
    annual compounded rates of return for
      portfolio of common stock, 28–30
    calculated of beta for stocks on, 138
    commission rates on, 11
    monthly returns on, 130
    share volume of, 7–10
New York Stock Exchange Composite Index,
    41, 44, 49
Niederhoffer, Victor, 76
90–day Treasury bills, 6
Nominal return, 180
"Normalized" earnings, 180

O

O'Brien Associates, Inc., 169
Officer, R. R., 21, 23
180-day Treasury bills, 5–6
Optimal portfolio, 129, 135
Optimization, 127
Options, 144–45
    investment strategies for using, 146–50
    market procedures, 145–46
    pricing of, 150–51
Options Clearing Corporation (OCC), 145
Osborne, M. E. M., 57, 59–60, 76
Out-of-the-money option, 146
Over-the-counter market
    quotation service, 8
    share volume of, 8

P

Patell, James M., 76
Pearson, Karl, 56 n

Pooling, 9
Portfolio
    efficiency of, 109–10
    efficient frontier, 118–22
    evaluating performance of, 154–63
    lending and borrowing, 122–26
    measuring different parts of, 163–65
    relationship of, to component securities,
        110–18
    riskiness of, 85, 109
Portfolio management, 108–9, 167
    degree of diversification, 84–85
    evaluation of, 154, 165
    functions of, 23, 86–87
    maintenance of desired risk level, 85
    riskiness of portfolio, 85, 109
    state of the art, 84
    tax status of investor, 85
    transaction costs, 85–86
Portfolio management theory, 132, 137, 164
    Markowitz contribution, 109–26
Present value of earnings stream, 5
Present value/worth, 180
Price-earnings (P/E) ratio, 92
Price fixing, role of SEC and Justice
    Department in ending, 11
Price pressure hypothesis, 68
Probability distribution, 111, 180
Professional investment management, 7, 73–
    77; see also Portfolio management
Put-call parity, 149
Put option, 145, 148, 180
Puts, 145

R

Raab, R., 30, 69
Random selection, 180–81
Random walk, 55–56, 99, 104, 181
Random-walk hypothesis, 57, 60, 62, 103
Rate of return, 13–15
    combining measurements of risk and, 159–
        63
    on common stock, 16–19
    and consumer price index, 16–19
    effects of commissions, taxes and
        weighting strategies, 28–31
    and evaluation of portfolio performance,
        154–58
    and inflation, 24–27, 29
    on long-term corporate bonds, 16–19
    on long-term government bonds, 16–19
    market's trade-off of risk and, 23–24
    on Treasury bills, 16–19
    variability in, 20–23
Rayleigh, Lord, 56 n
Rayner, A. C., 104
Real Estate investments, and inflation, 25
Regression analysis, 181
Regression coefficient, 181
Reilly, Frank K., 67

Reward-to-variability ratio, 162, 181
Reward-to-volatility ratio, 162
Risk
    allowance for differences in, 92
    beta as measure of, 138
    combining measurements of rate of return
        and, 159–63
    and evaluation of portfolio performance,
        158–59
    measurement of, 94, 138–40
    and portfolio management, 85
    transference of, 1
Risk aversion, 127–30, 132, 181
Risk-free rate of return, 5, 141, 181
Risk neutrality, 181–82
Risk premium, 182
Roberts, Harry V., 57, 59–60
Rogalski, R., 7
Roll, R., 34, 44 n, 65–69, 103, 163
Ross, Stephen, 140, 150 n
Round turn, 52
Rozeff, M. S., 7, 105
Rubach, Richard, 25 n
Rubinstein, Mark, 150 n
Rudd, Andrew, 144
Runs, 182

S

Salomon Brothers' High-Grade, Long-Term
    Corporate Bond Index, 17
Sampling, 41–42, 182
Samuelson, Paul A., 56, 63
Scholes, Myron, 68–69, 85, 93, 141, 148,
    150, 152
Schwartz, Anna, 6
Schwert, G. W., 25
Securities and Exchange Commission (SEC)
    monitoring of inside trading, 76
    sanctioning of fixed brokerage rates, 9
    Staff Report on the Securities Industry, 7 n
Security analysis, 167
    definition of, 96
    and earnings forecasting, 97
    implications of, 81–84
    and portfolio management, 120
    predictions of earnings, 105
    state of the art, 81
Security valuation, 81
Semistandard deviation, 182
Separation theorem, 125, 182
Sequential sampling, 165
Serial correlation, 182
Sharpe, William 74–75, 94, 118 n, 121–25,
    132–33, 135–38, 142, 162
Short selling, 97, 149, 182
Simulation, 168–69
Sinquefield, Rex A., 14–15, 17 n, 19 n, 21 n,
    23, 27 n, 29
Skewness, 182–83
Slope coefficient, 39

Smith, Adam, 63, 142
Speculation, 149
Spread position, 183
Spreading, 149
Sprenkle, Carl, 63
Sprinkel, Beryl, 6–7
Standard and Poor's Earnings Forecaster,
 105
Standard & Poor's (S&P) indexes, 17, 41–42,
 44, 48–49, 73–74
Standard deviation, 21, 23, 30, 112, 117,
 122, 124, 160, 183
Statistical independence, 183
Stigler, George, 38
Stock dividend, 183
Stock index futures, 52–53
Stock market
 effect of national economy on, 1–12
 trade-off of risk and return, 22–24
Stock market indexes, 33–54; *see also specific*
 names of indexes
 market model, 35–41
 methods of averaging, 44–46
 problems with, 41
 sampling, 41–42
 utility of, 33
 weighting, 42–44
Stock price index, as component of index of
 leading economic indicators, 2
Stock prices
 determinants of level of, 5–7
 effect of stock splits on, 34
 relationship between accounting earnings
  and, 99–103
 relationship of business cycle to, 2, 4–5
Stock splits, 183
 effect of, on stock prices, 34, 65–67
 and value weighting, 43
Stoll, Hans R., 69
Straddle, 149, 183
Striking price, 145, 183
Summers, Lawrence H., 25
Swary, Itzak, 93
Systematic risk, 38, 141, 183–84

T

Taxes
 effect of, on rates of return, 28–31
 status of investor and portfolio
  management, 85
 treatment of dividends, 92–93, 141, 155
Time to maturity, 150–51
Time deposits, assets in, 8
Time-series models, 105
Time-weighted rate of return, 156–58, 184
Timing problems, 165, 170

Tobin, James, 123, 142
Transaction costs, 85–86, 146
Treasury bills, U.S.
 and inflation, 25–27
 risk premium and inflation-adjusted
  returns on, 26–27
 variability of returns on, 20–21, 23
 year-end cumulative wealth indexes on,
  18–19
 year-by-year returns on, 16–17
Treynor index of fund performance, 184
Treynor, Jack L., 97, 161–62

U

Uncertainty, in investments, 1
Uncovered writing, 146, 180
Unsystematic risk, 139–40, 184
Utility function, 127–28, 184
Utility theory, 128–30

V

Valuation model, 99
Value Line 1,400 Composite Average, 50
Value Line index, 34–35, 44, 46
Value Line investment service, 105
Value weighted index, 42–43
Value weighted portfolio strategy, 28, 30
Variance, 184
Vertical spread, 149
Vinso, J., 7
VLA cash value, 52
VLA index value, 53
Volatility, 184

W

Warrants, 151
Watts, Ross, 97 n, 104–5
Wealth indexes, comparison of, for various
 securities, 17–19
Wealth ratio, 14–15, 15 n, 175, 184–85
Weighted average, 5, 112
Weighting, 42–44, 185
Weighting strategies, effect of, on rates of
 return, 28–31
Weil, R., 34
Wilshire 5,000, 50–51
Winn, Willis J., 14 n
Work force projection model, 170
Working, Holbrook, 57
Writer, 185
Writing a call, 149 n

Y–Z

Yield to maturity 185
Zero sum game, 146
Zimmerman, Jerold, 97 n

*This book has been set in 10 and 9 point Caledonia,
leaded 2 points. Chapter numbers are 24 point Caledonia and chapter titles are 18 point Caledonia Bold. The
size of the type page is 27 by 47 picas.*